C000258292

tales

of

the

tea

trade

'I've never grown or sold tea,
only shared a cup of a magical,
mystical Himalayan herb.'

Rajah Banerjee in conversation with
Michelle, 2017.

Michelle and Rob Comins

tales of the tea trade

The secret to sourcing and enjoying
the world's favourite drink

PAVILION

For Mum, thanks for all the teatimes.
For Clara, Esme and Ruen, be brave and be kind.

First published in the United Kingdom in 2019 by
Pavilion
43 Great Ormond Street
London
WC1N 3HZ

ISBN 978-1-91159-522-9

A CIP catalogue record for this book is available from the British Library.

10 9 8 7 6 5 4 3 2 1

Reproduction by Mission, Hong Kong
Printed and bound by Vivar Printing, Malaysia

www.pavilionbooks.com

welcome

Hi, hello and welcome to the wonderful world of tea! We are Rob and Michelle Comins, owners of Comins Tea, direct-trade fine tea merchants in the southwest of England. We trade pure, whole-leaf, unblended teas that celebrate origin, growers, production and preparation techniques. Our travels take us all over the world to fascinating places and wonderful people.

You might be at any number of different points in your own tea journey: perhaps you're an established tea drinker looking to gain a deeper real-life insight into the world of tea and the culture surrounding it; maybe you're right at the beginning of your exploration, keen to be more adventurous but unsure how to get started. Today, we are living in an era in which more people want to understand more about where their food and drink comes from. In this book we want to introduce you to the people making some of the finest, best-tasting tea around the world and tell you their stories, in what we hope is a refreshingly transparent approach to knowledge-sharing in the world of tea. We hope to help build a better connection with, and greater understanding of, a drink that most of us enjoy every day.

In these pages we invite you to look at the world of tea from a completely new perspective, by taking you on a journey with us directly into the lives of those who plant, pluck and process tea. Going beyond the standard tea encyclopaedia, this book offers a unique, first-hand insight into the lives, culture, ceremony, opportunities and threats surrounding this ancient drink. We'll look at the ways in which tea is grown, processed, sold and enjoyed in many of the major tea-producing countries, and examine its health-giving properties. Closer to home, we'll explore how Eastern tea rituals can find a place in our day-to-day lives and help you re-create tea ceremonies at home, all with the aim of making loose-leaf tea a simple, everyday pleasure.

Our hope is simply to encourage readers to take part in an ongoing conversation about the evolution of the tea industry, one that will excite tea drinkers about the role that tea can take in their lives. Once you close this book, we hope you'll feel inspired to start new journeys with tea. When you do, let us know! We hope they'll be as rich, rewarding and life-changing as ours.

A QUICK NOTE ON TEA BAGS, BLENDS AND TISANES

We source fine, unblended, loose-leaf teas (known as 'orthodox' teas in the trade); our work does not include mass-produced, commodity-type blended tea that is generally used in tea bags, or herbal 'tea' (more accurately defined as tisanes or herbal infusions). These are specialities in themselves and deserve exploration in their own right. We will occasionally touch upon the commodity tea market in the book, the context of which is important to understand in the wider conversation about tea.

our story

Michelle: I've always loved tea. It's been present and significant in my life for as long as I can remember – not in the way I know tea now, but in a way that many British people would recognize: at breakfast, when you get home from school or work and at family gatherings or times of relaxation. My first memories of discovering more than just tea with milk and sugar are the outings my mum and I used to make on a Saturday afternoon. We would walk together into Leigh-on-Sea, where we lived, to do some shopping and have tea. They were special times to spend together and, faced with the choice of several different teas, I started drinking Earl Grey, before moving on to Darjeeling. It was still in tea bags, but it was a first taste of something more delicate than standard builders' tea. It was the ceremony of tea that I fell in love with – not the classic Chinese or Japanese tea ceremony, just the act of sitting down with my mum, choosing a tea and spending time together.

Like my first experiences with tea, my upbringing was most definitely British, but I was lucky that my family was curious about the world and other cultures and we travelled extensively. I remember feeling a different energy inside me when I stepped off a plane, a mixture of excitement and slight anxiety at the unknown. I still get that feeling today when I travel and it's invigorating, a true sense of what it is to be alive.

My interest in tea developed. I recently found an ornate Japanese tea set my great friend Mariko (who also designed our logo) gave me when we were at school – an indication that in my teens I had talked about tea enough to warrant her bringing back an enormous box on the plane! Much later, having been to university and started a career in marketing, I called Rob from the commute and told him I wanted to open a tea room. The idea seemed ridiculous, but this was the moment the seed was planted. It took another 10 years for it to become a reality, but tea stayed with me for all those years.

By around 25 I was managing teams of people twice my age. A wise boss and friend of mine, Joyce, used to hold her meetings with me over a cup of tea. She told me that a cup of tea was more than a drink: it was an unspoken commitment of time to a person. Tea became an invaluable tool at work. Outside work, my fondness for the Saturday afternoon tea ritual lingered, even strengthened, throughout university and into my working and married life. I would always insist that Rob and I took time for tea, to talk, reflect and discuss our week, our direction in life, our goals. It was these moments over the years that started to shape our future in tea.

By 2007, the desire to find mental and physical space came to a head and, still dreaming of a life outside the office, I requested a sabbatical. Rob and I headed to India and took a life-changing trip to Darjeeling. We had no plans for the trip, other than to see where tea is grown. I remember it seemed such a strange concept that 'Darjeeling tea' was grown in Darjeeling. We had no idea how tea looked, grew or was processed – we were two complete amateurs starting our journey. We ended up staying in Kurseong, a hill station 1,458 metres above sea level, on the way to Darjeeling. This is the heart of tea country, with gardens along the mountain slopes and viewpoints offering glimpses of forests and villages. We had turned up out of season, so the tea fields lay dormant and the factories were closed, but we were staying very close to the famous Makaibari Estate and therefore, unbeknown to us, close to one of the best-known, most charismatic figures in Darjeeling tea: Rajah Banerjee.

It was on a very misty January morning that we decided to walk down the hill and knock on the factory gates. We both felt nervous. If someone answered what were we going to say? Hello, we're interested in starting a tea business, but we have no money and no idea how to do it… We were about to have our first experience of one of the reoccurring themes in tea: kindness and hospitality. I think the novelty of seeing two young English people standing on the other side of the gate gained us entrance, and it so happened that Rajah was on site.

The next two hours were like a dream. The factory was dormant, but that enabled us to get up close to the machines and meant that the factory manager had time to explain how everything worked, which is near impossible at the height of the season when factories are filled with people. At the end of the short tour we were ushered up to the office while a tea tasting was prepared, and we could hardly believe our luck. We did our best to look as professional as two people who had never properly tasted tea could, and even with our amateur skills it was obvious that we were experiencing a liquor far removed from the Darjeeling we'd tasted back home.

In addition to the incredible flavour was the revelation that there was more than one Darjeeling to try. It sounds ridiculous now, but until that point we had simply been offered 'Darjeeling' in the west. But now here we were with leaves separated not only by grade but also by picking date, variations in which resulted in distinct differences in the cup. Our next step was to meet the man himself: Rajah Banerjee.

Rob: This taste-changing trip took place when I was 29 years old. At this time I believed that tea wasn't for me – in fact, anything other than water and hot chocolate wasn't for me. At a young age, I remember my parents drinking tea made from tea bags with milk, and this was not to my liking. I also remember the pungency of their coffee. I therefore spent my childhood, school years, university years and an initial career in teaching declining all offers of tea and coffee, based on my perception that I had tried and disliked them.

That all changed with Michelle and the aforementioned trip to Darjeeling. Michelle had been trying to bring me across to the world of tea for quite a few years and I still wasn't convinced. I think I must have been suitably enthusiastic at the time, but without thinking that anything would come of it. Even when we decided that a large proportion of our Indian travels were to be based around a trip to Darjeeling, I have to admit that I wasn't in the same place as Michelle. However, I'd long had a fascination with the Himalayas, as my father had been on many mountaineering trips there when I was a child. This, and Michelle's passion, meant I agreed wholeheartedly to the plan.

I found the tour fascinating for different reasons from Michelle. I had a strong interest in machines and processes, so the tour around a tea factory caught my attention. Even though the machines were silent I could still grasp how they would be used and how they would process the tea; in fact, I can still vividly remember the factory layout.

I had been inspired by our tour so far, but I didn't expect what would occur in the famous tasting room and Rajah's office over the next few hours. First, we were shown into the tasting room and a perplexing array of teas labelled with names and letters with numbers. No amount of questions would have made up for our limited palates and experience that day, but to my surprise, my desire to understand the relatively small selection of fine Darjeelings in front of us was immense. After stumbling through the tasting we were invited into Rajah's office, and there my attitude towards tea changed forever.

We were served a pot of first-flush Darjeeling by Rajah's tea lady. There was no escape: I was going to have to drink at least a few cups, which of course I was very prepared to do out of politeness. After the pot had been refreshed several times I was still drinking and wanting more. I was suddenly talking animatedly about possibilities for opening teahouses in the UK. Ten years on, the feeling that was ignited that day still drives me forward.

When we finally stopped talking we were invited to take a walk through part of the estate. Having told us proudly that the majority of his estate was forest, Rajah also informed us that Bengal tigers and leopards roamed through it. This filled us with trepidation, but thankfully all we saw was a wild pig rolling in the the bushes. Rajah immediately shouted to a worker to get it moved on before it damaged the plants further. His care for his tea plants also became clear when we came across a group of workers resting after the morning's work. They had placed some of their clothes over the bushes to dry, something that was clearly not good practice, of which they were swiftly reminded. A sign in the factory said 'Tea is Our God', and this started with the plant. It was a message that would stay with us and infiltrate every level of our business.

We stepped outside the gates full of nervous energy. It really felt as though this was it, this was the life goal – but how to move forward? We reflected on the decisions that had brought us to Darjeeling and given us the courage to knock on the gate. Thirst for knowledge, bravery and an enquiring mind – yes, these would be the ingredients for our new life in tea.

The course we set ourselves that day in Darjeeling has seen us travel the world, and been amazed by the incredible kindness and open-heartedness of the people working in tea all over the world. At Comins we work only with pure tea, no blends, and the people who grow and nurture these leaves have shown great generosity and faith in us over the years, sharing their stories, their expertise – and more often than not, their homes. Often, when we leave their farms or homes, their last words are 'tell more people – share what we're doing here': after all, it's no good producing amazing tea if there aren't enough places where tea drinkers can enjoy and appreciate them. That promise is the motivation for this book. The best way we can repay these wonderful producers is by telling their stories and exciting you, the reader, about the possibilities that great tea can offer. Enjoy!

the story *of* tea

All true teas are made from a species of evergreen shrub called *Camellia sinensis*. The different types of tea we know today arise only from the different processes applied to the leaf once it's picked. The bushes cultivated today are descendants of wild tea trees known to have grown in one giant primeval tea jungle that covered an area including what is now Thailand, East Mayanmar, Yunnan, northern Vietnam and India over 50 million years ago.

EARLY ORIGIN STORIES OF TEA DRINKING

According to legend, the discovery of tea occurred around 4,750 years ago in southwestern China. Like many events in ancient China, it is surrounded by mythical tales. This one concerns the Chinese Emperor Shennong in 2737 BC. Shennong, who was named the 'Divine Farmer' or the 'Emperor of the Five Grains', was said to be a skilled ruler and herbalist who travelled the country discovering new types of herbs and plants, tasting them and noting the effects.

There are many versions of Shennong's initial encounter with tea, the most common being that one day, while boiling water, a leaf from an overhanging wild tea tree drifted into his pot. Shennong enjoyed the unusual delicious flavour and felt refreshed. In other versions of the story, he has a crystal stomach into which he could look to analyze the effects of the herbs he tasted. A more dramatic version has Shennong lying on the ground near to death, poisoned from tasting too many toxic herbs and plants, when a leaf drifts down from a tea tree into his mouth, reviving him. Whether or not any of these things happened, the symbolism of each story certainly rings true. In reality it's most likely that the tea plant was discovered many thousands of years earlier by indigenous tribes who would not have legends recounted about them. The Shennong legend may mark a point when the tea plant's use became recognized by the richer classes. Its properties would have been realized and documented, and in turn, its usage spread further afield.

There is another popular legend about the origin of the leaf from around 526 BC, when an Indian monk called Dharma travelled to China to spread the message of Buddhism. It is said that he meditated for many years without sleep, but one day, in a temple in Honan province, he became drowsy and fell asleep. When he awoke he was so disgusted with himself that he tore off his eyelids and threw them to the floor, where they miraculously grew into a tea bush, the leaf shape mimicking the shape of the eyelid. Another less gruesome tale describes how by chance he chewed the leaves from what turned out to be a tea bush, allowing him to stay awake to meditate.

What these tales show is that from the very beginning, tea had a profound effect on the people who encountered it. These unique qualities ensured its initial expansion across China and ultimately the world. Today, tea is currently grown in 62 countries and is second only to water as the most consumed beverage. In later chapters we look at the history of tea cultivation in just a handful of these countries – those we currently purchase tea from – to give a snapshot of the stories behind the drink. Religion, trade and politics all have their parts to play, creating a fascinating history that can only be touched upon in this book.

TEA ARRIVES IN BRITAIN

Tea first came to the attention of Europe thanks to the Portuguese in the early 1600s. They had reached China in 1557 and began trading tea in 1610. In 1611 the Dutch started trading tea from Japan, but the English did not show much interest. The exact date when tea first reached England is not known, but what we do know is that the first tea offered to the public for sale was by a coffee shop owner, a Mr Thomas Garraway of London, in 1657. Interestingly, the poster created for this historic moment focussed on the health benefits of tea, which worked very well, making the Dutch imported tea an instant success, if only among the rich initially. Converted into today's prices, one pound (454 grams) of the highest grade tea would set you back around £220. Garraway started the trade of tea, but the habit of drinking it was not established in court circles until King Charles II married the Portuguese princess Catherine of Braganza in 1662. She had developed a taste for tea in her home country.

TEA STARTS TO CATCH ON

Over time, tea drinking spread to the rest of society, but the new commodity led to a great deal of confusion, as its proper way to prepare and serve it was not well known. There are accounts of it being spread on bread, boiled and served with salt and butter, taken with nutmeg, ginger and salt, and even smoked. Despite this, demand was such that tea auctions began in London in 1679. By 1689, tea consumption had become so widespread that the British government started to tax it. By 1700, consumption was at 20,000 pounds per year. Tea continued to be sold in 2,000 coffee houses in London alone, but when these started to decline in popularity tea spread even further, and was recognized as the national drink by around 1750. During this time the East India Company had the monopoly of tea imports into England; remarkably, they held it from 1721 until 1833.

The growth in tea's popularity continued to inflate the tax charged until in 1773 it equated to 64 percent of the value of the tea, pushing the price beyond the reach of ordinary people. The result was a sharp increase in smuggling. Even so, tea was still expensive, which led to the extensive adulteration of tea leaves to make it cheaper. The addition of leaves from other plants, liquorice or even sheep dung all made the tea go further. Thankfully, this practice became unnecessary when in 1784 Prime Minister William Pitt cut import duties to 12.5 percent, making smuggling unprofitable. Tea's popularity grew again, and by 1785 consumption was at 1 million pounds a year.

A RITUAL AND COMMODITY

It was around this time that the ritual of taking tea started to take shape. This is often credited, along with the concept of afternoon tea, to the Duchess of Bedford. Certainly she and her husband were early promoters of tea, buying large amounts of tea and teaware for drinking it, but it is quite likely that many others had started the habit of stopping for tea in the afternoon as well. They may not have done it with as much finesse or as many fine cakes, but the principle was the same. Our experience of serving tea in our teahouses shows that this mid-afternoon period is still a time when tea and a cake are craved.

London remained at the centre of international tea trade until the end of the 1900s, thanks to the regular London Tea Auction, which ran for over 300 years and ended on 29 June 1998. This, combined with Britain's history of taking tea to its colonies, has indelibly stamped it with the title of 'tea nation'. However, when looking at British tea drinking habits from the 1950s onwards we question whether this title is accurate from a quality perspective.

During the middle of the last century, teahouses became expensive to run, self-service became fashionable and American influence was strong. Into this culture was introduced the tea bag, invented in 1908 by a New York tea trader named Thomas Sullivan. He prepared tea samples in small silk bags for his customers, thinking they would tip the leaves out before use. In fact, they placed the bag straight into the water and returned to ask for more. Sullivan replaced the silk with gauze and the tea bag was born. Over time the material and design has been modified, but the biggest change came when in 1953 Joseph Tetley and Co started mass producing tea bags. It is widely recognized that the flavour experience from a tea bag cannot compete with that of loose leaf. The tea used in most tea bags is in the form of very small granules that give out flavour and colour quickly. This limits the flavour, however, and increases the chances of over-brewing and creating undesirable bitterness. Despite this, in 2007 tea bags accounted for 96 percent of the tea market; in 1960 it was just 3 percent.

Today, new shapes, materials and designs have improved the tea-bag offering and consumers are being more selective about what is inside them. Interest in, and sales of, loose-leaf tea are growing too, especially with increasing concerns over plastic pollution caused by some tea bags.

WHY DO WE ADD MILK AND SUGAR?

Milk has been added to tea for hundreds of years, both in the east and west. Initially, this would have been because tea was more about sustenance than flavour. Centuries ago in China, tea was sold in blocks that were crushed into powder and then cooked. Ingredients, such as milk, were added to provide a nourishing drink or soup. Over time, as tea manufacture methods and drinking habits changed, this habit died away in China. In Britain, though, this copied habit prevailed, and was probably necessary due to the bitterness of the low-grade tea we were drinking.

Sugar is also used to soften the bitter taste of tea brewed using tea bags. Extensive use of sugar in tea began in the 1720s and was promoted because British colonies produced sugar and needed a market. Tea was an ideal partner, and one that was already popular. The workers of the Caribbean sugar plantations feeding this habit were slaves controlled by the Empire, which left a far less sweet taste in the mouth.

Many people nowadays are still using sugar and milk to soften the harshness in their cup, and most commodity (mass-produced) black tea blends are now designed to take milk and sugar. Blends vary in quality, but the focus on the colour in the cup rather than the flavour means that in the cheapest, most basic blends there is no need for the quality to be high. In contrast, when presented with a quality orthodox black loose-leaf tea to taste without milk, our experience shows that almost every customer will agree it does not need milk or sugar. The larger unbroken leaves in these teas release their flavours gradually without over-brewing and releasing undesirably astringent flavours that force people towards the milk jug. While tea bags have made the enjoyment of tea more convenient, they have also distanced us from the original plant, the growing country and process of making and the flavours we should expect – demand, in fact – as part of our tea experience.

MODERN-DAY TEA IN THE WEST

Today, around 165 million cups of tea are consumed in the UK every day, mostly at home or at work or as part of a growing out-of-home market. Tea has been at the heart of British life for hundreds of years, but the tea bags we now enjoy are a far cry from the tea leaves enjoyed by ancient Chinese scholars and early British traders. At Comins we believe that by understanding how and by whom tea is grown and processed, we gain a greater respect for its preparation and how it can nurture us.

The exciting news is that there's a world of tea out there that many know little about. Awareness and interest in orthodox teas and the different ways to enjoy them are growing in Britain. Loose-leaf tea is increasingly available in supermarkets and there are more specialist merchants. Most tea drinkers, however, do not understand tea's heritage and the basics of its preparation, which varies between types and according to how it has been grown and processed. This can make loose-leaf tea seem cumbersome and complicated rather than beautiful and ritualistic. But historically, one of reasons tea was absorbed into so many different cultures was the opportunity it provides for social interaction; it is rich with rituals and ceremonies that could also play an important and enriching role in modern western life.

A NEW RELATIONSHIP

The days of sitting around the kitchen table sharing a good old British 'cuppa' are fading. Traditionally a storecupboard staple, sales of traditional tea bag teas are on the decline; young people are twice as likely to enjoy speciality black and green teas than the generation before them. This change in behaviour is being driven by a number of factors against the backdrop of our increasingly frenetic lives, most prominently health and wellbeing. Coffee has become the perfect fuel for a fast and 'successful' modern life. But many of us are starting to realize the value of slowing down, a change in mindset that is perhaps reflected in the growth of the out-of-home specialist tea market. Studies have shown that over two-thirds of tea-drinking Britons agree that tea is an important element of social occasions. The same studies also show that in order to build on this appetite for connection, the quality and experience of drinking tea outside the home needs to improve.

Changing consumer habits, trade patterns, unpredictable weather and competition for land are affecting the lives of millions of people in the black tea industry, but we hear little of this story. Our consumer decisions, and the industry's ability to adapt, will dictate its future, and that of our daily cup. Scattered among the large-scale tea production are a number of modern pioneers breathing fresh life, new ideas and greater value into the orthodox black tea industry. The personal stories of dedication from these tea growers deliver us a sweet, flavourful elixir to connect with and linger over.

Away from the black tea industry, there is a world of tea the west knows little about, but that has much to offer. Exploration of the rich cultural heritage of tea in China, Japan, Korea and Taiwan reveals the continued domination of small holders whose generations of expertise have preserved traditional tea growing and production alongside ceremonial tea drinking. Back where the story of tea began in Yunnan, China, there is a unique market in which teas are picked from ancient trees, aged and sold like fine wines. In these markets, tea is seen as an investment; the experience is central to enjoyment, provenance is key, craftsmanship is celebrated and quality closely scrutinized. Tea here is certainly not a quick fix.

This overview raises some questions we encourage you to consider while reading this book. Firstly, as consumers turn away from tea bags, can the black tea industry, on which millions rely, persuade a new generation that there is more to black tea than milk and two sugars? We believe that with increased transparency, more tea specialists and more spaces for people to appreciate the flavour of quality black tea, we certainly can. If so, there is hope for a new relationship with tea producers in which we are prepared to pay more for tea of higher quality, great flavour, more clarity and a fairer distribution of value through the supply chain.

Secondly, what can we learn from eastern tea cultures rich with tradition, ceremony and flavourful teas full of reputed health benefits? Can the extraordinarily diverse range of teas produced there and the slower way of life they encourage offer a tonic for our hectic modern society? We believe they can. At our teahouses we regularly observe how bringing the stories of tea growers, ancient tea culture and modern tea drinkers together can turn a 10-minute cup of tea into a transformative two-hour experience.

Let's dive in to the world of tea, starting with an overview of the magical plant itself, to learn more and hear from the people who live and work in tea today.

the tea plant

To fully understand how the *Camellia sinensis* plant developed from a medicinal herb to become the mostly widely consumed beverage, after water, around the world, we need to examine the plant itself in more depth. The qualities of tea as a drink can be broadly attributed to three main factors: the variety of tea plant, its growing conditions and how it is processed, and we will explore these here.

VARIETY AND CULTIVAR

Camellia refers to the genus of the plant and *sinensis* details the species. This can be further broken down into varieties or cultivars. Varieties are the differences among the same species that are found naturally in the world; if they are propagated (bred deliberately) by the grower, they become cultivated varieties, or cultivars. This happens when a grower notices desirable variations in a plant (such as yield, or frost, insect or disease resistance) and chooses to preserve them through cultivation. This is done by using cuttings rather than seeds from the plants. Cuttings create identical clones of the mother plant, whereas seedlings do not always pass on their parents' desirable characteristics. This is because tea is a cross-pollinated plant. Pollination is caused by small insects with a short flying range, and pollination from an undesirable plant can occur. However, there are ways to control this.

The two main varieties used in the making of tea are *Camellia sinensis* var. *sinensis* and *Camellia sinensis* var. *assamica*. *Sinensis* means 'from China', and *assamica* is derived from Assam, the northern India state, reflecting the origins of each variety. Cultivars are created from these varieties. Take, for example, our Taiwanese Shanlinxi oolong. This can be accurately described as *Camellia sinensis* var. *sinensis* Qing Xin. The genus is *Camellia*, the species is *sinensis*, the variety is *sinensis*, and the cultivar is Qing Xin.

Camellia sinensis var. *sinensis* tends to have relatively small, light and narrow leaves and is thought to be native to western Yunnan, China. It has a greater resistance to cold and drought than other varieties, so outside China it is grown widely in Taiwan and Japan. A notable area of use is Darjeeling, India. When left to grow it reaches a maximum height of 6 metres. The characteristics of its leaf mean that it is mainly used to produce green and white tea.

Camellia sinensis var. *assamica* has much larger leaves that tend to be thicker. This is the variety that was first recorded as growing in Assam by the Scotsman Robert Bruce. It can grow into a tree of around 30 metres tall and thrives in more moist, warmer and tropical regions like its native Assam, and also Sri Lanka and Africa. It is most suited to making black teas.

Choosing the right cultivar

The question of which variety and cultivar to use is an important one for any grower. The decision is often dictated by growing conditions and the plants already grown in the area, but with modern cultivation methods and an increased understanding of the science behind growing, choosing the right cultivar has become more complex and is a process of continuous learning.

Pallab Nath, tea maker at the Kanoka garden in Assam (see page 133), described the pros and cons of the various cultivars they have planted when we visited. 'The choice of cultivar is extremely important for us to make a viable business. TV17 makes up 75 percent of the garden. We also have TV24, TV25, S3 and TV1, and have planted a seed nursery for a TV1 and S3 cross. S3 is slow-growing but good quality, TV1 delivers medium growth but the quality is not so good, but together they will make good tea. TV24 and 25 grow fast and produce heavier leaves with early production, however the fibre content is high in the leaf, making them hard to roll. We find that TV17 is much lighter.'

At Nuxalbari Tea Estate in the Dooars-Terai region of India (see page 143), careful observation of both the plants and the changing environment have driven decisions about cultivars. When the owner, Sonia Jabbar, took over from her mother in 2011, yields were declining. One of the first things she did was to uproot the old, unproductive sections and plant new sections. She found that the yields of 'Old Chinery' or *sinensis* bushes planted in 1890 had more or less the same yields as 40-year-old clonal plants but the older sections were less prone to disease and drought. They now have a mix of old plants and new. As Sonia explained: 'Our best green teas come from older sections. We have new sections with quality cultivars like AV2, TV1, Teenali, S3A3, Panitola, RR144, and a Japanese cultivar called Yabukita. However, the bulk of our new planting uses bi-clonal seeds that are key to our climate change mitigation program. New saplings from cuttings are shallow rooted and require a lot of water. Scant winter rains mean that, by April, irrigating the land runs our well dry. Bi-clonal seed plants grow tap roots and can withstand pest and drought conditions better than cultivars. I choose TS463, TS491 and TS520.'

Most tea-growing countries have specialist centres that, among other things, develop and register new cultivars for their growers and advise on their use. Opinions on these centres vary; we have met growers who welcome new cultivars as well as those that don't appreciate government interference.

One example of a cultivar that has enjoyed widespread acceptance is Kenyan Purple Tea (technically, cultivar TRFK306). During a trip in 2017, Rob learnt that many growers had replanted fields with this cultivar, so called because it has purple leaves. Purple tea was actually first discovered in Yunnan, China and Assam, India. It has also been cultivated experimentally in Sri Lanka and Japan, where it is known as Sunrouge. The Kenya Agricultural Livestock and Research Organization (KALRO-Tea) spent 25 years developing drought-, disease- and frost-resistant varieties. According to Lilian C. Kerio, a biochemist Rob met there, the distinctive purple colour is down to the leaf pigment, anthocyanin.

This pigment makes purple tea extra special, because anthocyanins are flavonoids, a type of antioxidant. Antioxidants may delay or prevent some type of cell damage within the human body and are therefore thought very beneficial to health (see page 184). There is still much to prove, as much of the research has been done on commodity tea (usually destined for tea bags), rather than the orthodox type that we specialize in. As well as the antioxidant content, though, according to Lilian the caffeine content in purple tea is much less than green and black – in fact, lower than most decaffeinated teas. The plant is high yielding, highly resistant to pests, diseases, frost and drought, and is thought to be widely adaptable and suitable for all designated tea growing regions. Clearly, these are all very positive factors for the farmer. In addition to this is the financial benefit: a higher price is being paid for each crop. So purple tea offers a crop that requires no extra resources to cultivate and offers benefits on every level. It is still developing its market, but it's an intriguing product and has a great flavour and health benefits. It's a good example of how and why a new cultivar is developed.

GROWING CONDITIONS AND TERROIR

Growing conditions are the next important link in the creation of the character of a tea. Just as with plant variety, there are enormous differences to be found. If the same cultivar is planted in contrasting conditions it will produce very different results, increasing the potential diversity of our finished tea. A farmer needs to have a well-developed knowledge of his land to understand what will grow well, what creates an interesting taste or how to develop the profile their clients desire. For consumers the term *terroir*, which is more commonly associated with wine, is helpful for understanding the effects of growing conditions.

Terroir describes how natural elements, such as the climate, soil, latitude and altitude of a growing region, impact on the character of a tea. Together with other factors such as irrigation, topography, tea plant variety and age, the presence of insects and of course cultivation methods, they create the leaf's unique properties. We have spent many hours in tea gardens around the world observing, questioning, learning and tasting to understand how the environment the tea has been grown in, and the decisions made during cultivation, affect the final flavour in our cup. Commercially grown tea plants generally produce viable tea leaves for between 30–50 years before they need to be replaced, so once a tea plant has been selected, it is terroir that, along with processing, has the biggest impact on a tea's quality and flavour.

Terroir also decides where tea can be grown in the first place. On a visit to Kenya, Rob's guide, Nick, explained how tea estates had initially been located within the constraints of the so-called Brown Lines, areas suitable for tea growing delineated in 1966 by a Mr Brown. These were based on ideal annual rainfall (1,270–1,397 mm) and distribution, cloud cover and humidity, temperature, soil acidity (pH 4.5–5.8), soil depth and indicator plants. The demarcation is found in and around the highland areas on both sides of the Great Rift Valley and astride the Equator within altitudes of 1,500–2,700 metres above sea level. Tea could be grown above these lines, but not below. The lines have shifted slightly with climate change and increased knowledge, but their limits for good growth still hold fairly true to this day.

A TALE OF TERROIR: WUYI MOUNTAINS, CHINA

Wuyishan, or Wuyi Mountains, a national park and designated world heritage reserve in northwest Fujian, China, has a rocky terrain and a long, rich history of tea cultivation. It is impossible to discuss Wuyi without talking about terroir: this region is blessed with high cliffs, weathered rocks, highly permeable and mineral-rich soils absorbed by the tea plants that grow here. The Rock Teas that come from here are classified according to their origin within the area. The Zheng Yan (original rock) classification refers to tea grown in the original area within the boundaries of the nature reserve. Pesticides are not allowed here, soils are mineral rich and the surrounding mountains create rich, biodiverse microclimates. Imagine yourself walking through this stunning natural environment; in the course of a 4-hour walk, you will encounter different environments at every turn, from high cliffs to narrow gorges to mineral-rich streams. Now you have to imagine how the light will hit and infiltrate each gorge at different times, and how water may drip and drain down their sides bringing rich nutrients and minerals to the trees that cling to their sides and grow at their base. Tea bushes grow in all of these biodiverse microclimates, surrounded by abundant plant and insect life, and you can imagine how each microclimate creates teas with different characteristics and quality in the final cup.

Within the Zheng Yan area some places are more famous for quality teas, because the combination of environment, water, soil (highly permeable, mineral rich with the correct pH, and so on) is optimal, and the presence of high cliffs that absorb heat in the day and release it at night creates a more constant temperature for the tea plants. If you read more widely about the tea produced here, Yan Cha, you will see varieties named after particular pits and gullies, such as Hui Yuan Keng, Niu Lan Keng, Dao Shui Keng, Liu Xiang Jian and Wu Yuan Jian, although there are many other areas that offer high quality and command high prices.

The areas outside Zheng Yan, which also produce Yan Cha, are well defined: the Ban Yan (half-rock tea) area lies around the edges of the natural reserve; the Zhou Cha area is around the nearby Nine Bends River; and the Wai Shan area is outside the mountains beyond both Cha and Ban Yan. These areas deliver widely different experiences in the cup – the teas from these outer areas are said to lack the 'rock charm' found with Zheng Yan teas. The further you go from the Zheng Yan area, the less sought-after the teas become; the high cliffs that create unique microclimates in the Zheng Yan are not found in the other areas. According to our guide, the Ban Yan area is not as closely monitored or subject to the same regulations as the Zheng Yan area, and many of the farmers we spoke to mentioned the difference in soil quality here. By looking at an area such as Wuyi we can see clearly how the same variety of tea, processed in the same way, may vary in quality depending on exactly where it is grown. In order that you, the tea drinker, can know and appreciate what you are drinking, tea needs to be clearly labelled and its origins explained.

SOIL

Soil and subsoil quality are crucial to the growth of the tea plant. The soil needs to support the roots and contain the nutrients, minerals and moisture required for growth. The prime conditions are an acidic soil of pH 4.5–5.5, a level that aids the absorption of the nutrients. A loose soil, covered in a good layer of leaf and plant litter, which allows a supporting root depth of just under 2 metres and drains well but retains moisture well, is also preferable. These elements differ vastly between regions, but the great adaptability of the tea plant means that it can thrive in very different conditions.

On our tea trips, the climate, latitude and altitude of a tea farm are clear, but soil is more difficult to understand immediately. Over time, the way a tea farmer feels about their soil and how they answer our questions about it has become a critical element in our buying decisions. It's a topic we've become quite obsessed with and we have thought a lot about how to engage consumers about tea and soil, since the tea fields are a long way from our doorsteps.

To better understand this topic it makes sense to bring it a little closer to home. One summer day we visited one of our partners, Deans Court in Dorset, where we met horticulturalist Teresa Costa. Teresa explained: 'Soil is a very complex and delicate system composed of water, a mixture of mineral particles, organic matter, gases, chemicals and a variety of living organisms.'

A healthy, thriving soil system, she told us, hosts a blooming community of soil organisms, has a high content of organic matter and balanced levels of chemicals, gases and nutrients. 'A healthy soil will allow plants to defend themselves from most pests and diseases and adapt to the surrounding changing environment. Thus the quality of the soil is intimately entwined with the quality of any crop.' Soil's capacity to produce abundant, high-quality produce is directly connected to the life present in it. If we disrupt this delicate system it will have serious repercussions on crop production. All over the world we see the soil associated with conventionally farmed land getting poorer, compacted and eroded. We are losing top soil every year at a rate never seen before, which jeopardizes wildlife, ecosystems and climate. Soil erosion is the biggest threat to the sustainability of agriculture around the world. Teresa made the solution clear: 'We need to take care of biodiversity and soil, to regenerate our farming systems and decrease our dependence on chemicals. Healthy soils support healthy plants, and healthy plants support healthy human life.'

FUKUOKA PREFECTURE: EATING SOIL WITH MR TOSHIRO

Rob: I will never forget my visit to Mr Toshiro's field in Fukuoka Prefecture, Kyushu Island, Japan. It was the first time I deliberately ate soil, which I was surprised to find I enjoyed. The field, an old mandarin orange field, was one of four making up Mr Toshiro's two-hectare farm, which is accessed by a road he built himself. Mr Toshiro started out as a fruit and vegetable farmer, but after a bout of ill health, and discovering the health-giving qualities of green tea, he set out to produce the healthiest tea he could, with no chemicals to be added. For him, this started with one thing: the soil. He explained: 'Soil feels elastic and smells sweet if it is supported by many kinds of microbes living together in optimal balance. Microbes increase minerals and other useful ingredients in soil, strengthen its resistance against pests and keep it in good health. Delicious vegetables grow in good soil. That is eventually good for your health too. This is why we dwell on soil cultivation.'

He described how 1 gram of soil contains 1 billion bacteria, and that the fertilizer he makes is for these bacteria, not the tea plants. Feeding the bacteria maintains the life cycle and balance of the soil, resulting in better tea plants. It was at this point that Mr Toshiro gestured me to to push my hand into the soil, which I did until I was past his elbow; the light, aerated soil offered little resistance. On removing my arm, I was instructed to taste the soil, which I did without hesitation. How could something that was growing such healthy plants be anything but good for me? It tasted sweet, soft and gritty. If it hadn't been gritty I would probably have gone back for another handful.

We walked around his picturesque field and saw where the wild boar had dug up a section and the deer had nibbled the leaves. 'This is nature,' said Mr Toshiro. He pointed out an area of wilderness at the very top of his field and told me that it was to prevent land slides: it absorbs the water and the trees binds the soil together. He showed me a sign indicating that the garden is Organic JAS (Japanese Agricultural Standards) certified, and tells me that his was the first tea garden in Japan to achieve this.

Mr Toshiro's approach has not been the easiest path. When he started, he told me, the surrounding farmers didn't understand about pesticides and organic cultivation, so the slopes were starting to get into bad condition. 'Growing organically is a life choice, so we spent five years building strongly, and over the course of five more years I finally made a tea.' He found, however, that the tea he was producing was not selling at all, so he worked patiently and continued to wait. But the number of customers increased little by little, they started visiting and a regular customer base grew. 'It took around 12 years to be successful,' he explained. 'I am sincerely thankful that so many customers are pleased with my tea and will continue to make safe and delicious tea.' We returned to his tasting room and sampled some of the most flavoursome Japanese teas I've ever tasted. And it all made perfect sense, because Mr Toshiro has control over every stage of production, undertaking the growing and picking himself and closely overseeing the processing at a nearby factory. He sells the tea himself online and wholesale to hotels and restaurants. One of his clients is the top hotel in nearby

Fukuoka, which is so determined to get the best tea that it sends 50 of its staff out to the field to help out each year, at a time when extra hands are very much needed. This is how valued his approach is.

CLIMATE

To thrive, a tea plant needs at least 5 hours of sun per day at an average temperature of around 18–20°C. Also preferable is plenty of rain (150–250 centimetres per year), a relative humidity of 70–90 percent and a dry season that is no longer than three months. This means that tropical or subtropical regions are best.

Variations in climate that are not too extreme develop flavour. The stresses caused by a drop or rise in temperature, or a period without rain, stimulate a reaction from the plant in order to retain chlorophyll, changing the flavour produced. We all know that the world climate is changing and tea-growing areas are located in high-risk regions for climate change. Planting varieties that are more resistant to these changes, as they do at Nuxalbari (see page 143), is one way that growers can prepare for the future.

LATITUDE

The latitude of a tea plantation controls the amount of sunlight a plant receives every day. In equatorial areas such as Kenya, sunlight is a constant 12 hours a day, meaning tea can be produced more or less all year long. As the distance from the equator increases, the amount and strength of daily sunlight starts to vary more, according to the time of year. At around 16° north or south during the winter months, the amount of daily sunlight drops to a critical level and this forces the leaves to become dormant for a while. This dormancy means that picking has to stop, but also has a favourable impact on the plants. When growth restarts the flavours are more concentrated due to the build-up of nutrients to create growth. The first spring harvests, such as the first flush in India and Nepal, the Shincha harvest in Japan, the pre-Qing Ming teas in China and the Ujeon harvest in South Korea, are often the most sought-after and expensive.

ALTITUDE

Many of the plantations producing the best tea are found at high altitude. The conditions here often slow the growth of tea plants, leading to a higher concentration of the aromatic oils and beneficial, flavoursome nutrients found in the leaves. At heights above 1,000 metres, days may start with mist followed by changing sunshine levels due to varying cloud cover and cool air, and then cold nights. This creates stress for the plant which is beneficial to the flavour. High-altitude teas such as those from Darjeeling

(600–2,000 metres) and High Mountain, Taiwan (1,000–2,300 metres), are considered among the best in the world for flavour complexity.

An excellent example of the how altitude affects flavour is Sri Lanka. The black Ceylon tea grown here is divided into categories: low-grown (up to 600 metres), mid grown (600–1,200 metres) and high grown (1,200–1,800 metres). The lowest grown plants are better used for very strong, smaller particle commodity teas often used for tea bags. Mid-grown plants provide excellent strength for strong loose leaf, while the high-grown tea plants provide leaves ideal for the most delicate aromatic black teas.

ORGANIC FARMING

Organic tea is produced by estates that sustain and promote soil fertility and ecosystems without using synthetic fertilizers, pesticides, antibiotics, growth hormones or genetically modified organisms. This requires an understanding of local biodiversity, ecological processes and natural cycles.

From the beginning we have been convinced that this natural approach to growing is the key to great-tasting tea. It is central to our sourcing and is not always shown by organic certification, which makes it even more important for us to visit in person and build relationships with tea farmers. There are various reasons why certification may not be beneficial in the local market, including cost and the lengthy conversion process, which may not be something a farmer wants to go through. This means that farmers may grow in a completely organic way, but if certification does not add monetary value or any other benefit it simply becomes an expensive paper-pushing exercise. For example, in smallholder systems such as Taiwan, where one farmer owns multiple pieces of land in different locations, certification would need to be undertaken on each individual plot, making it a very time-consuming and expensive process given the yield.

Organic tea estates vary enormously. Some are predominantly driven to organic standards to gain certification in response to market demand. Then there are those who grow organically because they care deeply about their land and the soil but may not be certified for reasons highlighted above. In many cases these are small-scale farms, aiming to increase soil fertility and therefore quality and yield of the tea over time. Mr Toshiro from Fukuoka in Japan, who we met earlier, is a great example of this.

'Producing organic tea is not a straightforward or easy path,' explained Mr Shen, who works in organic farming in Zhejiang, China. 'It's a challenge to manage the whole environment around the tea, and involves much higher costs and lower production rates, not to mention the education needed for everyone involved in the process, from farmers to workers to sellers, buyers and consumers, to appreciate the benefits of organic production.'

BIODYNAMIC FARMING

We have experienced the effects of biodynamic farming at several of the estates we work with, including Makaibari Tea Estate in Darjeeling, Idulgashinna in Sri Lanka and the Jamguri garden in Assam. The term 'biodynamic' comes from the Greek words *bios* (life) and *dynamos* (energy). Biodynamic principles and practices are based on the work of the Austrian philosopher, social activist and scientist Dr Rudolf Steiner. His methods are explained succinctly by the The Biodynamic Association: 'Biodynamic farmers strive to create a diversified, balanced farm ecosystem that generates health and fertility as much as possible from within the farm itself. Preparations made from fermented manure, minerals and herbs are used to help restore and harmonize the vital life forces of the farm and to enhance the nutrition, quality and flavour of the food being raised. Biodynamic practitioners also recognize and strive to work in cooperation with the subtle influences of the wider cosmos on soil, plant and animal health.'

Part of Steiner's methodology involves the creation and use of compost, together with special preparations to act as catalysts in the composting process. These harmonizing and vitalizing preparations are made and applied according to strict instructions. Steiner designed nine homeopathic preparations for his biodynamic fertilizer, including ingredients such as quartz crystal mixed with rainwater, yarrow blossoms, chamomile blossoms, stinging nettle, oak bark, dandelion flowers, valerian flowers, and horsetail plants. Cows are also central to the biodynamic system. Straw-free cow manure is filled into cow horns, buried in the ground for six months according to the biodynamic calendar (for example, buried in October, dug up in March) to make biodynamic preparations. These are then sprayed on freshly cultivated fields. The horn silica preparation, which is made in a similar way, is used to invigorate the plants in the harvesting phase.

The biodynamic calendar is based on the lunar calendar and other 'cosmic rhythms', taking into account the interaction of the planets and constellations with the earth. This includes the change from day to night, the seasons of the year as well as more subtle effects such as ground water rising closer to the surface when there is a full moon. These all affect the tea leaf in some way, and a greater understanding can help farmers know when to plant, fertilize, prune or harvest. One clear example is that there is more sap in the tea leaves when they are plucked at full moon, which benefits the flavour.

The brilliance of biodynamic methods is that they massively improve the health of the soil and overall crop by increasing the soil's micronutrients and trace minerals, while also reversing any damage to the soil from chemicals. This is vital with tea, as it is mostly grown as a monoculture in which large areas are planted with only tea bushes. They are picked all year, or in flushes throughout the year, meaning that nutrients are constantly being taken from the plant and therefore the soil. Crop rotation is not possible, so there is no variation in what is put in and taken out. Often this means that chemical fertilizers are applied, which are designed to raise crop yield rather than support the soil. Over time, soil quality declines and the need for fertilizers

increases. Biodynamic farming can prevent this downward spiral. Better soil means better tea, and our customers continually tell us that they can taste the difference in the cup.

THE IMPACT OF TEA ON NATURAL LANDSCAPES

There is no doubt that cultivation of tea has an impact on the land on which it is grown. People involved in the cultivation of tea all over the world have difficult and complex decisions to make every day, and these decisions will have long-term implications on the planet and on the tea we enjoy. Let's visit Taiwan and India to look at different scenarios in the tea world that illustrate the delicate balance that exists between tea and nature, and the work being done to try and find a sustainable balance.

RESPECTING THE MOUNTAINS: TAIWANESE HIGH MOUNTAIN TEA

Taiwanese high mountain tea (Gao Shan Cha) is grown at altitudes higher than 1,000 metres. This covers a great swathe of around 5,000 hectares in the central area of Taiwan, where there are several mountain ranges of over 2,000 metres at their highest. The teas from this area have complex aromatic properties and are therefore world renowned for their exceptional taste. Gao Shan Cha is, however, a relatively modern product. The first crops were sown in 1969 and the area's popularity took off in the 1980s after the world trade embargo against Communist China was lifted. But behind these highly desirable teas is a more complex story.

First is the issue of land ownership. Much of the land at these high altitudes was given to local government when the Japanese left, which then gave or rented small plots to veterans as retirement gifts. Much of it was designated National Forest Land at the time. Records were not always kept, which created confusion over ownership, and land was given on the proviso that the occupants developed a property and created 'forests'. At this time of economic growth this was interpreted as tea fields or fruit trees, but more recently the definition has changed to refer only to tall trees with long roots to secure the soil. This, of course, does not include tea bushes.

Secondly, there are the pressures of being a high mountain grower. It's quite a gamble to be a high mountain grower in Taiwan – high investments are required to get started, and then you produce smaller crops at a higher cost due to the terrain. The rewards are high if the tea is right, but with high stakes it is perhaps understandable that farmers are often cautious to do anything that would jeopardize the yield of their gardens.

Finally comes the subject of soil. Farming at high altitude is often considered to have a negative impact on soil due to the removal of trees and vegetation. This destroys vital ecosystems and weakens the land in mountainous areas where rainfall is heavier and winds stronger. The removed vegetation would have had deep roots that hold the soil together, which is very important in areas where, due to altitude and land steepness, soils can be thinner. All this results in erosion that has serious knock-on effects further down the mountains, especially in an country like Taiwan, known for its typhoons. In addition, it is often deemed necessary to use pesticides and fertilizers due to poorer soil quality, which can contaminate water sources and the land and reduce the soil's ability to hold moisture. Of course, some farmers are taking a different approach and integrating themselves with nature. They argue that their approach has little or no negative impact. Tea bushes planted without chemical pesticides or fertilizers develop deeper root structures in order to survive, thus negating that part of the argument.

All these factors came together in recent events in 2016. The highest garden in Taiwan was formerly said to be Da Yu Ling on the Tai Eight Road at around 2,600 metres on Li Mountain. The farm was dismantled by the Taiwanese government in November 2016, along with many others at this altitude. This all happened as part of a government policy to reduce high mountain agriculture as a whole. It was not just aimed at tea, but tea made up a large proportion of it. The programme to reforest many high-elevation tea farms and restore them to their pre-agricultural state started in late 2016. Many farms that had not complied with the new rules are reported to have been returned to nature.

This process is generally being seen as an attempt to protect the delicate high mountain environments, but to explore it fully from all sides requires an extensive study, which is beyond the scope of this book. It raises important concerns here and for tea cultivation in general, though, and reminds us of the importance of tea and nature existing in harmony. It also brings us back to how we should, as consumers, set out to educate ourselves about where and how our tea is grown, with the aim of understanding its impact to both the land and the people involved.

RESPECTING THE FOREST: SONIA JABBAR, NUXALBARI ESTATE
Sonia Jabbar at Nuxalbari estate in the Dooars has made several changes to her larger family garden in recent years (see page 143). Underpinning these is a deep passion and respect for the land.

Sonia: 'Soil is fascinating. We know this as children, but lose our love for it as we grow older. Healthy soil is very important. When we pluck leaves every week, the tea bushes are continually producing leaves in the top hamper (layer). This requires tremendous energy, and if you have hundreds of thousands of bushes extracting from the soil and all you are doing is adding chemical fertilizer, sooner or later your soil will become exhausted.

'In 2010 I converted 12 acres of our estate to organic after taking a course in Bhutan. Everyone, including scientists at the Tocklai Tea Research Association (TRA), said it couldn't be done because of the lush, tropical conditions, which are a veritable breeding ground for pests. The organic sections got very weak with repeated pest attacks. I lost crop. I got terribly disheartened. But then I stuck to good agricultural practices. I fixed the drainage, so that water did not stagnate. I regularly sickled the area, but I also observed very

TEA SEASONS AROUND THE WORLD

■ = NO GROWTH

	Jan	Feb	Mar	Apr	May	Jun	Jul	Aug	Sept	Oct	Nov	Dec
India (north)			1st flush		2nd flush		Monsoon flush		Autumnal flush		Occasional winter flush	
Nepal												
Assam		Frost teas (Nilgiri)		1st flush	Spring pick		2nd flush			Other grades		Some Picking
India (south)		South coast best picking	Central best picking					Ongoing picking				Frost teas (Nilgiri)
Sri Lanka	Dimbula best picking			Spring pick			UVA best picking		Ongoing picking			
Africa	Peak Growth		Ongoing picking		Peak Growth		Ongoing picking			Peak growth	Ongoing picking	Peak growth
China			Season begins	QING MING (before April 6th) YU QIAN (before April 20th)	GU YU (before May 5th) LI XIA (before May 21st)		Ongoing picking					
Taiwan			Early spring semi-rolled Oolong	LOW grown Oolongs (mostly Jades) and Baozhon	HIGH grown Oolongs (mostly Jades) and Bai Hao	Bai Hao	Ongoing picking			Gau Shan high mountain and mid-level semi-balled		
Japan				ICHIBANCHA including Shincha (April first harvest)			NIBANCHA (2nd tea)	SANBANCHA (3rd tea)	YONBANCHA (4th tea)			
South Korea				UEON (before the rain — picked before April 20)	SEJAK (small sparrow — picked before May 6th) JUNGJAK (medium sparrow — picked before May 21st)		DAEJAK (large sparrow)					

carefully. The British industrialized the agriculture around tea. So where in China you had small plots of tea grown between rice and other crops, here we grow acres and acres of tea, unrelieved by any other plant species except for shade trees. I observed the weeds and wondered why we were obsessed with keeping these sections "clean" and weed free. Apart from three or four species, most weeds have shallow roots and were hardly competing with the mature tea, whose roots went down to 3 feet. The weeds actually disrupted the monoculture of tea and encouraged biodiversity.

'Our planting scheme also meant uprooting many old trees, and though we planted many shade trees in our new sections these were not successful. Every time we uproot a tree we perform a ritual, acknowledging with gratitude what the tree has done for us. The *pandit* (priest) chants mantras in Sanskrit and we honour one tree that represents all the trees we are going to uproot. We offer it incense and flowers and pour milk on its roots. Then I make cuts and ask forgiveness of the trees and ask the spirits of the land, the protectors to bless and protect the new trees and teas we will be planting so that all sentient beings can benefit from them. It's very difficult even then. In order to address this, I took on Mr Mahato, a retired forest department tree planter. Together we have planted 25,000 trees of 11 different species this year. I want to do as many for the next five years, so we are talking about over 125,000 trees. The forests and the ponds I have planned are to create localized micro-climates and increased biodiversity. This will attract more birds and wildlife. And you can't have too much of that.'

PLUCKING

Plucking is the harvesting of the leaves from tea bushes by hand. For the production of quality tea there are clear guidelines as to which leaves should be plucked. This is generally called the 'plucking standard', and could stipulate just the leaf bud, the bud and a single leaf or two leaves and a bud (for white, green, yellow, black and *puer* teas), or up to three to five leaves and occasionally a bud (for oolongs). Today the best-known configuration is two leaves and a bud, mostly due to images of teas like Darjeeling. This sort of specification is known to have existed in China back in the Tang dynasty (618–907 AD) for top-quality green tea.

Knowledge of the plucking standard allows an evaluation to be made of a tea's quality, and therefore its cost. If an oolong is found to be made up of two leaves and a bud, or a black tea from five leaves, these may well be inferior teas. If they are consistent in their standard, their value will increase. However, particularly in the case of oolongs, plucking standards are harder to generalize, and can vary considerably in different areas and according to factors such as weather fluctuations and how quickly the leaves have grown.

Historically, there was more emphasis on specifying plucking standards in former colonial areas such as India, Sri Lanka and Kenya, where many of the systems that were introduced by the British still exist today, and black tea is the main type produced. In our experience of travelling around the tea fields, plucking standards for white, green and black teas from all countries are readily given, whereas for oolong growers it varies.

One very specific plucking standard is for a tea we will explore later, Taiwanese Oriental Beauty (see page 120). This special tea relies on a small insect to create its unique flavour. The plucking standard specifies the number of leaves to be picked as well as the fact that only the bitten leaves should be plucked. The rest are left, as they would adversely affect quality.

In most countries, plucking usually starts after the dormant period of winter. However in Africa, Sri Lanka and southern Indian areas, where it does not get cold enough for this to happen, plucking can occur all year. During the growth period throughout the year there are peaks associated with when rainfall and sunshine is optimal. These seasons have various names, depending on the country. The diagram opposite shows a generalized view of these seasons, since of course the harvest time can vary according to the climate.

For countries that do have a dormant period, the best tea often comes after this in spring. In China, this is called 'pre-Qing Ming', in India 'first flush', in Japan 'shincha' and 'ujeon' in South Korea. The quality results from a build-up of nutrients in the plant during the cold period in preparation for new growth. When the heat and longer days return, growth begins, releasing this store of nutrients and meaning that the leaf has a higher concentration of beneficial flavour compounds. Initially, the leaves are small and the bud is fat, but as growth continues the leaf gets larger and the bud skinnier, eventually opening out to become a leaf. This effectively dilutes the flavour compounds, reducing the quality of the flavour, so early plucking is key.

When the next peak in growth of the year occurs there is not the same store of nutrients, which changes the flavour possibilities in those teas. This is not necessarily a reduction in quality. The best Assam, for example, is deemed to be from the second flush, or the second peak in growth in the year when the leaves are thicker and have developed their characteristic malty flavour.

When plucking season arrives, farmers have to keep a keen eye on their fields to assess how growth is developing, monitoring leaf size and bud development. Buds can form and mature into leaves in a matter of days. Young leaves and buds have a greater concentration of aromatic compounds that is important for great tea, but their size yields a smaller harvest than it would if they were older and therefore larger and less aromatic. In all cases, the farmer's aim is to maximize both flavour quality and yield from their field for the tea they are making.

Teas such as first-flush Darjeeling require an early pluck before the leaf bud opens, but for some a later pick is needed. For oolongs, for example, more mature leaves are required for their fuller flavour profiles and added toughness in processing. The beautiful Chinese green tea Taiping Houkui needs long leaves, often in excess of 7 centimetres. To use shorter leaves would not create the same appearance, so farmers have to wait for the leaves to reach maturity before plucking, around 20 days after the bud appears.

Plucking can be delayed or brought forward due to yearly variations, with the farmers reacting accordingly. However, in some areas there are auspicious dates that control picking. In China, the Qingming festival ('Tomb-Sweeping

Day') occurs in spring. During its duration it is meant to rain. This means that the pre-Qing Ming tea is more desirable than that picked after the ceremony because the rain speeds up growth and reduces the tenderness of the leaf. In recent years, pre-rain teas have often been classified pre-Qing Ming teas even if the rain did not come during the festival.

Hand plucking and machine picking

When examining tea it is important to distinguish between leaf plucked by hand and machine-picked leaf. Most of the tea we buy is plucked by hand, but some of our Japanese tea is machine picked. How does this affect the finished tea?

With hand-picked tea the pull and snap of the 'pluck' is important, as this breaks the cell walls in the stem and creates a chemical reaction that benefits the flavour. This does not happen to the same extent with mechanical cutting. Good hand plucking requires great skill and speed. A good picker, depending on the chosen standard, can harvest anywhere up to 24 kilograms of fresh leaf in an 8-hour working day. This equates to tens of thousands of plucks in a day, which is only achievable with immense speed, focus and accuracy. In many areas, pickers are paid by what they pluck to the specified plucking standard. If picked leaf does not comply it may be discarded.

This is not the case in machine picking. The machines vary from hand-held trimmers with a large bag to suck up the leaf, to wheeled vehicles that straddle the bushes and cut to a desired height, shooting the leaves into a container. Machines are currently not selective in what they pick or how they cut, meaning that leaves may not be whole and particle size may be inconsistent. In many countries this method is used for lower-grade tea where leaf size does not matter but cost does. In Japan they are used because of high labour costs. In fact, in all stages of tea production machines have had to be developed to reduce the amount of labour required. The machines we saw on our recent trip to Japan are certainly not low-tech and achieve very good results. Laser-guided systems allow the cutting to be made at pretty much the same place for each crop. New growth comes from the previously trimmed level, which over time can be more accurately cut to be more consistent.

On our tea trips we are often told that labour costs are rising, and that the younger generation don't want to become tea pickers. This means that mechanized harvesting methods will have to be used more in the future. Judging by other machines developed to aid processing, we suspect that much better results can be achieved in this area, but there's a long way to go to achieve the quality of hand-plucked tea.

PROCESSING

There are generally considered to be six types of tea that can be processed from the *Camellia sinensis* plant: white, yellow, green, black, oolong (also called *wulong*) and dark, which we will learn more about later. Developments in processing have spread gradually over large areas, over hundreds of years,

passed on by farmers who all had their own techniques. As we've seen, terroir and plant variety create wide variations in the finished teas. This generates enormous scope for complexity in how tea is defined, described and evaluated.

Today, as tea processing knowledge and cultivars have been shared and spread worldwide, any country that grows tea (all 62 of them) can in theory produce any type of tea, although the end result will depend on many factors. Today you can buy white tea from Malawi or India, green tea from Sri Lanka or southern India and even oolong from New Zealand, all of which are areas not traditionally associated with those teas. Although many are exceptional, at Comins we believe that as a starting point it is vital to understand the key countries and areas of countries synonymous with the development of certain types of tea, so that core characteristics can be understood. Taking this approach, you would look to Taiwan for its reputation with oolong; India, Sri Lanka and all African countries for black tea and China for all types, but especially white, green, yellow and dark teas.

This all means that the options for the consumer are vast, which is hugely exciting, if not a little daunting. In the west, we tend to want to categorize tea neatly into boxes, but the huge variation means this is simply not possible. What is possible, however, is to gain a base level of understanding from which we, as tea drinkers, can build and start exploring the many wonderful complexities of tea.

History of processing

Tea processing methods have changed a lot since Shennong's 'discovery' centuries ago. From a bitter herb it has transformed into a fresh and fragrant beverage valued around the world. In China, as early as the Zhou dynasty (1046–256 BC), drinkers had started to experiment with how to turn this plant with its health qualities into something that actually tasted good.

Initially, this developed from eating the raw leaves to eating the boiled leaves and then drinking the liquid. During the Zhou dynasty, distinct progress was made with the start of sun-drying the leaf for storage. In the Tang dynasty (618–907 AD) the steaming of tea began: the leaf was mashed up and formed into cakes before being baked to dry. It was in the Song dynasty (960–1279) that this steamed tea was processed in a loose leaf form, and whisked powdered tea became popular. This died out in China soon after, but was taken up and refined in Japan. The final method, pan-fired tea or roasted tea, was first written about in the Tang dynasty, but it was during the Ming dynasty (1368–1644) that this technique was truly refined.

Until the Tang dynasty, the tea produced was all green in style. Around this time it was realized that varying the time left between plucking the leaves and heating them by the sun, steam or pan affected the flavour. Experimentation with this, along with the style of heating and variations in the moisture content of the leaf, was what created the different types of tea we know today: white, yellow, green, black, oolong and dark. They are still evolving to this day and provide an almost endless variety of taste and aroma as producers strive to unlock the full potential of this incredible plant.

Location of processing

The work of tea producers takes place in a wide variety of tea-farming systems and factories around the world, from the single farmer with half a hectare to the largest commercial estates. Some small producers farm their land and sell their leaf on to a local factory, while others grow, process and sell from their own garden. Then there are medium, family-owned, self-contained estates such as Nuxalbari, and finally larger estates that have their own land and factory, but also buy in tea from the surrounding small holders. Some add value to tea bought from other producers, such as Yuwen in Taiwan. At Comins we buy directly from small and medium-sized tea farms that we have built a relationship with, and who produce high-quality orthodox teas.

The process itself

Let's imagine that the tea leaves have been plucked and are entering the factory, which could be a small hut or an enormous building, and look at the many processes the fresh leaf goes through in order to become a particular type of tea. This can only ever be a very generalized look, since tea production is complex. Not every tea undergoes every stage, and for some teas the order changes or certain processes are repeated. The only way to know exactly how the tea in your cup has been processed is to visit and speak to the farmer directly, or deal with a tea merchant who works directly with them.

1. WITHERING

Withering reduces the moisture content in the plucked leaf, thereby developing flavour and aroma compounds. It can be done in many ways. In a Taiwanese tea factory we visited, we helped lay fresh leaf out in large, shallow bamboo baskets outside. Left in direct sunlight, the large, stiff, shiny leaves soon lost moisture and became wilted, limp and matt.

Other methods see the leaf being spread outside on smooth, clean floors, or placed inside in long mesh-bottomed troughs where air is blown under the leaf. No matter what method is used, the leaves must be treated delicately and spread out uniformly to make sure withering is consistent. The process decreases moisture content by about one third to a half and can take anywhere between 1 and 24 hours, depending on the tea.

2. OXIDATION

Oxidation occurs naturally and starts the moment a tea leaf is plucked. A series of chemical reactions begin that, over time, darken the colour of the leaf from green to brown to black. These create the aroma and flavour compounds in the leaf, which benefit the character of the finished tea. It is vital to control oxidation once it has begun. For some teas (such as green) it is stopped straight away, but for others (oolong, black) it is controlled for a period of time, then stopped. Note that oxidation is not the same as fermentation. It used to be assumed that the browning of the leaf was due to fermentation, but modern science has shown that this is not the case.

Control of oxidation occurs through the choice of temperature, humidity and the way the leaf is handled. Around 25–30°C is considered an optimal temperature, with high humidity to keep the leaf fresh. The leaf is then either bruised, rolled or chopped to expose the insides of the leaf cells to oxygen in the air. It is done deliberately by the tea grower in a variety of ways, depending on the type of tea. No matter the method, great care has to be taken: if the leaves are accidentally damaged, oxidation will start and the finished tea may be unevenly processed.

For delicate teas, the leaves are often placed on large bamboo trays, then gently turned regularly over many hours, which lightly bruises the leaf. A slightly more intense method involves the use of large cylinders to tumble the leaves, resulting in a slow and gentle oxidation. Another is rolling, which delivers faster oxidation and is usually done using a rolling table or by hand on a bamboo mat. The most aggressive method is to macerate or shed the leaves, chopping them into smaller particles which exposes much more of the insides of the leaves to oxygen. Maceration is typically used in mass-production methods to create CTC (cut-tear-curl) tea or broken-leaf teas used in commodity teas and tea bags. For rolling and maceration, the leaf is then spread out in piles to allow the chemical reactions to take place up to the desired stage. The smell of the leaf during any of these processes is intoxicating, and always stirs a feeling of excitement.

3. HEATING/FIXING

Once oxidation reaches the desired level, the process is halted by heating or fixing. The heat applied changes the enzymes responsible for oxidation and stops them working by denaturing them. This process is called *sha qing*, a Chinese term that translates as 'kill-green'. A high heat of at least 65°C is applied to the leaf for a short period, adjusted depending on how much leaf is being processed, along with its thickness and size.

All the original Chinese methods of heating leaf over time are still in use today. Sun-drying came first, but was then developed into the use of ovens to bake the leaf. After that, large metal wok-type pans heated by fire were used. Finally, steaming began, by which steam was forced through tea leaves. All these methods create their own characters.

Oxidation is never completely stopped, just slowed to a very slow speed. Drying slows it further, but it will always continue while oxygen is present. Over time it will reduce the flavour quality of a tea, and therefore impacts on tea storage. Tea should be stored in air-tight containers. We receive many of our teas from our farmers in vacuum-packed bags to completely eradicate the presence of oxygen. This results in fresher tea.

4. ROLLING

For certain teas, rolling is used to release aromatic oils as well as form the shape of the finished tea. These shapes can be needle, twisted or curly, flat or balled. Rolling can be done using mesmerizing, mechanized rolling tables, or by hand.

5. DRYING, FIRING AND BAKING

To stabilize the leaves, their water content should be around 3–5 percent. Removing this residual moisture stabilizes oxidation, if it has occurred, and also the aromatic oils released during rolling. It is done in a variety of ways, including passing the leaves through an 'oven' on a conveyor belt or placing them in a heated rotating cylinder. The blast of hot air combined with the sweet aroma of hot tea leaves is a very special experience. Firing is usually the final procedure to ensure the moisture content is as low as possible. In some teas, however, this can be happen weeks after the processing took place, and in the case of 'baked' oolong teas, such as Taiwanese Dong Ding, its purpose is to have a dramatic effect on the flavour.

BAKING TEA AT COMINS

The more we travel and experience tea processing, the greater our desire has become to get a little more involved. For us, the answer has been baking our own oolong teas here in the UK. On his first trip to Taiwan, Rob fell in love with oolong, particularly the baking of the finished tea. This originated as an extension of a method used by farmers and producers to dry out a finished tea; over time the changes in flavours were noticed and baking became a process in its own right.

Traditionally, oolongs are baked by tea masters using bamboo tea bakers over charcoal fires. It takes many years to gain the experience and expertise needed to maintain the temperature of the fire for the long periods of time needed to bake consistently. Each tea has a unique baking programme, which consists of a series of temperature adjustments to bake the tea from the inside out; some can take upwards of 18 hours. Adjustments are made at each step after tasting, always with a specific taste goal.

On seeing this process Rob immediately wanted to try it himself. The modern-day equivalent of the bamboo bakers is the electric baking unit. These large oven-type devices control temperature for you, meaning that the expertise lies in sourcing the correct teas, developing baking programmes and learning to adjust them according to the tea's variations – still not at all simple, but achievable at least! Most importantly, this process is not time critical, and it does not have to be done with the other processing. Given the right equipment and knowledge, it was a process we could undertake at our tea base in Dorset, England.

For the equipment, it was merely a case of finding someone who would ship an electric baking unit to the UK. The knowledge was a little trickier. Luckily, during my trips in Taiwan I'd had the privilege to talk to farmers, experts and scientists. Dotted around the country are five Tea Research and Extension Stations (TRES). These put the science into every part of the tea process, including baking. With effort and a little pestering I was able to gain a greater understanding of the baking process and the types of baking programmes. So one of our dreams has come true, and we are now working on our own range of British-baked oolong teas.

6. SORTING AND SIFTING

Sorting and sifting are the last processes before packing. These terms are used in different ways around the world but refer to the separating of the finished tea into grades, the naming of which varies between countries, according to the size of the leaf and the removal of anything undesirable such as dust, twigs, fibre or other residue. However, some teas may be broken leaves or stems. These processes are done by hand, using sieves of varying sizes, or by machine.

TEA PROCESSING IN ACTION: A MEDIUM FACTORY IN KHONGEA, INDIA

Michelle: I visited the Khongea Estate in Assam in 2017, and saw first hand the complexities of the factory and the many factors a tea maker must consider.

Looking over the large withering beds, the factory manager Diwakar explained that once withered to about 70 percent of its original weight, the leaves would be removed. Those destined for CTC (cut-tear-curl) tea pass into the machinery that will eventually deliver the fine particles used in tea bags. The orthodox leaves pass to the rolling tables, where cell breakage takes place, stimulating enzymes from the nucleus and cytoplasm to react in the presence of oxygen. The sap concentrated in the leaf from the withering process is released, coating the tips and giving them a golden hue. Diwakar told me that you should be able to see the sheen on the top of a good-quality leaf – a sign of good processing – something I certainly observed later at the tasting table.

While all this is happening, the leaves are shaped. The style is determined by the pressure, which is controlled by the large wheel to the side of the roller. Every 10 minutes, pressure is applied and then released, getting heavier with each cycle. The amount of pressure will be determined by the leaf type. The leaves then pass to the oxidizing room where they are left on the floor for 2 hours. This is an extremely important part of the process, in which the chemical changes in the leaf develop and several external factors must be considered, including the weather and the conditions in the room.

The final stages of the process involve removing dust, getting rid of stalks, fibre and flaky leaf and then, of course, tasting. Diwakar and his team taste the teas twice a day in a space at the heart of the factory, something I was allowed to partake in on my visit; it was quite an experience! Early samples are tasted to see if any improvements can be made, and packing samples are tasted to ensure quality before the teas are packed to ship. Diwakar explained how they always taste the CTC first, followed by the orthodox, looking at the appearance, infusion and the cup. On the dry leaf they are looking for tips, leaf glossiness and size and the presence of stalks. For the CTC teas they are looking for fullness (how thick the tea is in the mouth), briskness and the astringent qualities in the tea. The brightness in the cup is confirmed when you add milk, so we tasted all teas both with and without.

Handmade or machine-made?

We hope that the importance of the human touch in making tea is by now very clear. Processing methods, whether by hand or machine, must be understood in the context of why and how they occur. Many machines have improved on the traditional method, as they can be more consistent in their movement and accuracy. Some can speed a process up, not always to the benefit of quality, but definitely to a financial benefit. Some processes are wholly dependent on the human touch, or create such distinctive variations that the customer demands it is done that way.

In Taiwan we have watched oolongs being baked over charcoal, while in the room next door the same thing is being done using modern electric ovens. Both can have great results, but they will have different characters. Appreciating the dedication required to bake an oolong for 12 hours or more over a charcoal fire enhances the enjoyment of a tea; keeping a fire at a constant temperature for hours on end while assessing the tea is an incredible skill.

In Japan we have seen heavily mechanized production, with only a small number of producers making 'traditional' handmade tea. However, despite the reduced emphasis on hand skills it is still the tea master who must decide how to utilize the machines, using their senses to draw the best out of the leaf and producing some incredible high-quality teas. The results of all these approaches depend on the skill of the processor, so each tea should be judged on its individual merit.

Purely handmade teas are sometimes referred to as 'artisan' teas. Here, one country's producers in particular are considered the most skilled with their hands: China. This is particularly noticeable in green tea, where appearance is an important factor in purchasing, and beautifully shaped and finished leaves are expected. Travelling around China, we have seen the craftsmanship in rural villages, where knowledge and skills are passed through the generations and highly skilled tea makers carefully watch over the tea-making process, using all their senses to determine when the process is complete. Often the window for producing these teas is very short, while demand and prices high. So how do you know if you are getting the real deal when you purchase famous teas that are traditionally handmade and, indeed, does it matter?

We believe it does. Earlier we put forward a case for demanding more transparency in the black tea industry so that gardens could be recognized and rewarded for the efforts they make to produce high-quality, great-tasting, sustainable teas. We also believe that details about the production methods should be made available to consumers, which would enable them to understand the craftsmanship behind particular teas, the impact this has on price and availability and the difference it makes to the flavour profile. Access to this information would allow the drinker to assess the tea properly and set the expectations of what characteristics it should have. Drinkers would understand what they are buying and appreciate the skills and dedication needed to produce what they have in front of them, and in some cases would promote and maintain age-old traditional skills. Knowledge of where a unique and desirable flavour comes from creates demand, which may help retain the rich heritage that began with the early pioneers in China all those years ago.

THE HUMAN TOUCH: TAIPING HOUKUI

Taiping Houkui or 'monkey king tea' is one of the top ten teas in China and is produced in the Houkeng area of Taiping county at the base of the Huangshan mountains in Anhui province. We have long been fascinated by this tea and the manufacturing process that results in the long pressed leaves that often measure up to 6 centimetres and deliver a beautifully delicate fragrance and smooth, mellow flavour. Our trip to Houkeng village in spring 2017 to meet Mr Xiang and his family and learn more about Taiping Houkui revealed the dedication needed to produce some of the most famous Chinese teas. What we saw perfectly demonstrates the great impact that the human touch has on a tea. The delicacy that can be achieved, the feeling of the leaf and the decades of experience can never be matched by a machine.

Michelle: As we trekked through the area on a gloriously bright day we saw boats zipping across and along the water. The three main villages for Taiping Houkui production are Hou Keng, Hou Gang and Yan Jia. We chose to base our visit around Houkeng. The teas from the three main villages fetch the highest prices, with variations according to altitude and location. The most sought-after teas come from areas that have the optimal combination of favourable ecosystem, sun and shade. At this time of year practically every house in Houkeng village becomes a small processing unit with families sitting together in their homes producing teas to take to market. Beyond them in the hillsides, areas of land are marked out for each family and each family often has multiple pieces of land dotted around the hillside.

After a stop at a *Nong Jia Le* or 'happy country home' (a small restaurant in the home of a local that has popped up to cater for travellers passing through the area) for a delicious lunch of tomato and egg soup and fresh village vegetables and rice, we were ready to head up into the hills for what we thought would be a short walk. Three hours later we had trekked through bamboo forests and tea fields to see the location of Mr Xiang and his father's land, which is around 700 metres above sea level. Location is everything, and higher tea surrounded by the more diverse ecosystems in their own micro-climate protected by the surrounding forest is considered to be the best. Teas growing on the edges of the bamboo forests are also said to have more aroma.

Visiting these beautiful places and drinking hand-crafted teas little known in the west can lead us to romanticize life in tea. The reality is that the picking, processing and selling windows for teas such as Taiping Houkui are very short, the work hard and the returns unpredictable. This means that tea pickers and producers must find other work: Mr Xiang is no exception, and when the season has finished he returns to his work as a painter-decorator for the rest of the year. We found it humbling that the family comes together every year to undertake this intensive process – I'm grateful they do.

We stopped just off the road to visit the first of Mr Xiang's small factory units. This is one of the things we love about sourcing tea in China: one minute you're driving along a pretty nondescript road, then you pull up and look around – still no sign of anything – then you approach a building that looks a little bit like a garage, walk in and it is full of people making tea, often from one extended family.

The first process we saw in the small processing unit was the production of partially handmade Houkui, easily identified from its wider finished leaf and light green appearance. When the fresh leaf arrives it is placed in a small heated metal tray to prevent oxidation. The tray's shape and movement allows the leaves to only briefly touch the hot metal, while also shaping them. The leaf stays at 150°C for 8 minutes and is then placed on a table to be sorted. When the leaf for this tea is plucked it contains one bud and three or four leaves; these are now re-plucked to leave one bud and two leaves. The excess stalk is also removed before the re-plucked leaf is straightened ready for pressing.

The ladies lay the leaves out flat on a plate that will go into automated pressing machine to remove the moisture. This 'plate' is essentially a wooden frame fitted with a tight wire mesh to make a screen. Another wooden frame is placed on top, pressing the leaves flat. This screen is then placed on a rolling or pressing table. This part of the process was mechanized: the person in charge simply had to press a pedal for the roller to automatically slam down onto the leaves. The result of this is more pressure as compared with a fully handmade tea. Once the pressing is finished, the complete frame is placed into the dryer at around 100°C, starting at the bottom and moving up and away from the heat filament before being pressed again and then removed from the tray.

The next thing we saw was the fully handmade process. The room was full of chatter and laughter as the extended family sat around hand making the tea. On the left the father of the family, who was in charge of the whole process, put the fresh leaf straight into a more traditional machine, a sort of hot wok with a paddle, for the 'kill-green' stage (see page 37). Once the leaf came out and cooled the ladies swiftly and skilfully hand-shaped the leaves and lined them up on the trays ready to go onto the press.

Once full, the tray was placed onto the press table, covered with brown cloths and pressed with a roller using human rather than machine pressure The tray was then moved across to the dryer for the same rotation as before. After the first rotation with the press and dryer the leaf has 70 percent of the moisture removed. When it goes through again the tea maker is trying to get it closer to 100 percent. Once finished the tea is taken to the market for sale.

In the cup, the fully handmade process maintains more original nutrients in the leaf, resulting in a more flavourful tea, something we definitely experienced in our tasting. We also had the chance to enjoy a delicious but extremely expensive handmade tea made in a garden high up on the slopes dotted with pine trees and bordered by bamboo forests. Mr Xiang explained how it takes the villagers one or two hours just to walk up to these higher areas before they even get to start picking. This combination of terroir and hand-processing took us to a whole new level once again.

The best way to enjoy Taiping Houkui is in a tall glass where you can admire the leaves as they 'dance' when you add the water. This is not just tea – it's a performance, an experience. As we enjoyed this ritual with Mr Xiang at the end of our visit we expressed our gratitude for his time. We have been to many tea gardens all over the world, but this family, with their camaraderie and dedication to continuing these tea-making traditions, has stayed with us.

the main types *of* tea

Here we outline a brief description of each of the main six types of tea, along with an overview of their processing method. This can only ever be a generalization, as every producer has their own method, depending on the leaf they use, the machines or equipment they own, workers they have and outcome they desire.

At the back (see pages 200–203) you'll find a directory of the individual types of tea made by the people we meet throughout the book.

WHITE TEA

White tea is a lightly oxidized tea produced from the withering and eventual drying of fresh leaves. This leads to delicate and subtle floral, sweet flavours. After careful plucking, the leaves or leaf buds are withered. This is a complex process involving both outdoor and indoor withering and careful control of the temperature, moisture level and ventilation. The leaves are spread on bamboo racks and are left whole and unbruised to wither for up to three days. Fans can be used to speed up the process. The timing depends on weather conditions, and is critical. During this time oxidation occurs (about 8–15 percent), but is not promoted. Too much oxidation will lead to a brown colour, too much handling causes the leaves to turn red or even black and if they are not dehydrated correctly the finished tea will taste stale or oxidized. After withering, the leaves are sorted according to the desired grade. Broken leaves are often removed.

White tea is thought to have originated in the Ming dynasty (1368–1644) in Fuding County, Fujian province, and quickly spread to nearby Zhenghe County. Initially it would have been just the downy leaf buds in the form of Bai Hao Yin Zhen, meaning 'white hair silver needle' after the silvery white hairs on the buds. From this developed the other types we know today of Bai Mu Dan, Gong Mei and Shou Mei. These, unlike the Yin Zhen, are made from a mixture of buds and leaves. Bai Mu Dan consists of two leaves and a bud, whereas the latter two have fewer buds with broken and older leaves.

One tea worth a special mention is Fuding white tea, and the increasing interest in aged white tea. On Michelle's first trip to Fuding in spring 2015 she first noticed the compressed white tea filling the shelves of the shops in the local tea market. Discussion turned to aged white tea, something completely new to us at the time. One of the merchants explained that aged white tea is not necessarily meant to be consumed fresh, like green tea, but rather aged, much like *puer*. In order to aid storage the tea is compacted and pressed into cakes, and grows more complex in flavour over time. The tea is often aged for around a year before the leaves are steamed to make them pliable enough to be pressed into cakes. The exact conditions for the storage of these cakes are important in order to aid fermentation and deliver the tea's complexities.

YELLOW TEA

Yellow teas have been through a unique process called *men huang*, which means 'heaping' or 'sealing yellow', and causes slight oxidation. Yellow teas have a distinct matureness with a sweet flavour. Processing varies dramatically between yellow teas, but the most common process is as follows. After plucking the leaves are withered lightly, then heated to prevent oxidation. The *men huang* stage comes next, when the leaves are lightly steamed and then wrapped in damp cloths and left for 5–10 hours. The wrapping creates gentle heat, causing light oxidation and developing aromas. The leaves are then dried for a short time at a high temperature to bring moisture content to around 5 percent. It is then sorted.

To show the variations possible, we look to Mr Zhang, a tea farmer located in Zhao Qing Wan village in Anhui province. Mr Zhang and his team make their Huo Shan Huang Ya yellow tea at their 1.7-acre tea garden. After plucking the tea enters the primary factory. Once inside it then goes through a process called *tan fang* for half a day: the spreading of freshly picked tea leaves on the ground or the dustpan, to let them take the withering and fermentation. This illustrates another difficulty in defining a tea: how to translate a very specific process into our vocabulary, in which we do not have the words required. 'The leaf is spread out and left in the style of withering, but for a longer period of time – not long enough for the chemical reactions that cause oxidation to start, but long enough to allow fermentation to occur. After this the leaf goes through the "kill-green" stage (see page 37) in an electric heater. Then it is back to *tan fang* for around 2 hours, before the leaf is shaped for 30 minutes on a machine and returned to *tan fang* for 3 hours. The next part takes place in the refining factory, where the leaf is baked for 1 hour before a much longer tan fang period of around 24 hours. The leaf is then rebaked for 30 minutes before a further *tan fang* time of 12 hours, then a final 15-minute bake to stabilize the tea completely.'

Yellow tea believed to have originated in the Tang dynasty (618–907) in China, which is still the only producer. It is a relatively uncommon type of tea, as green tea is easier to make and in more demand. It can be classified into the three grades of bud, small leaf and large leaf. The best-known types are Meng Ding Huang Ya, Huo Shan Huang Ya and Mo Gan Huang Ya, after the areas in which they are found.

GREEN TEA

Green tea is made when oxidation is stopped in the leaf very soon after plucking. This leads to a range of flavours from grassy and vegetal to toasty, sweet and umami. After plucking, the leaf is lightly withered, heated to prevent oxidation, rolled and then dried. Tea leaves slowly begin to oxidize as soon as they are plucked, so the 'kill-green' heating stage must occur within a couple of hours in order for minimal oxidation to occur. Therefore, unlike other teas, oxidation is not promoted in any way.

When introducing it to the customers in our tea houses, we describe the process with the example of an apple cut in half. If it is left it will go brown through the same process of oxidation that happens in a tea leaf. However, if the apple is sliced and baked in a tart, it will not go brown, as the oxidation was prevented. The heating can be done in a variety of ways, depending on traditions or what kind of tea is required. Pan-firing is the preferred method in China: the leaves are pressed or tossed in a dry, hot wok for 1–2 minutes. Examples of teas processed this way are Gunpowder and Long Jing ('Dragon Well'). Oven baking and sun-drying can also be used. Heating by steaming is more prevalent in Japan, where the leaves move through a rolling, steaming tunnel for anything from 20 seconds to over 1 minute. *Sencha*, *gyokuro* and *matcha* are examples of teas produced this way.

After heating, the leaves are rolled to release their aromatic oils, and also to begin to shape them as desired. Hand- or machine-rolling can form the leaves into needle-like shapes (as for Japanese *sencha*), balls (as for Gunpowder) or twisted (as for *bi luo chun*). Finally, the leaves are placed in a drying room or an oven to reduce their moisture content to around 3–6 percent. This stops any further chemical reaction and stabilizes the tea.

Two teas worth a special mention in this category are *genmaicha* and *houjicha* (*hōji-cha*), which both always gain attention in our teahouses, initially due to their appearance, but also in their flavour profile. *Genmaicha* is a mixture of green tea and roasted rice, although it is considered a type of Japanese tea rather than a blend. *Genmai* means 'brown rice'. There are many tales about its origin, but the most likely reason is that adding rice (which was in plentiful supply) made the tea go further, making it a cheaper drink. It is thought to have started in the early twentieth century, either by a canny tea seller or by families who didn't have the funds to produce pure tea. Despite the translation, it is white rice that is used. It is soaked, steamed, dried, roasted and cooled before being blended with the tea. This blend has the beautiful astringency of Japanese green tea along with the nutty, savoury flavour of roasted rice.

Houjicha is a roasted Japanese green tea invented in the 1920s. It is commonly made using *bancha* tea, which is roasted at about 200°C and then cooled quickly. This changes the leaf colour from green to a reddish brown and gives it an incredible roasted fragrance. The roasting process reduces the caffeine content to often negligible amounts as well as reducing catechins present. Catechins are naturally occurring chemicals found in many plants, including tea, that have powerful antioxidant effects. This makes it a mild, easy-to-drink tea which, because of its low caffeine content, is popular with children and the elderly.

OOLONG TEA

Oolong (*wulong*) teas are those that are partially oxidized. Oxidation in oolong tea can range from around 15–80 percent, depending on the production method. This helps explain the variations in flavours, which range from light, fruity and sweet to woody, strong and roasty.

After plucking, the one bud and 3–5 leaves are briefly withered before oxidation is promoted. This can be through light turning for lightly oxidized oolongs, to tumbling and rolling to highly oxidized ones. This process is repeated with pauses in between to allow the oxidation to occur. When the right level is achieved, heating occurs, either by the use of hot pans or rotating cylinders. Then the leaves are rolled and shaped. Depending on the variety, they can either be the long and curly 'ribbon' style (such as Wuyi Rock teas), semi-rounded or semi-balled (such as Taiwanese Dong Ding) or fully rounded (such as Anxi Tie Guan Yin). For the latter two, the shape is achieved by placing the leaves in a cloth that is tied into a tight ball. This is then rolled in one direction, usually by machine, twisting the leaves inside. The cloth is untied and the leaves tumbled to separate them, before being retied in the cloth and rolled again. This process is repeated many times until the ball shape is achieved. The tea is then dried or fired at a high temperature for a short time to stabilize it. Some oolongs are then baked, often many months after the initial process. This uses heat for an extended period of time and produces a distinctive style of 'baked' oolongs, something we at Comins tea are starting to produce our own version of (see page 38).

Oolong teas can be traced back to the end of the Ming and the beginning of the Qing dynasty around 1644, and to the Wuyi Mountains of Fujian province. The term 'oolong' is derived from *wulong*, which means 'Black Dragon Tea', because of the dark, twisted leaves of some varieties.

One oolong tea worth a special mention due to its unusual processing is GABA tea. This relatively new type of tea was first produced in 1987 in Japan by Dr Tsushida Tojiro while researching food preservation. GABA stands for gamma-aminobutyric acid, an amino acid that occurs naturally in the human body (as well as the tea plant) and is the main inhibitory neurotransmitter found in the nervous system.

The tea involves a unique processing method instead of the traditional 'kill-green' stage, which increases the levels of GABA in the tea – hence the name. Processing starts as normal and requires high-grade leaves, as these have the higher amount of natural glutamic acid needed for conversion into GABA. The tea plants are often shaded for about 10 days prior to being picked, as this has been found to increase levels of glutamic acid even further. The fresh leaf is placed in a stainless steel container and one of two methods is used. The first involves pumping in nitrogen to remove the oxygen and then exposing the tea to this anaerobic, nitrogen-rich atmosphere and a temperature of over 40°C for around 8 hours. The second involves sucking the air out to create a vacuum and leaving the leaves in this state for around 24 hours. These methods both result in the conversion of the glutamic acid in the leaves into GABA. This process can be performed in all types of tea, leading to GABA green, GABA oolong, and so on.

The benefits of the increased level of GABA are said to be mostly health related. In addition to all the healthy benefits of tea drinking, it's claimed by many that increased GABA decreases stress and anxiety, helps to improve memory and alertness, aids in weight loss and acts as a natural sleep aid.

With all health claims we like to err on the cautious side, and some experts disagree with these claims. Doctors at New York University's Langone Medical Center have observed that 'when GABA is taken orally, GABA levels in the brain do not increase, presumably because the substance itself cannot pass the blood-brain barrier and enter the central nervous system'.

What cannot be argued is that GABA tea has a distinctly different aroma and flavour profile from other teas made in the same style. The process raises the level of catechins, called gallate esters, in the leaves, which are responsible for the aroma of many fruits, spices and herbs. These unique GABA aromas and flavours are what we think will help continue its success in the long term, rather than the reputed health benefits.

A Taiwanese producer, Mr Yu, makes the GABA tea we sell at Comins. At the time of writing we are selling a Mi Xian GABA oolong, which is a truly unique tea. Mi Xian means 'bug bitten', which refers to the same green leafhopper bug that is critical in the creation of Oriental Beauty (see page 120). Mr Yu is based in Nantou, an area not known for these insects. However, due to global warming farmers at higher altitudes are discovering that these insects are visiting them. Mr Yu discovered the insect-bitten leaves and decided to make GABA from them, therefore creating a truly unique tea that may never be recreated again.

BLACK TEA

Black tea is a fully oxidized tea, giving strong, robust, invigorating, sometimes malty teas with higher but varying levels of bitterness. Once the leaves have been plucked they are withered for anything from 3–20 hours, before being rolled to promote oxidation. They are left until the right level of oxidation is reached, which can take up to 5 hours for Indian-style black teas and up to 12 for Chinese. When this is achieved the leaves are dried to stop the oxidation and stabilize the leaf. The finished leaf is then sorted.

Oxidation levels vary between black teas and is actually never 100 percent; the producer chooses the optimal time to stop oxidation to maximize the flavour characteristics, rather than waiting until no further oxidation is possible. Full oxidation would lose most of these desirable flavours.

In our teahouses our customers are generally surprised by the range in colours found in the leaf of the black teas. These go from the browny greens of a Darjeeling up to the jet-black colour of a Ceylon. The lighter colours are generally found in higher-grown teas and indicate lighter oxidation and a longer withering period, chosen by the producer to bring out the more delicate flavours of the tea produced by growing at altitude.

Black tea is the youngest type of tea, originating from the sixteenth century. The first was Zhengshan Xiaozhong from Fujian, China, which is more commonly referred to as lapsang souchong in the west. Qimen in Anhui province followed on, creating another tea famous to this day in the form of Qimen Hong Cha. *Hong cha* means 'red tea'; in China the colour of the liquor is referred to, rather than the leaf. It wasn't until the nineteenth century that

black tea started to be grown in India, Sri Lanka and Japan.

There are several teas worthy of special mention due to their processing. The first is Sandakphu Ruby Vine. Processing begins in the normal style, but after the firing the tea is placed in a jute bag and left outside, exposed to the Nepalese weather, for a year before finally being fired. This creates slight fermentation, leading to the tea being described as 'semi-ripe'. The flavour is somewhere in between a black tea and a ripe dark tea.

The second is lapsang souchong. The lapsang profiled in this book is made by Mr Wu in a small factory in Tongmu. Lapsang souchong originated in the Ming dynasty in the pine forests of Wu Yi Shan, northern Fujian province. To be authentic it must be made from gardens located around Tong Mu Guan village, within a protected nature reserve. The most favoured of many origin stories suggests that it was first produced by accident, when an army passed through the village and the freshly picked leaves were trampled. After the army departed, the farmer realized that the leaf could no longer make his usual green tea, as the trampling and passing of time had caused the leaf to turn much darker. In an effort to make something of the leaf he dried the leaf by burning local pine wood below the tea. The resulting 'black' tea took on the smoked flavour and lapsang souchong was born. Today, the leaf is lightly smoked during the withering stage. Pine wood is used to create smoke, which is drawn into a smoking shed where the fresh leaf is laid out. The smokiness should be gentle and balanced with a slightly sweet floral and fruity flavour. Some modern lapsang is smoked after oxidation, which leads to a much stronger, smokier flavour.

DARK TEA

Dark teas (*hei cha*) are fermented. They vary enormously in their processing and therefore flavour, but many are earthy, rich, smooth and complex. Broadly speaking, they involve withering, heating, rolling, heaping and fermentation. Heaping is a process called *wo dui*, when the leaves are piled up and covered in an environment where the temperature and humidity can be controlled at a high level from 1 hour to 20 days. This is necessary because the rolled leaves are quite tough and coarse and take time to ferment.

Dark tea is one of the earliest styles of tea and can be traced back to the Tang dynasty (618–907). There are many types, but the most famous include Liu Bao from Guangxi, dark tea of Hunan, Old Green tea of Hubei, Frontier tea of Sichuan and *puer* of Yunnan. This last category is the most famous and we will focus on this specifically. In some areas, though, *puer* is considered a different category altogether.

There are two types of *puer*: *sheng cha* (raw tea) and *shu cha* (ripe tea). The initial process for both is much the same as that of green tea and creates a type of tea called *mao cha*. For true *puer*, large leaves (with var. *assamica* lineage) grown in Yunnan province must be used. Once the leaves are plucked they are withered briefly and heated by pan firing to 'kill-green'. During this process the temperature is key, as the function of some enzymes must be maintained to ensure long-term ageing; too high and this will not occur. The leaves are then rolled by machine for the best results before being sun-dried for a couple of hours and then sorted. At this stage they can be sold as a loose-leaf tea or used to create *puer* or other fermented teas.

Sheng cha is the original style, whose character is created by natural fermentation over time. For *sheng cha*, the *mao cha* is first sorted into grades from the smallest leaf to the biggest leaf. Several different types are often blended together to create the perfect mix. They do not go through the *wo dui* process. The leaves are lightly steamed to soften them and tied up in a cloth bag before being pressed under a stone or mechanical press. The cakes, or *bings*, are cooled in the bag, removed and air dried, then finally individually wrapped in paper. Storage now becomes very important. They are packaged in sevens and wrapped in bamboo bark. At this point they the appearance is of compressed green tea. The *bings* must be aged for many years, ideally in the dark, at a consistent temperature around 25°C and 65 percent humidity. These conditions begin fermentation, when the microscopic organisms found naturally on the leaf break down the carbohydrates and amino acids within. It also causes some oxidation to take place, which combined with the fermentation gives *puer* tea its distinctive flavour. It normally takes 5–8 years before the colour is acceptable and another 2–3 before they are ripe enough. Therefore, most *sheng cha* are not considered aged until they are at least 10 years old, and are not mature until 30 years have passed.

The more modern style of *puer* is *shu cha*, which was introduced in the 1970s to meet a developing demand for *puer*, but is now considered a category of tea by itself. *Shu cha* is made by speeding up fermentation to reproduce the flavours and characteristics of *sheng cha* in a much shorter period. To achieve this it goes through *wo dui* (heaping) for 1½–2 months, greatly speeding up the fermentation before the final compression. The leaves are then sorted before being compressed. *Shu cha* is also available in loose form.

Each type appeals to different drinkers. *Shu cha* offers an increased smoothness and lower bitterness straight away, whereas *sheng cha* takes many years to develop a similar character. Both types can be aged further, but *sheng cha* will develop a greater complexity over time. *Shu cha* will not develop dramatically over time. Another major difference is cost: aged *sheng cha bings* sometimes sell for thousands of pounds. In fact, there are *puer* collectors who have long wish-lists of named vintages from various established makers, which are rare and highly regarded.

PUER: A JOURNEY TO YUNNAN

Puer is named after the prefecture town of Puer in Yunnan, a province in southwest China that borders Laos, Vietnam and Myanmar. Local growers developed the technique of compressing the tea, in part so that they could more easily transport it by horse. On one of our tea trips we visited Mengku, an area that lies to the north of Shuangjiang Autonomous County in Yunnan. **Michelle:** The 12-hour journey was particularly epic, but anyone who has been to Yunnan looking for tea will tell the same story; to find the best tea always means taking a bit of pain! We were there to meet Mr Ni and his wife

Mrs Zhao, who rent land from around 20 farmers in this area, which is well known for high-quality tea. They explained how in the area there are more than 400 ancient tea trees over 500 years old, more than 5,000 trees that are 200–400 years old and more than 1,000 trees over 100 years old. This is a beautiful and special place. This area and the other famous *puer*-growing areas in the region have gained a cult following for the teas they produce, which has completely transformed these once-poor farming communities. This has been driven by the economic boom and the emergence of a new middle class keen to connect with their cultural heritage. *Puer* is also associated with a number of health benefits, including weight loss and stress reduction, which further increases its appeal. The hype around *puer*, its rise in popularity and the status of certain tea-producing areas means you need to know what you are buying, which is exactly why we were here.

Arriving at the small factory, we saw that it was a simple operation but it had all the key ingredients to make *puer* tea: raised flat bamboo mattresses in the outside area while undercover a set of around six fixed woks, a rolling machine and some flat bamboo baskets. Mrs Zhao explained that withering time depends on temperature, with decisions on when it is ready to move to the next step guided by sight and touch: looking at the leaf texture, smelling the leaf and assessing the water content.

The team had been eagerly awaiting our arrival and ushered us into the undercover area towards the woks. This is where they do the *sha qing* or the 'kill-green' stage. It is all done by hand, and therefore by touch. We put on some white gloves and they fired up the woks with wood from the local area. Over the next 20–30 minutes I had a go at heating the leaves. There is a real skill in constantly turning them to ensure an even heat, a process designed to destroy the enzymes responsible for oxidation and reduce water content. Throughout, the temperature is controlled by putting in and taking out firewood. Temperature is very important in *puer* production because you want to preserve the most temperature-resistant enzymes, which are critical to the long-term ageing of the tea. Stored properly, it will take years for these remaining enzymes to oxidize the leaves fully.

Mrs Zhao next showed us how she hand-rolled the teas; there was also a small rolling machine in the courtyard that they use for this part of the process. Hand-rolling the leaves is extremely physical and as a result Mrs Zhao explained that it can be hard to maintain a constant pressure, so the machine can actually be more effective. Rolling has a variety of purposes: shaping is one, but more important is how the approach affects the final profile in the cup. At Mr Ni's the rolling is applied after the 'kill-green' stage to encourage the release of the polyphenols responsible for aroma and taste. Mrs Zhao explained how a hard roll could result in a tea with more bitterness in the early infusions, versus the more delicate roll that produces a *puer*, which will release its component over many infusions. These characteristics will only be revealed when the infusion is finally prepared and enjoyed. After this extremely active demonstration we were taken to see the tea drying on mats and baskets. The leaves stay here for about 2–3 hours; the exact decision on when to bag up the teas is again driven by human touch and experience.

teahouses

Historically, teahouses have always been places to meet up and connect, whether purely socially, for debate and discussion, or for business. Over the centuries, the formal rituals and ceremonies that have developed around tea have needed physical spaces to facilitate them. The earliest evidence of teahouses as spaces to gather is in Song dynasty China (960–1279), when they became very popular. This was taken much further by the Japanese, who created beautiful teahouses surrounded by elaborate gardens where the focus was on spiritual rather than social connection.

In Britain, coffee arrived before tea, and the first coffee shops opened in the early 1650s; tea was served from around 1660. These establishments were frequented by male customers who used them instead of inns to socialize or do business. There were different houses for each profession – politicians, businessmen or clergy, for example. Intellectual conversation was a common feature, so much so that in 1674 the King's Chief minister considered them a 'hotbed of political intrigue' where opponents would hand out provocative material. He tried to close them down, but the resentment and commercial impact were so high he decided not to.

We at Comins are increasingly interested in tea as a connector of people. The best spaces to enjoy tea are rarely in prime commercial locations. Our fondest teahouse memories are of our hosts, the beauty of the experience offered and the spaces that allowed us to escape and purely appreciate tea. Here are two of our favourites:

RAISED TEA HOUSE, MANG JING, YUNNAN

Michelle: It was late evening. As we walked back through Mang Jing village after dinner there was no-one to be seen, and total silence apart from the odd car and the local wildlife. Down a side track we spotted a lit building against the night sky that looked a little like a bar in an Alpine-style lodge. We decided to investigate. Upstairs on a covered deck was a long table framed by shelves stacked with tea. The table was crowded and the air electric with conversation. Suddenly self-conscious, we were grateful to be ushered in to take a seat. It turned out that this was a guest house and this tea area, open to all, hosted a random gathering of visitors to the region, most of them strangers travelling here for the tea season. No one was in charge; the role of tea maker passed seamlessly between people and we were warmly welcomed with bowls of incredible *puer*. Although I could not follow the conversation, through translation it transpired that it was full of politics, arts, travel and, of course, tea. I fell in love with that moment.

SOREKARA TEA HOUSE, KYOTO, JAPAN

Rob: Hidden down a long alleyway, behind a traditional Japanese fenced entrance, Sorekara teahouse was a magical discovery that took me a long time to find. The owner was delighted to see me. I think he could scarcely believe I had found him. He and his one customer had just slightly more English than I had Japanese. I took a suggestion from the customer and hoped for the best. An incredible marshmallow-like *wagashi* sweet was followed by the most perfect bowl of *matcha* I have ever tasted.

We stumbled through a conversation, but the connection had been made. The experience mattered to all of us, despite not having the language to say so. Tea has been doing this for centuries and that day reminded me how special it can be.

THE COMINS EXPERIENCE

Our teahouse began when we bought a house with a shop attached in the small market town of Sturminster Newton in Dorset. Away from the pressures of modern life, the space has attracted tea lovers from all over the world. As we write, you can also find us in Bath – a larger city but the same concept. You won't find us on the high street, and we are more certain than ever that we don't belong there. Great tea is all about discovery and connection, both at origin and at the point of enjoyment. Comins is all about creating time and space for tea, a modern British tea experience worth venturing off the beaten track for. We believe that great tea should be an everyday pleasure, not just for special occasions or for rarefied, elite enjoyment. We aim to present our teas with the same openness, grace and enthusiasm with which they have been shared with us.

The design of our teahouses is minimal; here, the tea takes centre stage. During our first trading weeks in Bath we were told that our interior was too stark, but a few years on, people really enjoy the quiet, contemplative space.

Our menu is global, inspired by our heritage and travels. We bake all our own cakes and serve dumplings, hoppers (a type of rice flour pancake) and Indian and Japanese ice creams. Our teas are pure and unblended, served in a way that celebrates their origin while offering glimpses of our British heritage. We always check if our customers are familiar with pure, unblended teas or are newcomers. It is also interesting to know why they have come to take tea with us; do they want to be warmed, nourished, refreshed or just comforted with something familiar, and based on their answer we can then make a recommendation.

Over time, a tea community has developed, keen to experience, learn about and enjoy fine tea. Lone tea drinkers feel comfortable to enjoy peace and tranquility, a moment to themselves. At their most sociable, tea drinkers offer tastes of their chosen tea to complete strangers, conversations start, topics are debated, connections made.

the international tea industry

The way that the international tea industry functions varies from country to country. For example, in China, tea is often taken to the local market and sold direct to consumers or to buyers who will pass it into a more complex chain. In India, much of growers' tea will pass to auction and be sold to brokers and then to big companies, often to be blended. In our case, we meet individual tea farmers or medium-sized enterprises with the intention of making a personal connection and building a long-term relationship.

THE DIRECT-TRADE MODEL

This is our model at Comins. Our year generally follows a pattern; we travel, on and off, from February until October. In some countries we simply do all this ourselves, and in others we work with a very small number of trusted partners who help us with logistics, travel with us, translate and ultimately purchase teas, since many farmers don't have the facilities to accept payments from us. We do it like this in order to bring tea drinker and tea producer closer together thus developing a transparent supply chain where everyone benefits. Every sourcing trip takes at least six months to plan and at least 50 percent of the trip is unknown. Quite simply, you never know what you're going to find and the story that follows is a perfect illustration of this.

Michelle: We visited Huangshan, Anhui provice, in April 2017, home to four of the top ten Chinese teas. We were looking for ecologically produced Huangshan Mao Feng green tea. The landscape was breathtaking, with forest-covered mountains divided by rivers and interrupted by villages. Coming to a bend in the road, we pulled over. What stood before us was pretty surprising: a large building that we were told was the largest green tea manufacturing plant in Asia. With four processing lines, this factory processed most of the leaf from the surrounding villages. Despite the huge volumes being processed the supervisor told us that all the leaf came from within a 5-kilometre radius of the factory. Pick-up times are staggered so that the leaf can be dated and assigned to a particular set of farmers on the mountain, providing transparency on date and terroir even at this scale.

By now I was wondering why the farmers chose to send their leaf here rather than processing it themselves. It transpired that this mountainous area faces many challenges. The first is a familiar one: a labour shortage. The tea bushes here cover undulating forested terrain, which requires hand picking. The leaf then needs transporting down to the villages to process and on to market for sales. Second, in the current *mao feng* market, much of the value is in marketing and branding, something most farmers have little expertise in. This means their hard labour in getting the product to market is rarely rewarded. A partnership between the factory and the village cooperatives ensures the leaf will be accepted by the factory and the farmer will be paid a rate in line with the local market. The farmers are free to sell direct to others if they wish.

Despite the size of the operation I realized that we were definitely in the right area to find some great tea – we just needed to make direct connections with tea farmers. Over lunch I discussed this with my neighbour, a dynamic lady called Sooha. Interested in our direct sourcing model, Sooha told me that her family were tea farmers, and we were the first westerners she had met who had any interest in building relationships with smaller growers.

Unfortunately, by the time we met Sooha her family had sold their tea for that season, so I returned the following spring. Staying in Yancun village, surrounded by Sooha's extended family, I was introduced to one of the most incredible woman I have met in tea, Du Xing'er, Sooha's mother. Together we walked the hills – her very quickly, me very slowly – and laughed about the softness of my hands, which showed I was clearly not a woman of the land. We discussed the exact specification of the tea we wanted and over the course of the weeks to come I received multiple updates of Du Xing'er climbing ever higher in pursuit of flavoursome, naturally grown wild *mao feng* leaves, which she personally processed for us in the village tea factory. Of course, this is just the start of our relationship, but such partnerships have the potential to make a larger impact. On our recent travels to India and Japan we've seen several small companies starting to help farmers build networks that increase their chances of delivering better returns on their labours.

THE AUCTION ROOM

Michelle: In July 2017 I was excited to accept a generous invitation to visit J. Thomas, the oldest and largest tea auctioneer in India. At Comins we don't buy through the auction system, but most of us will have drunk tea that has passed through these doors at some point. We were welcomed by Anindyo Choudhury, the vice president at the time and now a buyer and blender at Tata Global. The auction house is designed to function as a single-supply source for commodity buyers. Just like orthodox tea, the larger commodity market also needs to be quality assessed and valued before sale. It is logistically impossible for bulk commodity buyers to individually visit gardens and make personal evaluations, so they rely on the skills of highly trained tasters and brokers at houses such as J. Thomas to provide that service.

It takes three weeks for a sample to pass through the system at the auction house. When a sample arrives, it is evaluated by the brokers and then sent out to high-value customers. The selling price is the prerogative of the seller, but set in agreement with the auction house. 200 lots will be sold every hour.

What does the future hold for the large-scale tea market in India? In Anindyo's view: 'The domestic market is exciting: rising consumption, people queuing up for speciality teas with rising per-capita income. Price is no barrier for the Indian consumer looking for his or her best cup of tea. On the other hand, MRL (Maximum Residue Level) issues concerning pesticide residues in tea, competition from neighbouring Nepal, rising costs for the estates, increasing wages, insufficient availability of workers for timely plucking, all these pose challenges on a day-to-day basis.'

china

China is undoubtedly the centre of the tea world. It was where tea was first discovered and has a distinct culture based around tea drinking that spans over 2,000 years, influencing tea production and drinking around the world. Tea is part of the fabric of Chinese culture. Several millennia of tea production in China has also led to a vast range and diversity of tea types not found in any other country.

The discovery of tea occurred in southwestern China in an area named Bashu, which covers modern-day Yunnan, Sichuan and Guizhou. Although Emperor Shennong is widely credited with the discovery in 2737 BC (see page 11), use of the plant would have started thousands of years earlier. There are no specific records of the usage at this time, but tea was initially used for its medicinal qualities as well as in rituals. It was chewed, boiled or simply eaten and wouldn't be consumed as a drink until around 1000 BC. The word for tea was not included in a dictionary for another 1,300 years after that.

The earliest record of tea cultivation was recorded in the *Hua Yang Guo Zhi* ('Chronicles of Huayang') in 1046 BC, which says that King Wu of Zhou ordered that tea should feature among tributes given to the emperor. Tea was 'a divine drug capable of healing a good many diseases'. During the Zhou dynasty, tea started to become popular as a drink, rather than being taken as a medicine or eaten with food. Around this time tea also became popular with Buddhist, Confucianist and Taoist monks, who found that the bitter drink kept them awake during long meditations. This helped the spread of tea as a drink around China and to other countries.

During the Western Han dynasty (206–25 BC) there is evidence that tea drinking was widespread in the Bashu area, certainly in the upper sections of society, and that tea was being used as a commodity. But the next key era for tea was the prosperous and culturally progressive Tang dynasty (618–907 AD), which created the ideal climate for a culture around tea-drinking to form. The first text specifically about tea (*Ch'a Ching*, or 'Classic of Tea') was written at this time by Lu Yu. This relatively short text gave structure to the study of tea by examining the origin, picking, processing, tools for making, brewing, drinking and legends of tea. Published in 780 AD, it vastly increased the popularity of the tea drinking, and its impact on tea scholars and connoisseurs remains strong today. During the central period of this dynasty, there was a surge in production scale, great advances in processing technology and large expansion of tea-growing areas. A tax was levied on tea for the first time, at a rate of 10 percent. Another stimulus for development was the rise of tribute teas. The Tang royal court had started paying great attention to the production of tea, making tributes compulsory and centralizing control. A special department was set up to supervise the manufacturing and supply to the Emperor, and imposed rigid standards.

This had the effect of increasing innovation and quality in tea production, to the great benefit to Chinese tea in general, which became an art form to be enjoyed by all social classes. However, most tea at this time still took the form of tea cakes made from steaming fresh leaf that was pounded, compressed into moulds, then baked. To serve, these were softened, crushed to dust and boiled in water, so the flavour was not as we know it today. It was often mixed with rice, orange zest, ginger, onion or even salt water before boiling. Knowledge of tea started to expand beyond China and trading soon began. Tea bricks were even used as currency, the most famous use being in the trade of tea for horses along the 2,500-mile Tea Horse road that linked China with Tibet.

The Song dynasty (960–1279) was the next significant era in tea. Artistry was added to the production of the tea, and 'Dragon' and 'Phoenix' cakes become the most popular style, named for the designs imprinted into the cakes at the time of moulding: dragons to represent the King and phoenixes for the Queen. This era also saw the development of tea whisking. Tea cakes were ground into a fine powder, which was then whisked using a bamboo whisk in an intricate process that involved adding water in seven stages. Great skill was needed to add the right amount of water each time and to whisk with the appropriate force. Such was this skill that whisking competitions were established among all classes. This was taken further in the form of the 'Fencha game', the art of relishing a tea: while whisking, scholars would compose a poem inspired by the images and shapes created by the infusion and froth of the tea. Alongside these games, tea had become a staple of life, ranked alongside firewood, rice, salt and other necessities. Teahouses became more than just places to drink and buy – they evolved into public spaces for events, games and connection. Tea culture as we know it today was developing quickly.

The Ming dynasty (1368–1644) was when tea drinking became recognizable to us today. Foreign rule during the Yuan dynasty (1279–1368) under the Mongolian empire formed by Kublai Khan had erased many aspects of Song culture, including whisked powdered tea. Early in the Ming dynasty, Emperor Zhu Yuanzhang enforced change by effectively banning tea cakes. Instead, he stated that only loose tea should be given as tribute tea, fundamentally changing tea habits. Loose tea had to be infused with boiling water. This simpler, more natural method was seen as offering a better taste, aroma and overall experience. It brought people closer to tea and consequently tea drinking spread rapidly. Black tea and scented teas also appeared. The tea up to this point would be considered as green today, but the production of the first lapsang souchong in around 1590 (see page 50) led to leaving the leaf for a period of time that created another type of tea we now know as black tea. This process is called oxidation.

The Qing dynasty (1644–1911) was the time of tea as a commodity and the era of the tea trader. Confined initially to the domestic market, the number of teahouses increased dramatically, boosting the tea economy and pushing makers to develop new teas and perfect current ones. By the late seventeenth century China had well and truly opened trade with the international world – but this was not without its problems.

By 1684 the British East India Trading Company, founded by Queen Elizabeth I, had established its first trading post in Canton, with tea as the main export. There was massive demand from Britain, but there was a problem: China did not want to trade goods for tea, it wanted payment in cash. China was self-sufficient and did not need any of the goods Britain was rich in. The solution was found in high-quality Indian opium, to which the East India Company had access, and China needed to supplement its own lower-quality opium crops. Contrary to popular belief, China already had a long-established opium trade, albeit a domestic one. The lucrative trade continued until the famous Opium Wars in 1840–2 and 1856–60, but by this time China's monopoly had been broken and Britain was no longer dependent on China for tea (see page 130).

Sadly, in the 1900s tea culture suffered in China. Invasion by Japan, the civil war, communist revolution and the Cultural Revolution all resulted in decline. Growers were utilized elsewhere, and with less production the teahouses closed. Mechanization increased and quality therefore declined. In the latter part of the century there were distinct improvements to this terrible situation. Driven by scientific research stations and supported by university courses on tea, the market has regenerated, with teahouses opening, museums being constructed and cultural events that celebrate tea gaining popularity. Today, China's production of tea dwarfs that of other countries: 2.35 million tonnes were made in 2016. It has a buoyant domestic market and consumption is growing, in contrast with some of the other countries discussed in this book. As buyers, we see this in the competition for great tea: clear evidence that after a brief lapse, Chinese tea has most certainly found its feet.

Our China

Michelle: In 2014 I was travelling extensively for my work, including to Shanghai for the first time. China started to become less intimidating and more familiar, but at that point I had never travelled outside the confines of comfortable corporate surroundings. I had been in email contact with a friend of a friend who had been helping us to track down organic teas (a long and frustrating process) when I discovered that we would be in China at the same time – me for business, him for tea travels. An invitation to come on a tea trip to Hunan seemed too good an opportunity to miss. So, with the simple instruction to meet at Changsha airport and carry a photo of him with me in my purse, I boarded a plane. When I arrived in Changsha the plan started to unravel. I had no Mandarin, there was no one to meet me and no way to contact anyone. I had been standing in the small greeting area for several hours when a young guy appeared, looking relieved. We managed to establish that he had been sent to collect me, and we travelled out into the night. After two more nervous hours of standing in a larger hotel foyer the next morning, the face in the photo finally appeared and we bundled into the mini bus and headed out to tea country.

Three years of spring travels have seen those early lessons of patience and having a little faith tested again and again. Both, it turns out, are key ingredients to happy and successful tea explorations in this diverse country. Experienced through the lens of tea, we have discovered a country, a culture and a people that have challenged my westernized views of China, and offered me opportunities to slow down and embrace connection in whatever form it may present itself. While researching this book I have met a number of extraordinary people who, had it not been for tea, I would most likely never have encountered. Freya Aitken-Turff, CEO of the China Exchange in London's Chinatown, is one of those. We connected over a shared passion for China and pondered how we could inspire others to shake off their western preconceptions and approach travel in China with an open mind and heart.

'We have an exotic view of Chineseness,' Freya told me. 'This means that expectations are often challenged when a visitor first arrives. How can we best experience a country with 5,000 years of continuous culture and civilization? How do we appreciate contemporary Chinese culture alongside its traditions and heritage?

'In a country where life can be incredibly fast-paced, the gentle custom of sharing a pot of tea is welcome. Tea provides those moments of calm. It allows us to enjoy and absorb something that has been part of China's culture and daily life for a few thousand years while connecting us to the country's contemporary experience. China now produces over 500 types of tea, from the fluffy buds of white tea to many types of black tea. Tea – in cities, in the countryside, up mountains, in the deserts, on trains, planes and everywhere in between – is an essential part of daily life.

'Tea drinking is a solo as well as collective pastime,' Freya explained. 'Across the country, from CEOs to street sweepers, tea is carried in tall glass jars containing tea leaves that are filled with water repeatedly throughout the day'. There are elegant tea bars serving *gongfu* tea in sophisticated teaware, an art form in itself. *Chayi*, or 'tea art', is a concept that we understand only vaguely in the UK, and we have no equivalent custom. It goes beyond using your best china or brewing up loose-leaf tea in a pot. *Chayi* describes the act of brewing, serving and savouring the moment of the tea and a heightened sense of the changes between the sensations and tastes of the first, second, third brews and so on.

It is tea, in all its forms, that helps connect the past to the present. In this section we'll introduce you to the world of Chinese tea through the lives and words of four inspirational people working in tea that we have met on our travels. Their stories highlight the diversity of tea in China and remind us that we must enter this world with a fully open mind, a willingness to challenge our perceptions of Chinese tea and an appetite to learn. The reward is some of the finest tea in the world and a tea culture that can offer us precious time and space in a busy life. Take a moment, make a cup of tea, open your mind and let us take you somewhere quite extraordinary.

THE ENTHUSIAST AND EDUCATOR: VINCENT HU AT THE TEA MUSEUM, QIMEN

Michelle: When we talk about tea in the west we often focus on the grower, but many other inspirational people help shape the way we view and enjoy tea. In 2017 I travelled to Qimen County to learn more about the tea this area is renowned for: Keemun. This black tea is one of China's ten most famous teas and was first produced in 1875. It known for its distinctive flowery, honey-like and fruity aromas and mellow, sweet taste. Hungry for more knowledge, I was very happy to find a small museum where I met Vincent, who introduced me to a world of tea making that brings together age-old methods handed down through generations and modern brand-new factories.

Vincent: 'My job in the museum is to spread the culture of Keemun and Chinese tea. I love green tea and oolong tea and my family owns a very small plantation in my home village of Huangsiwu.

'The history of tea in Qimen County dates back to the Tang dynasty. Of course, it was green tea then, as it was not until the late Qing dynasty, in 1875, that people in these areas started to produce black tea. This change was driven by a decline in the market for green tea, which forced diversification into black tea production. To facilitate this, a tea maker from Jiangxi province was hired to process black tea in Qimen. The tea maker had learned his skills from Wuyi Mountain, so there is a special relationship between Keemun and the black tea from Wuyi. Keemun gradually developed a very complex refining and processing system by around 1900.

'By 1936, black tea production was thriving, with 128 factories in Qimen. With its highly distinctive aroma and balanced flavour, it was a key ingredient in English Breakfast tea. But locals only really started drinking Keemun in the last 10 years. The whole area is the designated growing area of Keemun, and the most famous comes from Likou.'

Vincent explained that there are three factors that contribute to the special qualities of Keemun tea: 'First, the unique environment of the whole county. Qimen covers a area of 2,257 square kilometres and is 88.6 percent forest. Most of the landform here is hills. The red soil of Qimen contains a lot of mineral substances, especially potassium and copper. Secondly, the special tea cultivar, named Qimen, is another important factor. During the rolling process the leaves release an aromatic compound called geraniol, which contributes to its rose-like aroma. Thirdly, the unique processing method can also influence its quality.

'For the traditional Keemun *congou* that we know and enjoy in the west, there are ten grades, three made by hand and seven made by machine. The difference between *congou* and *maofeng* is determined by whether the tea is refined or not. After primary processing, we call the teas *maofeng*. During the refining process the *maofeng* tea is broken into smaller particles and different screening methods are used to separate out the leaf based on weight and length, which produces various grades. Compared with *maofeng*, *congou* is more mellow in flavour, yet *maofeng* is richer in floral scent. We call the processing method of *congou* the traditional method, but if you visit some villages in Qimen you hardly find the traditional method because *maofeng* is much easier to produce. Only big companies have the ability to produce *congou*.

'About 4,000 tons of Keemun are produced every year in Qimen. Most of them, around 60 percent, are low-grade teas used for export. Most of the high-level teas (level 1 and special level) are for the internal market.'

THE ENTREPRENEUR: MR ZHENG, FUDING WHITE TEA, FUJIAN PROVINCE

Michelle: White tea, a lightly oxidized tea from the buds and leaves of the *Camellia sinensis* plant, is a key part of my daily tea routine. Fujian province, and in particular the hilly Jianyang, Fuding and Songxi counties, are the centre of white tea production in China. Quality white tea produced in this region is my first choice. I met Mr Zheng in 2015 on my first trip to Fuding and was immediately intrigued by him and his story; his passion for his brand and quality organic white tea is infectious. This is the story of how he made it happen, evidence that entrepreneurial journeys are similar, no matter where you live in the world.

Mr Zheng: 'I retired from the army in 2004 and returned to Fuding. I had a vision of starting my own business and I was friends with the boss from an import-export company in Xiamen. We talked about the tea business and he suggested that I start in tea – specifically, in organic tea.' When Mr Zheng saw Fuding white tea being given as prestigious gifts at the 2008 Beijing Olympics he felt sure it was the right area to be in. 'Until 2009 I was working for someone else, but that year I started to look for land for myself. I bought about 130 mu [around 9 hectares], and a year later I created my brand, which was called the "stone and orchid" tea factory. The garden was not organic. I started to wonder why Chinese people drink unhealthy tea; many people need better health and white tea has a long history as a healthy product. I also want the people who work for me to think about their health, so that became my goal. I cut the tea trees right back and started to follow organic practices, such as using organic manure to feed the soil and planting osmanthus among the tea bushes, which attract insects. When they eat the osmanthus they forget about the tea! Investing in organic certification for the garden has not been an easy path. It costs a lot of money and it's hard to convince people it really is organic. All my tea is hand plucked and a lot of people think I am crazy because it involves a lot of work.

'My day starts early, when I go up into the mountains with the pickers at around 5 or 6 a.m. I collect the fresh leaf at around 10 a.m. and 4 p.m. and I come back down to check the factory at lunchtime. It is important for me to oversee the whole practice. My gardens contain the three main cultivars Fuding Da Bai, Fuding Da Hao and Xiao Chai Cha. The predominant cultivar is Da Bai.

'The first garden I bought, Da Gang Tou, is still the best. I like drinking the tea from this garden; when I drink my own organic tea I can feel confident in the quality. There are many reasons why people should drink Fuding white tea. White tea is one of the six famous teas of China, it has many medicinal uses and China is the true origin of white tea. The environment in Fuding is perfect and at a good latitude for the tea. There is a lot of rain, which is not too drying for the tea, and no pollution. The ideal day for white tea is a north wind, a temperature of 20–25°C and humidity of 20–30 percent.

'If you have never had white tea before I suggest drinking an aged Shou Mei, which is full-bodied and sweeter. If you have never tried tea before, very fresh, new white tea is a great place to start – it is very light and delicate like water. If you are more experienced I suggest a vintage Bai Mu Dan or Shou Mei, my best-selling tea. The future for white tea in Fuding looks bright: the market is hot and rising but there are still relatively few organic white tea producers. I will be focusing on cooperation with other tea farmers to gain more land for the tea, but they need to be convinced of my methods. My learning is continuous; I got a certificate in organic tea farm management from the China Tea Research Institute last year and I make it my aim to oversee every detail.' Mr Zheng is certainly dedicated to the cause.

THE SPECIALIST: MR WU, WUYI ROCK TEA, FUJIAN PROVINCE

Michelle: Ah, Wuyi. As our tea travels in 2017 were coming to an end we decided to finish by visiting one of the most spectacular natural landscapes in China: Wuyishan (see page 20). This was not my first visit here – I had visited in 2015. Two years later, a little older and a little wiser, I was returning to reunite with

Mr Wu and continue my education in rock tea. Mr Wu has the most spectacular office overlooking the reserve in which I have spent many hours tasting tea. As we taste we often enjoy long periods of silence, but we have also learned much about each other. This is the story of one man's journey to produce high-quality rock tea in one of the most famous areas of China, and shows just how complex some tea-growing regions in China, and the teas they produce, can be.

Mr Wu: 'In my first career I was a teacher, but tea was my hobby and around 2005 – a time when the tea industry was going through a bad patch, with areas being left to go wild – I decided it was time for a change. At this, tea's lowest point, I rented a 100-mu [7-hectare] plot. I had to borrow a lot of money and my family thought I was crazy. I had to clear the land to gain access and retable the tea plants, which took me 2 years. Even once I could pluck the tea, I had no facilities for processing so I had to engage someone else. In the first year I sold no tea, and in the second I sold only half of my output. Only in the third year did I get lucky and find a big customer. I gave the boss some of my Lao Cong (old bush) Shui Xian tea and he thought it was so good he purchased the entire output, plus a fixed order every year that followed.

'It was time to refocus. From the original piece of land I rented, I kept 20 mu [1.3 hectares] in the Hui Yuan Keng area and gave back the other 80. I decided to specialize in Zheng Yan teas (see page 20), so I rented some land in the Shui Lian Dong area, and later added some in the Hui Yuan Kung area. None of the areas were attached; I simply rented them with ten-year leases. The rental prices are shooting up, and all of this money goes to the farmer who originally owned the land. In 2010 I decided to rent some more land in a cooler valley location (Wuyishan is on the golden latitude and the east–west valleys are the best) with trees on both sides, a rocky stream running through it and plants near the base of the rocks. As in so many places, the quality comes back to the soil. The high mineral content in the soil is excellent, and there is no clay so the tea trees have good drainage and the roots can breathe. Water is there, but it is not stagnant.

'I also set up my own small processing unit in my building, which I still use today. That building is where my daily life in tea begins, and a tea day for me starts around 7 a.m. and ends at 11 p.m. I help get the workers to the mountains – only registered vehicles are allowed in the national park, so I drop them off between 7 and 8 a.m. and they walk for an hour up into the fields. They start picking at 9.30 a.m. until around 4 p.m., coming down with the leaf twice in the morning and twice in the afternoon. Across the areas, around 14 cultivars are planted and plucked. I have reached the limits of what I want to do – to plant and manage more cultivars would be too diversified for me. Half of my planting is Shui Xian, one of the earlier varietals to become popular, which is very stable.

'If the weather is good, we wither the tea leaves outdoors for 15 minutes, breaking the plucked leaf into two batches in order to do this. If the weather is bad we are forced to move inside without the initial sun drying. The processing takes 8–10 hours and will involve indoor withering, bruising, wok frying and shaping, followed by a light initial bake. The tea is then dried to get the *mao cha* (crude tea), which is then sorted. Once the picking season is over we enter a 5-month period of roasting. Throughout the season I spend every morning and afternoon tasting teas from the previous day. I am a professionally trained tea taster, and I'm looking to pick up deficiencies so that I can advise my team on what needs to change. It is a team effort: attention must be paid at every part of the process. We keep a record of the teas: when they are picked, what time, which area, what the weather was like, the weight, type of tea and the grade, and so on. We refer to this when we begin the baking later in the season. This starts with what I call a "foundation" baking from 7 a.m. to 3 p.m. From then onwards I taste the tea every hour. The appearance of the tea is a critical component, as is the "feel" and the smell; if you over-bake the tea you can lose the fragrance. Customer preference and my experience guide me in how to produce the best tea.

'The best part of my job comes from feeling I have made a great tea. Done well, the tea gives back to me. The camaraderie of sharing a good tea with other producers is special. The most challenging part is the marketing and sales: people's tastes are changing, regulations also constantly change and the competition increases. Once people try the true *zheng yan* teas they soon realize that the mass-produced tea that bears the same name is very different.

'If you're new to Wuyi rock tea, I recommend Huang Mei Gui (yellow rose), which is highly fragrant, and Qi Lan, which is highly fragrant and lightly baked. I would probably build up to the Rou Gui and Shui Xian, which are more heavily baked. I drink the yellow rose from 2016 and also the Lao Cong. I think the way the Wuyi market is developing is good – the market for good tea is growing. I see the middle market becoming commodity based, which I am not interested in, so I am moving away from it.'

THE PRESERVER OF TEA CULTURE: MR NANKANG, YUNNAN PUER AND BLACK TEA, YUNNAN PROVINCE

Michelle: In April 2016 I travelled to Yunnan for the first time. Flying in to Kunming, the capital of Yunnan province, it took a gruelling 9 hours to reach Jinghong in the far south. This is a region well known for its rich and diverse styles of tea, and it was the *puer* tea, a unique style that originated in the region, and the black teas, in particular Dian Hong, that I had come to see. Yunnan province is a land very different from the modern cultivation and terraced tea fields you see in other parts of the world. Here, ancient tea trees, some hundreds of years old, are cultivated in natural forests rich with biodiversity. I was interested to meet the people living here who, I had been told, had formed a traditional, sustainable method of ancient tea cultivation in natural forests where you need a ladder to climb the trees and pick the leaves. The experience was to be a magical one, and it was Mr Nankang who inspired us to write the book. This is his story and the story of harmony between tea cultivation and ancient forest ecosystems.

In about 180 AD, the Blang ethnic minority group migrated through the area and discovered tea. Limited available land meant that they started to cultivate tea trees in the forest, gradually mastering the growing and processing skills that would be passed from generation to generation to this day. The area is now the largest and best-preserved cultivated ancient tree plantation in the world. The largest of the 14 major *puer* ancient tree mountains, it is 1,250–1,550 metres above sea level and covers just under 1,067 hectares and contains about 1.13 million ancient tea treas. The oldest is around 1,400 years old; most are around 200 years old. An incredible multi-layered ecosystem naturally preserves soil fertility and reduces pests and disease; the forest canopy reduces unwanted plant growth as it restricts the light reaching the forest floor. Its fallen leaves also act as natural fertilizer, slowing the path of rainfall to the soil, thus protecting against soil erosion on steep slopes. No expensive terracing is required, in sharp contrast to many tea plantations around the world, intensive monocultures that can lack biodiversity.

These prime conditions only exist because of the understanding gained by the farmers through studying nature over time. Tea gardens and natural forest blend seamlessly into each other, and due to this connection, fifteen plant species have been discovered in the tea forests that are considered rare and endangered in natural forests. This connection is shown by the annual tea ancestor festival in mid-April. This year's was the 1,711th such event, which shows how important tea is to the rich ethnic culture of the Blang people, a celebration and spiritual expression of the coexistence between humans and the land. Village elders pray for a good harvest for the coming year and villagers go to an altar in the tea forest to make offerings and dance. The oldest tea tree in each family-run plot is worshipped throughout the year to ensure good production and success.

Our day at Mr Nankang's started with tea on a platform overlooking the spectacular forest. We travelled out to the villages, walked through the ancient tea forests and ate lunch with the locals in a picture-postcard setting. Knowing the high prices that *puer* tea can fetch, it would be easy to assume that individuals in these communities must be thriving. It is clear that the tea here is high quality and highly valued, requiring no pesticides or fertilizers. However, Mr Nankang explained how the local people, with limited processing and marketing skills, lose out in the value chain. Realizing the amount of work and additional resources needed to go it alone, we learned that many locals have now formed a cooperative in Mangjing with Mr Nankang as their executive. Mr Nankang explained that 6 villages (570 houses) are part of the co-operative, an area that includes arable land, tea terraces, tea forests and natural forest. By working together to process and market their own teas they can realize more of the profits and gain support on matters such as forest protection and tea forest conservation, which they work on with the support of scientists. The cooperative also purchases fresh leaves from members at a guaranteed price, rewarding them with a dividend at the end of each year. As we walked through the forest, Mr Nankang explained the importance of the ancient forests to the villages and community. They provide much for the area – not just in terms of cultural heritage, which can help them to market the teas and build other eco-tourism sources of revenue, but also in terms of protection against landslides and water course conservation.

At the end of our visit we tasted some of the teas made here. We were each invited to take turns in the tea making, which was surprisingly nerve-racking in Mr Nankang's company. Working together, the co-operative produce handmade teas using traditional methods, but they are also embracing modern methods. The collection and processing of tea is closely monitored and recorded to ensure high quality and to prevent the mixing of tea harvested from forests with that from terraces, enabling them to be processed and sold separately. As we tasted our way through their teas, it felt as though we were being invited, through the tea cup, to join a wonderful club, a club more connected with the earth and the environment than anywhere else I have ever visited.

It is clear to us how important Mr Nankang and others like him are in maintaining the authenticity of tea areas and their connections to traditional cultures. Modern-day pressures mean that only sustainable economic thinking will ensure the future of these amazing forests. This is something Mr Nankang fully supports – by gaining funding and driving forward various initiatives he has ensured that this region has been extensively restored and that organic farming practice is understood by modern farmers. He even helped with a submission to declare the area a World Heritage Site. As we left, and he took my hand, I promised to share the story of his work more widely.

THE PREPARATION & ENJOYMENT OF CHINESE TEA

Michelle: Every time I visit China, I always wander around the tea market in Shanghai at the end of my trip. I never really buy anything – it is simply a ritual that marks the start of my return to the real world. Once, walking along a particularly empty row, one shop, lit by a faint glow, drew me in. Once inside I was not disappointed; it belonged to a group who produce and sell beautiful cultural objects such as teas, cloth and pottery, and on that day a woman named Chuanchuan sat near the back, making tea. I can't explain what drew me to Chuanchuan, but it was powerful enough that I asked if I could return the next day to take tea with her, something I never normally do. Conversation flowed easily as we discussed the pressures of modern life in China and the west, our shared passion for tea and how she and her group approach their work. She told me: 'We spend a large amount of time practising our heart instead of thinking simply of our products' appearance. We believe that the art and crafts come from real life, and that people who can be satisfied with the current moment can produce great simple things.' I was captivated, and over the years Chuanchuan has explained how the group has collected many friends who share the same values, including tea makers and tea masters deep in the mountains.

The tea ceremony forms an integral part of their everyday practice. 'It is crucial to present the quality of the tea. To taste tea really well requires people to have a peaceful and compassionate heart. The physical will never be more important than the metaphysical. So this is how we devote most of our time in practising our heart by meditation-related activities.'

Chuanchuan's words provide an excellent moment to pause in our journey between tea the plant and tea the drink. Her words paint a picture of a buoyant Chinese tea market in which knowledge and close relationships with growers are critical in order to secure quality. They also provide food for thought on teaware, tea preparation and tea ceremonies. Sourcing beautiful tea and choosing beautiful teaware is just the start of your tea journey.

Chuanchuan: 'The tea ceremony is the step of awakening the tea leaves. After all the processes have been done, how to present the tea? What is the right temperature? How long should the water stay with the tea leaves before each pour? This requires very rich experience. Sadly, I feel we have much less knowledge about tea in China than French people do about wine. Maybe this is related to our Chinese Zen culture – we prefer not to record the essence of the *tao* of tea, since we believe that the "essence" of cooking the best dish is something that can only be communicated beyond language.

'How to achieve that? By daily practice, which allows us to become more experienced and more self-disciplined. With greater concentration we find ourselves able to relax and therefore exist more peacefully. Through this practice and our good intentions to become more "whole", the beauty will start to happen by itself. This is the intention of our group – by simply living with and practising tea our knowledge of each tea's character will grow, and each year our ability to prepare the tea will get better and better. This is a possibility open to all of us, if we choose to follow this path.'

Chinese teaware

People have been particular about the wares they choose for brewing tea since ancient times. The choice of teapot, tea cup and utensils offers the tea drinker the opportunity to express their individuality and create their own unique tea ceremony. When people come into the teahouse for the first time, much of the teaware we use is new to them. We always explain how the pieces we use are beautiful but also functional. We have travelled to the most remote parts of China, sat on mountain tops and in remote villages and had tea prepared in a Yixing pot or Jingdezhen porcelain *gaiwan* (a lidded bowl). Sometimes, the table is set with a beautiful cloth and fine utensils, but more often than not the teaware is used, loved, chipped, much like the pieces we find in our cupboards at home. At the heart of each interaction, whether ornate or simple, is something universal and beautiful – a shared moment with tea, the leveller of people, at its centre.

Even in the most famous tea-producing countries, people are still learning and experimenting as they build their own unique tea ceremonies, and in this section we aim to equip you for that journey. First, we will travel to two important centres for teaware in China, Jingdezhen and Yixing, before looking at how to use these wares to prepare and enjoy tea at home.

JINGDEZHEN: THE PORCELAIN CAPITAL OF CHINA

Michelle: Jingdezhen is in Jiangxi province, southeast China. When you look at its location, in a remote and hilly region, you question how it gained its fame, until you realize that Jingdezhen is close to the best-quality deposits of *petuntse* (porcelain stone) in all of China, as well as being surrounding by pine forests to feed the kilns. Better still, it also has a river system flowing north and south, which has provided easy trade for its fragile wares. Jingdezhen has been described as a 'fantasy land for potters' where 'specialists in every aspect of production from moulding to glazing to firing are found', and I would challenge any tea lover not to feel the sense of intrigue and excitement that I felt when first visiting the area in 2017.

Baixu Xiong, co-founder of the renowned RedHouse ceramic studio that I had the honour of being shown around in 2018, explained some of the history of Jingdezhen porcelain.

Baixu: 'Jingdezhen has been the centre of porcelain production in China since the Song dynasty, around 1,000 BC. Most of the porcelain pieces you see in museums all over the world were made in Jingdezhen. For over a thousand years, Jingdezhen has never stopped manufacturing porcelain. It started with the discovery of the material kaolin, or China clay, in a small village called Dong Pu, about 40 kilometres from the city centre. Jingdezhen porcelain is a magical and mysterious material, a clay body that has translucent properties, creating pots that are pure and white, delicate to hold and often painted with very skilled and exotic eastern decorations.'

'After the founding of new China in the 1950s, the government put an emphasis on developing export businesses to build the country's foreign exchange reserves. Jingdezhen introduced modern factories to accelerate porcelain production, which reached its peak in the eighties. However, as other, perhaps more geographically suitable ceramic industrial cities in China rose up in the nineties, Jingdezhen lost its chance to modernize and expand further. The factory workers of Jingdezhen hit hard times as the country focussed on industrial expansion and demand for their skills fell away.

In the 1990s, Baixu Xiong explained, Taiwanese tea was introduced to mainland China through Fujian province, and Taiwanese oolong tea products enriched the Chinese market: 'Tea took on a new importance, and the way to best appreciate its value became more essential, involving methods of brewing, tasting and sensing the tea, along with how to create and enjoy the whole process and atmosphere of drinking tea. Particular environments were created for sharing tea together, which often came from observing traditional paintings, poems and philosophies.'

In the early 2000s demand for tea continued to increase, as Chinese people started to think, question and redefine what tea meant in their own culture. Many ceramic factories made the decision to change their production into tea markets, and Jingdezhen saw new opportunities to become alive again after the depression of modern industrialization. 'Just like coffee, wine or any kind of drink or food, tea needs its own objects to help express its meaning. In China now, refinement and elegance are key to appreciating tea. These two elements seem to be in the forefront of peoples' minds when purchasing tea sets. Colour, volume, size and pattern and even the weight of the ceramics are also all considered. Many private and small workshops now thrive in Jingdezhen, each producing highly individual items. The energetic and innovative environment in Jingdezhen suits the new diversity and dynamism of the tea industry – customers are curious and fond of its ceramic culture and history; it is a special place whose rich history brings additional value to the products made here.'

CERAMIC CADDIES AND MORE: YANGYANG LI, YUNBAI STUDIO

Michelle: I love tea caddies, and the scent of tea you get each time you open them – a sensory marker for the journey ahead. When I saw some small, beautifully decorated pieces on a stall in the corner of the Taoxichuan market in Jingdezhen I had to take a closer look. This stall, it turned out, belonged to the YunBai Studio run by Yangyang Li. They use pottery clay, or porcelain clay, or both in different proportions, with different clay materials revealing different characteristics after firing. Careful thought is given to the composition of each piece.

Yangyang Li: 'Porcelain clay expresses freshness and brightness, while pottery clay expresses unsophisticated and sober feelings. Using them in different proportions can express many other different feelings. Some of our glazes just come from the ordinary shop but we mix them in our own way and grind some with aerolite or other special stone. In general, our pieces will give you a sense of nature after firing. You will often find me making while enjoying a rock tea or orange peel *puer*!'

We love the style of Yangyang Li's pieces and have since returned to Jingdezhen to visit her studio. As a result we have moved beyond caddies into other pieces. She receives many requests, and if she needs help the close-knit community of Jingdezhen makes collaboration easy. 'When my clients ask for something too big or something I'm not good at making, I will ask for help from local craftspeople – that's the great thing about working somewhere like Jingdezhen'.

'ZHI YE' TEA CUPS: XING XIANG, STUDIO JINGDEZHEN

Michelle: The tea cup is just as important as the tea itself: a chance for the tea drinker to express themself and make tea time a beautiful, satisfying moment. On my first trip around Taoxichuan, the vibrant night market in Jingdezhen, I came across Xing Xiang and his wife, and their 'Zhi Ye' ceramic tea cups drew me in. Xing Xiang is one of the new generation of young ceramicists who want to develop a new take on traditional ceramics and continue the tradition of Jingdezhen. His wife Kiki told me about his approach. Born in 1987 in Jingzhou, Wubei Province, Xing Xiang followed the teaching and guidance of Professor Sun Ji Dong, focusing his research in the Buddha Arts of the Wei and Jin dynasties and graduating with a bachelor degree from the University of Yan Shan in 2012. After traveling he settled in Jindezhen to continue his research in ceramic materials, vessels, and the art of Buddha sculptures before establishing his studio in 2014 to create and research Buddha sculptures, tea wares and various other utensils. He spent three years researching the glaze art of 'Zhi Ye', successfully developing his own specific glaze, which he applies to his artworks.

Kiki: 'We only use Jindezhen's natural mineral clay that contains iron element to produce the vessel body. Different types of clay and glaze have an important influence in tea making. The clay affects not only the pure taste of the tea, but is also important in setting the right aesthetic moods for tea tasting in different environments.' At home and in the workshop Kiki and Xing Xiang explore tea widely. 'Generally, as we enter the autumn, we will choose cooked *puer* tea, sometimes we add a plum making it taste even better. This seems suitable for times when we lack appetite or our intestines and stomach are uncomfortable. Black tea is a year-round favourite, especially Yunnan black tea; we love the scent of sweet potato, and in the winter we may choose to add milk. We generally like to cook white tea in the summer. Jingdezhen is a humid city – it can be very wet – and for us white tea has the medicinal properties that help us overcome summer colds with a sweet bitterless taste.'

Back in the studio Kiki explains more about the 'Zhi Ye' glaze. 'Our glazes are self-made from natural materials, which are fired to the ceramics at 1300°C. The appearance of the "ink and wash" patterns in the final vessel are due to the randomness of how the glaze absorbs the heat and carbon during firing. The resulting patterns are unpredictable – some look like smoke, some like clouds, others are just like ink and wash scenery paintings. Each cup is unique. They are natural, pure and simple.

'We create "Zhi Ye" ceramics out of pure enjoyment. The artist can follow his heart with freedom in each process, from clay preparation right through to seeing the finished artwork when the kiln door is opened. This freedom and enjoyment comes from the balance between setting high standards and accepting the randomness of nature. We do not chase perfection preferring to concentrate on continuously improving ourselves – applying the skills we learn to create new pieces, without forcing each piece to look identical to previous ones. The enjoyment and excitement we experience is tremendous each time a new artwork comes out of the kiln. You see the heat and smoke imprint and transform every work into a unique ink-and-wash art piece.'

SETTING THE TABLE FOR TEA: LIAO YI, JINGDEZHEN AND JIANGXI

Michelle: For us, the simple task of setting the table for tea has taken on a whole new meaning. In China you often see beautiful tea tables set with fabrics, teawares and utensils, and as I walked the side streets of Jingdezhen I was drawn to a shop specializing in a traditional fabric called *xia bu*, made from ramie, a perennial Asian flowering root herb of the nettle family, which means 'the fabric of summer'.

This shop belonged to Liao Yi, aka 'Knife', who explained that *xia bu* has been a speciality handiwork of his home town, Wanzai, JianXi province, for thousands of years. In 2009 it was granted the status of National Intangible Cultural Heritage. Liao Yi: 'I love this fabric, it's beautiful and we need to let more and more people know about it so that they too can appreciate its special beauty'.

Xia bu is often used to dress the tea table. Liao Yi explained how this originated in Taiwan, 'a way to make the tea table more beautiful and show off the oriental aesthetic celebrating the ritual of tea'. *Xia bu* is still handwoven from the ramie plant that mainly grows along the Yangtze River. More absorbent than cotton, breathable and resistant to bacteria and mildew, ramie is one of the strongest natural fibres, even when wet.

'We harvest ramie three times every year. We cut down the plants, remove the stalk and green skin and get the fibres. After processing, they are set on bamboo pieces in a wooden frame, which is sent to families in the countryside. They use traditional Chinese looms to weave the *xia bu*. Depending on the quality of the fabric, it takes three days or even a month to weave just 25 metres.'

As I leave I ask Liao Yi what role his cloths could play in encouraging traditional tea drinking in the west: 'This is the first time I have the chance to show my cloths to Europe. *Xia bu* is so different to the machine-made cloths people have become used to – I think European people will love it just as much as I do.'

Yixing: the home of zisha teapots

Michelle: Inspired by the beautiful pots we have seen on our travels, we now use such teapots in our teahouses. As we place the small pots on the table and remove the lid so that people can see the leaves inside, conversations stop, minds become inquisitive and the stage is set for a new experience. Ours come from Yixing in the province of Jiangsu, famed for its purple clay from which the pots are often formed. China is a world where tea is an experience, not just a drink, and once you have tasted great tea from a *zisha* teapot you too may be unable to turn back.

Teaware made from *zisha* clay has been prized for centuries; its high percentage of clay quartz and iron is considered to be perfect, resulting in teapots that have high permeability and allow the appreciation of the colour, smell and flavour of tea perfectly. They are often adorned with poetry and paintings, each a unique combination of art and practicality, earning the *zisha* teapot the name 'the king of teaware' in China. A *zisha* teapot cannot be rushed; it can take several weeks (or even longer) to make just one pot, and if it is not perfect it will be destroyed. Competition is fierce, with many hundreds of people making pots in the streets of Yixing. As with tea, the quality and craftsmanship will vary – you need to know what to look for.

Joyce Ji is the fourth generation of a family of top craftsman making *zisha* teapots. Her father, Master Ji, still has a workshop on the south street of Shu mountain in the old downtown of Yixing. Joyce explained what is so special about *zisha* teapots: 'The first thing is the *zisha* clay, found only in my hometown Yixing. The Green Dragon and Yellow Dragon Mountain are the most famous areas. These two mountains are located face to face at the centre of Dingshu town, with a lake between them that has been formed as the clay has been removed over time. The second thing is the artists themselves. The way of making the teapots is special: they are handmade, not using machines, and this way of making teapots is only found in our home town.'

Zisha clay varies in colour, which is why you see a colourful array of teapots on sales in the shops of Yixing, and is subdivided into many different types, each with its own qualities. Handling the pots in the shops in Yixing, it became very clear that *zisha* pots vary in texture, which is informed by the size of the particles used; these are separated into different sizes using screens that resemble large sieves with varying mesh types. A teapot made from a 100-mesh screen (0.15 mm) will be as smooth and fine as jade, while one made from particles from a 60-mesh screen (0.3 mm) will be coarser.

Once the *zisha* powder has been chosen, the teapot maker starts the process of transforming it into *zisha* clay in a process called 'hammering'. Every teapot maker has his own formula, resulting in unique teapots of different texture and colour. Once made, the traditional method involves wrapping the clay in a tarpaulin and placing it in a sealed jar for at least half a year to let the carbonates and organic matter decompose so that water can be absorbed into the clay and evenly distributed. Afterwards the clay must be repeatedly hammered to remove the air bubbles and ensure the particles inside are compact, resulting in a clay which, when cut, has a smooth and compact surface. Joyce explains how modern machinery is used to shorten this part of the process.

The main step of forming the teapot body is called *da shen tong*. The maker taps the clay with their hands while spinning the wheel and tapping the teapot body, aiming for geometric symmetry. The next step is called *ga shen tong*, which involves taking the hollow teapot and using an arc-shaped tool to trim the lines to the desired finish. Finally, the handle and the spout: the inside of the spout must be perfectly smooth for the water to flow easily, and only an experienced maker knows how much strength you need to apply and how to make a suitable hole. The final part of the process is to trim the lines without leaving any flaws. In the words of Master Ji: 'Making a teapot is easy to learn but hard to master. The difference between a technician and master is in how skilful and creative one can be in making teapots. Masters can transform this simple material into something of great artistic value.'

MR FAN AT ZHI YUAN JING FANG WORKSHOP

Michelle: As we walked along the streets of Yixing we came across a shop that felt quite special. Out the back, a lady sat carefully crafting pots, a not uncommon sight in many shops. The shop was tidy and uncluttered with glass cabinets neatly displaying teapots like works of art, and just one large tea table sat on the side. This was Mr Fan's shop, and I rather liked his pots.

Mr Fan: 'My wife has now been making Yixing teapots for 25 years, and makes all the pots for our store. In 1996, my sister and I started studying in the top teapot factory in Yixing, and by 2004 we felt ready to open our own workshop and establish our brand, Zhi Yuan Jing Fang. We mainly focus on Yixing *zi ni* purple clay. A big part of the popularity of Yixing clay for brewing tea is historic – it became well known through its use by the royal family.'

Mr Fan sells pots in different shapes, sizes and finishes, and you can buy off the shelf or commission pieces to order. He explained: 'Different people buy different types of pots. If you were starting out in tea the best one to start with is a simple round or *fang gu* shape. Spend less money, use it often and enjoy it before you invest in the more expensive types. White *duan ni* clay is more suitable for light tea, *zi ni* clay is good for Wuyi rock and oolong teas and *jiang ni po* clay is suitable for *puer* tea. These pairings are based on their impact on the cup of tea, which is down to the make up of the clay. For example, the pore size is different in different clays – the teapots are still breathing – and larger pores result in a different flow of air compared with a pot made with denser clay. These differences affect heat distribution, which impacts on the final cup of tea. Regardless of what pot you buy, you need to take care of it. First, once you make your purchase you need to put it into boiling water and soak it. This is mainly to get rid of the dust from firing and open the pores of the clay before you make the first infusion. After using it you must clean out the leaves and rinse it in hot water, then dry it well before putting it away.'

We buy a number of pots and small jugs from Mr Fan, and it's amazing to think they are all made by his wife in the shop I visited. Knowing him and the origin of the pots certainly adds to the flavour of the tea brewed in them. He is pleased with the partnership too: 'I'm really excited that there is growing interest in our work in the west, and that people can see beyond it simply being a teapot to being a beautiful and essential part of the tea ceremony.'

japan

Japan holds a special place in the history of tea and, as with China's story, there are many different tales to tell, far too many to detail here. We will instead focus on the key moments that shaped this wonderful country's tea culture, and ultimately the flavour in your cup.

The introduction of tea can be traced back to Buddhist monks, who brought leaf tea back when they returned from study in China as early as the sixth century. They made special use of tea, realizing that its stimulating yet calming effect aided their long meditations.

The first record of tea is found in the Heian period in the 815 writings called *Nihon Kôki* ('The Chronicles of Japan') and concerned the scholar and monk Eichû, who, alongside fellow monks Saicho and Kukai, accompanied Japanese envoys to China. Eichû returned from Tang dynasty China with tea seeds and knowledge of the production method for tea. Eichû is said to have offered tea to the Japanese emperor, who then decided to encourage its drinking in the imperial court. This had limited success, due to a decrease in desire by the Japanese to imitate the Chinese, the fact that access to tea was limited to monks and noblemen and, ultimately, that it did not taste that good. However, this all changed after 300 years when the first major step towards what could be called a tea culture was made with the help of another Zen monk called Eisai (1141–1215). On returning from China in 1191 he planted tea seeds in the Sefuri mountains in what is now Saga Prefecture in Kyushu. This is thought to be the first tea grown in this area. More importantly, he also gave seeds to the Kazanji temple in Kyoto. The high priest at the time, Myoe, greatly appreciated the gift and when the seeds grew he replanted them in Uji, which was more suited to tea growing. These transplanted seedlings became the basis for tea production in Uji, which became the traditional hub of tea growing in Japan. Many techniques and technologies evolved from this area, impacting greatly on tea production.

In addition to these advances, Eisai's biggest contribution is seen as the introduction of the beginnings of the tea practice or *chanoyu* as we know it today. Fundamental to this was his knowledge of the technique for powdered tea making, developed by the Chinese Song dynasty in the tenth century. This method fell out of favour with them, and ended up being used only in Japan. The method uses green powdered tea, which is scooped into a bowl and hot water is added and whipped into a frothy, bitter-tasting drink. Eisai also wrote the first Japanese book about tea, *Kissa Yojoki* ('How to Stay Healthy by Drinking Tea') in 1211. It gave details of the value of tea for many uses, for example as a medicine for many ailments, for stopping fatigue, quenching thirst and improving brain function. It also integrated Buddhist teachings with Chinese philosophy and tea practice, honouring humility, simplicity, imperfection, and emptiness of ego: 'Tea is the ultimate mental and medical remedy and has the ability to make one's life more full and complete'.

The book proved to be the catalyst for a more formal use of tea when Eisai managed to introduce the benefits of it to the Samurai warrior class in 1214. On hearing that the shōgun Minmoto no Sanemoto drank too much alcohol, he presented his book to him with some tea. Tea drinking then spread down to the shogun's enforcers, the Samurai, where it became a key part of life. Over time, this spread outside of the confines of Kyoto and created a demand for tea estates nationwide.

The start of the formal tea practice as we know it today is credited to Murata Shuko (1422–1502). He took the large, busy practices performed at the houses of warriors and simplified them. He created a specific tea-room design, smaller in size to accommodate a reduced number of guests, surrounded by gardens. He had been taught by the famous monk Ikkyû and it was this influence that instilled the spirit of Zen into the practice. This form became popular among rich merchants, but did not spread widely.

Widespread popularity was to be achieved by Sen no Rikyû (1522–91). He established a tea practice for the general population to enjoy called *wabi-cha* or 'sober tea', thus spreading the enjoyment of tea to everyone. He defined seven rules for the *chanoyu* or 'way of tea' and the *sadou* or process, made the room smaller and simplified the design and the accessories used. Importantly, these objects were to be made in Japan, not imported from China. Powdered tea was still used, now in the form called *matcha*. One key addition was the *nijiri guchi*, which is the small entrance that forces all guests to bow their head on entrance. Despite all this, Rikyû's life ended sadly when he was sentenced to commit suicide for treason.

After this the *chanoyu* and *sadou* developed quickly, becoming part of Japanese culture, synonymous with hospitality. It can be summarized by the Zen Buddhist term *ichigo-ichie* ('one opportunity, one encounter'), meaning that every meeting in the tea practice should be treasured and treated with the utmost sincerity, as they will never recur. Over time the practice has developed as different ideals became important, becoming more ritualized and subtle. Among the wealthy and cultured, *chanoyu* became an expression of tranquillity, purity and harmony, in sharp contrast to actual life at the time.

Alongside the development of *chanoyu*, which was still mainly the domain of the more privileged classes, tea was being drunk by those in the countryside. This would not have been *matcha*, but teas made using a wide range of more rudimentary methods. Leaves would have been dried in the sun and then boiled or baked. This resulted in what is now called *bancha* or 'coarse tea', which has many forms; the term refers to any steamed-style tea made from large leaves harvested after the more premium first harvest.

It wasn't until the Edo period (1603–1868) that tea developed beyond this. Japan had begun a more peaceful period, when the warrior class was not in control and the fixed form of tea consumption was beginning to be challenged. Merchants and intellectuals were becoming more powerful and wanted something less rigid. This coincided with a time when Japan separated itself from the world. From 1641 to 1853, this self-imposed isolation, or *sakoku*, meant that there was no contact with the rest of the world, including in the trade and development of tea. This isolation contributed to the uniqueness of the Japanese tea and tea culture.

Inspiration for a new type of tea had begun slightly before this time in the form of Chinese style pan-fired teas called *tô-cha* (today in the form of *kama-iri cha*). These teas were infused in leaf form and therefore produced an attractive liquor instead of the opaque broth of *matcha*. The desire for infused leaf led to the birth of *sencha*. In 1738 Nagatani Sôen, a producer from Uji, used his knowledge of making *matcha* and *kama-iri cha* to make this new style of tea. Instead of pan-firing the leaves he heated them with steam to stop oxidation. There were many others doing the same process at the time, but he has a place in history because he offered his tea to a local shop, where it was very well received. Despite this, *kama-iri cha* was still very much in favour, but in 1835 the next development came in the form of *gyokuro*. This higher-grade tea is unique due to the shading of the plant prior to plucking, which increases the sweetness and umami depth of the finished tea. Unfortunately, all these new teas, like *matcha*, were still expensive and only enjoyed by a minority of wealthy customers. Everyone else had to be content with banchas, the most widespread being the pan-fired *kama-iri* type.

After the period of isolation ended, trade began with the world, with good success. At the end of the nineteenth century, black tea (*koucha*) began to be produced, but this did not continue long as Japan could not compete with the low production prices of India, Kenya and Sri Lanka. Gradually, it died away in the 1970s with the focus more on domestic distribution.

Since then, Japan has increased tea production considerably with the use of mechanized picking and processing. Focus has mainly been on green teas, 70 percent of them *sencha*. In recent years there has also been a big growth in tea-based products such as flavoured food, toothpaste and ready-to-drink bottled tea. In 2016 around 77,000 tonnes of tea were produced, making it the eleventh largest tea grower in the world, but very little is exported. As the younger generation turn to coffee in greater numbers and domestic consumption declines, there is growing awareness of the need for the development of foreign and alternative markets.

This task is not a simple one, as tea drinkers in the west are not used to the taste or brewing style of Japanese green teas, or aware of the range that is possible. The most common green teas consumed in the west tend to be pan-fired Chinese ones, like the gunpowder-style tea that is often complimentary in restaurants. These are easier to produce in volume, simpler to store and keep fresh and are more sympathetic in brewing. In our teahouses, Japanese tea always provokes a strong reaction. Japanese green teas are the ones that people are most likely to have a strong opinion against, but conversely they are the teas that, once discovered and loved, attract more dedication than any other tea. An education of what to expect from this country's unique styles and flavours of tea, how they became that way – and also how to brew them – will go a long way towards preparing the consumer for the experience. With this educated approach we see a bright future for wonderful Japanese teas.

Our Japan

Rob: A fascination with Japan, Japanese tea culture and Japanese life more widely has seen us return again and again. On our first trip in 2009 we explored the Uji tea region and experienced *chanoyu* at cultural centres in Kyoto while also visiting Kagoshima, Takayama and the Noto Peninsula. Returning again in 2012, again to Uji, we focused on learning more about Japanese tea in order to gain a greater appreciation for the history of tea here and its modern interpretations. Exploring the uniqueness of what Japan has to offer was to be a key part of the most recent 2017 sourcing trip. With more contacts and Japanese friends willing to help us, this was the most in-depth of our trips here and included trips to some stunning tea houses in Kyoto.

First on the itinerary was the island of Kyushu in the south, then on to Kyoto and Wazuka in central Japan. Yame and Kagoshima in Kyushu are highly respected tea areas, but their teas have a very different character to the more traditional style teas of Uji, as do the teas from Wazuka further to the north. Yame and Kagoshima are considered to produce stronger tea than Uji, particular in the umami character. This is the so-called 'fifth taste', after sweet, sour, bitter and salty, and is a highly desirable savoury, brothy taste also found in some mushrooms, Parmesan cheese, tomatoes and seaweed. Nothing can prepare you for the first experience of true umami, but if you enjoy Japanese green tea, that's what you crave – it's the unique element of Japanese tea.

Kyushu's hotter, more tropical climate and therefore earlier flushes than the rest of Japan has often lead to its *aracha* (unfinished tea) being sent to Shizuoka and Uji for finishing, to be sold as Uji or Shizuoka tea. This results in a higher price because of the famous area name plus the incredible taste. One exceptional estate that strives to maximize this special character in its tea is Mr Sakamoto's farm in Kagoshima, see below.

How to sum up Japan? There is beauty everywhere you turn in this country. On every trip we are met with amazing hospitality, stunning teas and beautiful teaware. Back in the west there is rising interest in Japan and we are determined to do our part in spreading the knowledge of Japanese tea and tea culture. Here, we have given you an introduction to modern-day Japanese tea through the lives and words of two inspirational tea farmers, Mr Toshiro and Mr Sakamoto, who we have spent time with on our travels. They both demonstrate how tea farmers in Japan are adapting to secure their future and the future of Japanese tea as a whole.

THE GYOKURO GURU: MR SAKAMOTO, KAGOSHIMA

Rob: Mr Sakamoto and his brother cut an inspiring presence, both in smart white denim 'uniforms' that set the tone for our visit from the outset. The calmness, warmth and quiet expertise they present is common to many tea farmers, but they also give out an incredible energy. I soon realize that this comes from a deep passion for the farm, its soil, the plants and the organic manner they have chosen to adopt.

Mr Sakamoto: 'Our family has 80 years of history in tea, as our grandfather used to grow tea to sell to customers in the local town. We built our factory 45 years ago and use the same machines today. My brother and I took over the farm when we graduated from high school around 30 years ago. When we took over we decided to reduce the size to concentrate on making high-quality tea. Kagoshima tea is second in quality after Yame. The soil and climate give excellent flavour to tea, especially *gyokuro*, which is the only type we make. The land is better for sweeter teas. We started the Sakamoto brand three years ago to sell our tea abroad and in Japan. We continue to work in tea because we want to drink better tea and make healthy tea. My mother, sister and other relatives have been lost to cancer and tea can help to prevent this in others. 'On the farm we grow Saemidori, Yabukita, Okumidori and now the new Kirari 31 Haruto and seimei cultivar. They all have the sweet characteristics for the making of *gyokuro* and are resistant to insects and frost. We use machines to pick our tea and make only *gyokuro*, but also *gyokuro* powdered tea and *gyokuro matcha*. From the 3 hectares we have this year, we will produce 3 tonnes.

'Our tea is organic. We make our own *bokashi* fertilizer on the farm from sesame fibre, rapeseed oil cake, mineral from rocks, silica and a mixture of fermented fish stock and black vinegar. We also sell it to other farmers. This is put on the fields mostly in autumn, but also in spring. We pick only once a year, as more picking will take too much from the plants. After picking we prune the bushes by around 30 centimetres, and these cuttings are left on the ground as compost to feed the good bacteria and promote the soil.

'The tea fields have to be weeded by hand as we can't use herbicides, mostly between the new plants and around the other fields. Very little is made of the plants themselves.' Instead, Mr Sakamoto shows me the earth. The aeration is demonstrated by pushing a 180-centimetre cane down into the soft soil in one fluid motion until only a tiny bit sticks out. It's a sign that his organic fertilizer is doing its job, feeding the organisms in the earth that break everything down and release the nutrients. Not for the first time on the trip, I am told that the fertilizer is not for the plants, it's for the soil.

The effect of good soil is not just how the plant grows. 'The minerals help with antioxidants. If there is less mineral content, the tea will oxidize fast and go off quicker. An organic tea full of minerals will be able to keep fresher than one grown using chemical fertilizer. It is better in production and its cell density is better. More minerals means that the plant molecules are more densely packed, which make them harder for insects to eat. Unfortunately, compared with 60 years ago the soil composition has completely changed. The mineral content has dropped, so we need to reintroduce it through properly made organic fertilizer. Some organic farms grow without this fertilizer but they can't grow good tea with umami in this way.'

When you drink Mr Sakamoto's tea you taste all of the above. That umami flavour is magnified, so it rolls around your mouth, zapping your jaw and continues to change in the aftertaste for a long time. Every decision he takes is to create that moment for his drinkers. In the changing market of Japan, he has put himself firmly in control, determined to make the best tea he can and create interest domestically and abroad.

'We worry about natural disasters, but that's all. The best feeling is when we harvest the new leaf and we get the tea we were aiming to make. As vice-president of the Kagoshima Tea Association I want to represent the farmers and allow tea in this area to thrive. We make the best tea in Japan, and we want to make the people of the world happy and healthy with it.'

THE SIXTH-GENERATION TEA PRODUCER: KOJI NAKAYAMA, YAME

Rob: One producer in Yame has created a whole new market for his tea. His story shows the importance of adaptability in tea producers. The man in question is Koji Nakayama, a sixth-generation tea producer whose family business dates back to 1865. His factory is near Yame city in Fukuoka.

Koji Nakayama: 'I used to work as a trader in Tokyo, but when I was 27 the stock market crashed and I decided to join the tea business. When

I joined, the tea business was going down. I decided that we must sell to foreign countries and over the internet to keep going. We decided to sell to the Middle East and east Asian countries, so we became halal certified. Unfortunately, selling to these countries didn't work very well, as they are too hot for Japanese green tea.

'However, since then I have made connections with distributors in Europe, Australia, Malaysia and Singapore. Our powdered green tea for use in cooking has done well, and an ice-cream company looking for halal tea found us. In Japan there are only four companies that can make halal powdered green tea.

'When it comes to business, selling the tea is the hardest part; making it is easy once you know how. Our tea is very good because our factory is small and we make small amounts at a time. To sell we need to try new, challenging things and think about each market when we try to sell to them. This is difficult. In the future I would like to find more markets for my tea.'

THE PREPARATION AND ENJOYMENT OF JAPANESE TEA

As we have travelled, we have become more and more interested in the role tea plays in the daily lives of people that we meet. We often ask tea farmers and their families 'What is your favourite tea?', 'When do you drink it?' Or 'What do you eat with it?' Judging by the puzzled looks we get, these are not questions that many tea buyers ask.

In Japan, where we are often told about the decline in tea sales in the domestic market, the role of tea in modern Japanese life has been a topic of particular interest to our customers. We spoke to a few Japanese ladies about their memories and experiences of tea, which provided a fascinating insight into everyday Japanese life.

MY RELATIONSHIP WITH TEA: HANAE OMORI

'I was born in Tokyo, but my parents had spent time living in England, so they were accustomed to English tea at breakfast. I still prepare it for my family. The person who got to the kitchen first every morning was obliged to boil hot water and prepare tea. Even though each member of the family had breakfast at different times, the breakfast tea was a family ritual, and is something we all carry on doing, although we all live in separate homes.

'Our day always ended with Japanese green tea (*ryokucha*) or roasted green tea (*houjicha*) after dinner. But we didn't only drink them after dinner. After we took our bath, we would come to the dining table for a cup of Japanese tea. It may have been a custom to prevent dehydration, but for me it was like a cool-down ritual to sum up the day. It was mostly then that I would sit down and talk over with my mother any small problems I had. My parents would read the paper or a book and relax over tea before they went to bed.

Cont'd

'Tea also played a role on special occasions. Having powdered green tea (*matcha*) is quite a special event for us. On New Year's Day, when we visited our grandparents, my grandmother would sometimes call her granddaughters to gather at the *tatami* guest room. She would hold a little tea ceremony for the girls. For me, tea ceremonies were something of a "higher world", a tense and formal event, but I remember feeling a sense of accomplishment afterwards. For a young girl, pure green tea was way too bitter, but the seasonal Japanese sweets that accompanied the tea were something to look forward to. I always admired my grandmother's mastery of Japanese tea.

'In modern Japan, I think tea still plays an important role in socializing. The verb *ocha-wo-suru* (to have tea together) in colloquial Japanese does not simply refer to the action of drinking tea, but refers to having a talk over tea. Regardless of age, we all like to *ocha-wo-suru*. From teenagers to mothers and retired people, it's a universal pastime, a fun and fruitful moment for all of us.

'Tea is an important factor for keeping healthy. I must admit, I am a big coffee drinker too, but tea is like home. Tea is probably one of the core things that make up our Japanese identity.'

MY LIFE IN TEA: AKIHO HORTON

'I am from Kyoto, Japan. I grew up both in Japan and South America (Bolivia and Argentina) and now live in Hertford in the UK. Having tea has been an essential part of my life. My mother used to take me to tearooms very often, even before I could drink tea and coffee – I just had a glass of water but felt so happy to sit and watch people having tea surrounded by nice décor. In Japan we call such tea rooms "kissa-ten", which literally means "tea-drinking shop". They are still my favourite places in Japan to have tea with a book to read or listen to music. I drink English tea in such tearooms. They rarely serve Japanese green tea, which is regarded as something to drink at home.

'Drinking tea after dinner was very important at home. We enjoyed talking a lot over a cup of tea. We tended to drink Japanese green tea (*ryokucha*) or roasted green tea () with sweets or fruits and discuss things that happened at school, work or books you have read. Rather than the taste itself, I just enjoyed the time with my family. I think no matter what type of tea, it has some magic to make people happy and relaxed.

'In Japan we don't have "afternoon tea" like the UK, so having tea is not regarded as a "treat" for me. However, going to a tea ceremony was, and still is, a special occasion. I didn't enjoy the tea ceremony when I was a child as I found it too formal with too many rules and protocols to remember. I still get a little bit nervous to be invited to a tea ceremony, but I can now enjoy more about the tea, artworks, and the whole procedure of the ceremony. It is very beautiful to watch, how the tea is served and without speaking a single word; we share something special during the ceremony. I find it a very philosophical and spiritual way to

enjoy the tea. At the tea ceremony, you have matcha tea with Japanese seasonal sweets. There are two types of matcha tea, usucha (meaning "thin tea") and koicha (meaning "thick tea"). Usucha is much easier to drink for beginners and it is regarded as more casual than koicha.

'In modern-day Japanese life tea connects people, provides a platform for new encounters and at the same time strengthens old bonds. That is how I see the role of tea (tea-drinking culture) in modern Japanese life. For me, tea makes me relax and provides a platform for quality time with my family and friends.'

Japanese teaware

Japan has been making pottery for thousands of years, and its artistic traditions have been much celebrated in the country's culture, eventually becoming an intrinsic part of *chanoyu*, or tea practice (see page 87). Earthenware is the oldest form, dating back to Neolithic times, with stoneware arriving in the third century when the first potter's wheel arrived from China. The Japanese developed their own unique style from the beginning, eventually creating two distinct styles. The first is the simple, roughly finished, traditional pottery in the *wabi-sabi* aesthetic. This philosophy requires a book of its own but, simply put, celebrates 'perfection in imperfection'. The second is the later porcelainware that is highly finished and has a much more complex design. Both these styles lend themselves to teaware.

Much like the development of tea in Japan, early Japanese pottery was inspired by the Chinese. During the Heian period (794–1185) Chinese-style, Japanese-made pottery was very popular and high-quality Chinese pottery was still being imported in large amounts. Chinese pottery was preferred for the early forms of the Japanese tea practice in the thirteenth century. This all changed when in the sixteenth century Sen no Rikyû simplified the *chanoyu*, demanding a simpler aesthetic. Teaware became more accessible to the less well-off, which increased demand and therefore became the focus of many more makers in place of the more standard jugs and vases.

During the early seventeenth century, porcelain was made for the first time in Japan, in a place called Arita. It used the methods of Korean potters and initially emulated the blue-and-white style of Jingdezhen in China (see page 75), but over time it evolved away from this to develop its own unique character. Today, there are six main 'schools' of pottery dotted around Japan, based around major kilns that developed thanks to a region's particular character of clay. These are Bizen (located in Okayama), Echizen (Fukui), Seto (Aichi), Shigaraki (Shiga), Tamba (Hyogo) and Tokoname (Aichi). Of course, thousands of other ancient kilns have existed over time, but these six are still in existence and have historically been considered the most significant as the birthplaces of important design traditions. They are often described as the 'six old kilns'.

We are especially interested in the Tokoname region as it is considered the teaware capital of Japan. This area's link with pottery dates back to 1100 and is believed to be the oldest in Japan. However, it wasn't until the start of the Edo period (1603–1868) that this area became important. In early times it focused mostly on vases and jars, but this period also produced the early *matcha* bowls in the form of *yama-chawans* (mountain tea bowls). These were coarsely finished bowls with little refinement, but beautiful in their simplicity.

Today Tokoname is famous for its redware teapots (*kyusu*), introduced in the early 1860s. Other teapots for green tea had been produced from early in the nineteenth century in Tokoname, but this new style became very popular. Again it was influenced by China, whose own redware teapots were the typical teaware used at this time. The name comes from the deep red, iron-rich clay from which it is made. Its use in Japan had a big effect on Tokoname's ceramic industry, with an influx of new potters who specialized in making redware teapots. This was helped by the visit of a Chinese potter called Jin Shi Heng who, in 1878, was invited to teach Chinese techniques for making teapots, greatly accelerating development and increasing quality. This, combined with a period of rapid industrialization, eventually meant mass-production hit Tokoname towards the end of the nineteenth century, with much small-scale domestic production replaced with industrial-scale manufacturing. However, Tokoname today is a place of great diversity, incorporating both small and large-scale manufacture.

The teapots we use for every day service of Japanese green tea in our teahouses are redware Tokoname teapots. There are three possible forms, categorized according to where the handle is sited. A *yokode kyusu* has it on the side, an *ushirode kyusu* has it at the back and an *uwade kyusu* has a handle on the top. The most typical modern type is the *yokode kyusu*, which is the one we use at Comins. This style can be traced back to the end of the Song dynasty (960–1279) in China for the preparation of powdered tea. It has been adapted perfectly over time to meet Japanese needs, incorporating a fine mesh to prevent the fine particles of tea from coming out. Each one is balanced according to the potter's preferences. Customers often comment how simple yet effective their design is, not knowing that the concept has not really changed in 900 years!

MEETING THE MAKERS

Rob: If you have been fortunate enough to have watched or taken part in a Japanese tea practice you will know that it is a very intimate occasion. During the time spent focussing on each movement of the host and the response that each one requires, a connection develops. The calmness of the process, the smoothness of the movements, and the delicate swish of the matcha whisk create an atmosphere that is both meditative and focussing.

In this section, we look at two very different ceramicists who make bowls (*chawans*) used in this unique process. The *chawan* has played an integral part of *chanoyu* for many hundreds of years, and still does to this day.

The Miyagawa family line of ceramicists began 330 years ago. Initially, the family was concerned with restoration using ceramic firing techniques, as at this time ceramics were very expensive. Around 200 years ago they started to create ceramics full time. The youngest Miyagawa is an eleventh-generation potter and also a *chanoyu* master.

The family specializes in making chawan bowls for the *chado* (*matcha* practice) as well as bowls for *sencha* leaf tea. International recognition began when the family won at the Expo 1876 Philadelphia, and has continued with numerous prizes at other world fairs, such as Gold at the Paris Expo of 1900. The family's work can be found in many permanent collections throughout the world. In the last 100 years their main focus has been on *chanoyu*.

When I visited Kyoto, where they are based, the newest generation and the drive behind the business, Shinichi Miyagawa, was in the USA getting ready for an exhibition. I was welcomed into their family house, studio and kiln by his father Kousai Miyagawa, a man with enormous experience. After walking over the just-washed stones of the path I entered through the cloths hanging in front of the house's small wooden sliding front doors. I was ushered into one of the family's two tea rooms. When they built the house 50 years ago they understood the need to greet their guests properly and show their wares off. I was served *matcha* in a beautiful bowl by the lady of the house. Thankfully, by now I knew what my part in this ritual should be. I thanked my host, turned the bowl in my hands, drank and then turned it back. I then replaced it onto the *tatami* mat and carefully examined it. This is part of the process, but I would have done it anyway, as the bowl demanded to be looked at. I was informed that it was a family bowl made by his grandfather.

We exited the house and went down to the family studio, a remarkable light and airy space that felt energized by the craft that took place there. Every aspect was beautiful to look at, from the wooden shoes Mr Miyagawa was wearing to the clay-covered work benches and piles of delicate tools. I asked him how it had begun for him.

'I was twenty-six when I became a potter,' he replied. 'Before that I wanted to be a calligrapher, but that was not to be and I joined the family business. Up until I was thirty I felt the pressure to learn, but my ancestors let me be free to do what I wanted. I don't believe I am talented, but I definitely have something inside that helps.

'I have always made *matcha* bowls, but in the last 50 years people are getting tired of old Japan, which is *matcha*. They want new things, so we started making *sencha* bowls as well. There is not the same level of history in making a *sencha* bowl. Just recently we started making stone bowls as a new challenge, but I like clay better, as there are more techniques that you can use. My son likes clay, but in the future we'll make both. We have always tried to keep pace with the progression of styles and taste over time, but our work follows on from the past work.'

Mr Miyagawa looked content and as he moved around his studio and I could see that, even after making pots for 50 years, he still loves what he does. I asked whether he would ever stop. The reply was an emphatic 'no' and that as long as he can move, he will be in the studio. He told me that what he doesn't enjoy is the business part of the work, making the same things over and over for big orders. He makes pots every day and enjoys making a living from it. When I asked him about the future, he said: 'The growth of the Japanese economy is not very rapid at the moment. Japanese people are not buying enough, so we need to grow in foreign places. This has happened before in the 1900s when Japan was poor – we had to export to foreign countries then as well. This was when the Victoria & Albert Museum in London bought many of our pieces.

'We began overseas development again about ten years ago, concentrating on our unique techniques developed through history and tradition combined with the spirit of *chanoyu*. We held a tea practice and lecture meeting in London and Paris last year, which was attended by many people with a deep knowledge of Japanese culture, including country ambassadors, curators and collectors.'

Until this point I hadn't directly asked about tea, as I didn't want the conversation to move away from ceramics. But now I asked how deep the connection was between the *chawan* and the tea. 'It's a big challenge because of how the bowl needs to be,' he explained. 'It must have a weight that is heavy enough in the hand, but not so much that it can't be held and turned with ease. If it is too thin it will lose its heat too quickly, but too thick and it becomes awkward and will not let any heat through to the drinker's hands.

'The important parts of the bowl are the foot (*kodai*), which is the base it sits on and must be the correct size for the host to hold with their thumb and fingers. Next, the inside of the bowl must be smooth and consistent so as to not damage the delicate bamboo whisk. Finally, the rim of the bowl must be the correct thickness and be smooth, so it can be wiped clean and is not sharp to the mouth. It is a big challenge, as the chado is very important to Japanese people.'

Mr Miyagawa also pointed out that different seasons demanded different *chawans*, with wide, flatter shapes being used in summer time, and smaller, deeper ones that don't lose heat so quickly are used in winter times. In fact, there are *chawans* for every season, every occasion and even importance of the guest. Another key feature important for the bowls' use in *chado* is that of the 'face'. This is a distinctive form that is deemed to be the most beautiful part of the bowl. It could be a drawing, glaze pattern, distortion, dent or anything distinctive that is chosen by the host or in some cases, the maker. During *chado* this is pointed at the guest by the host, and is the reason for the turning of the *chawan* by the guest. You must not drink from the face – instead you must turn it to face the host. It must then be turned back before returning the bowl to the floor.

We ended the tour by visiting a small *tatami*-floored room with 20 or so exquisite *chawans* laid out humbly on the floor and finally with another *matcha* back in the tea room in the house. Walking to the car, my companion informed me that I should be pleased. I agreed, but then asked why. 'Because a host matches their choice of *chawan* to the guest,' was the response. 'The *chawan* you have just been served was even more beautiful than the first one you were given.' I decided I would accept the compliment without any argument.

THE FOURTEENTH-GENERATION POTTER: JUN KAWAJIRI

Rob: Jun Kawajiri is a fourteenth-generation potter based in Kyoto. His kiln is to the east of the city in an area where traditionally kilns were concentrated. I first met Jun in the car driven by Mr Yutaka Kinoshita, my amazing guide, who collected me from Kyoto Shinkansen station (bullet train) after a superfast but nonetheless quite long journey from Kagoshima in 2017.

Yutaka had kindly agreed to guide me around Kyoto as well as take me to meet a farmer in the Wazuka tea fields near Kyoto. Jun joined us on the journey to Wazuka and we chatted in the car about how he became a potter.

Jun: 'I decided to be a potter sixteen or seventeen years ago, I was a graphic designer before. I realized that pottery had many aspects of painting and sculpture. Previous generations of my family created very traditional pieces, but I am interested in contemporary; there was no pressure to continue the lineage of potters or even their work. I strive to do new things, but the colours and glazes that I use come from the traditions of my ancestors.

'I think that Japanese art has a special sense of beauty and an interesting feel to it. For example, there is the art of finding beauty within creations that appear to have nothing to do with beauty. We cherish crooked and chipped teacups and teapots that seem poor at a glance, and prefer imperfect objects to the perfection of perfect circles or symmetrical forms. This sense of beauty originated with the practice of *chanoyu*.

'In the history of Japanese Yamato-e paintings, there is no sign of pursuit or desire to represent the real space on a two-dimensional surface with extreme preciseness; it never followed the laws of perspective. As a result, painters placed motives freely on the screen and painted in an extremely flat style with deformation, creating an open-hearted art that generated the gem of a movement called *Rinpa*. I love such sense of beauty and feel it is unique to Japan; I have been creating works as a proof of love and respect for them.'

After our trip to the tea fields, high up in the Wazuka hills, we returned to Kyoto to visit Jun's studio. We parked up next to a vintage car, several motor bikes and a number of large kilns in a corrugated iron-clad garage, which led to a series of dusty, crowded rooms. Everywhere I looked pottery was stacked – glazed and unglazed, traditional and contemporary, restaurant ware and unique pieces. Even to my untrained eye I could see the variations in clay used. I was led to a table where a jumble of pots were placed, all unlike each other and all beautiful in completely different ways. I was also drawn to a shelf of rough-textured, oddly shaped *chawans* that were painted in bright, bold colours. These were the same as those I had seen in my research, and of a style that had been produced in Japan since the seventeenth or eighteenth centuries. They were in sharp contrast to the perfectly smooth round ones I had seen at the Miyagawa family studio.

Further exploration showed that Jun was equally skilled at making smooth-finished pots as well as the deliberately imperfect ones from coils. 'When people try to make a pot look unbalanced, it looks too unbalanced,' Jun said. 'It has to be a natural process. If you do it a thousand times rather than ten, you understand the way the clay wants to react.' This is a recurring theme in Japan.

THE BRITISH-JAPANESE POTTER: YO THOM

Michelle: Closer to home in Dorset, I first encountered Yo Thom's work in a gallery in Shaftesbury, Dorset, before I met the wonderful lady herself. I love Yo's work because it is beautiful but functional. Whenever I visit I am offered Japanese tea in one of her *yunomi* teacups, which we use in our teahouses. They are a great reminder to take time, savour and enjoy Japanese tea every day. This is Yo's story and her thoughts on the enjoyment of Japanese tea.

Yo: 'I was born in Tokyo in 1973. When I was growing up, my mother was always making pots as a hobby – she was taking the pottery class run by my art teacher at school. I knew I wanted to work in 3D so took a product design course. When I visited the ceramics department I was instantly captivated; I knew that it was what I wanted to do and nothing else.

'*Yunomi* is the term for everyday tea cups used for green tea. They are narrower and taller than a *matcha* tea bowl, and generally people hold it with one hand, whereas a *matcha* tea bowl has to be held with both hands. *Yunomi* don't have handles, as green tea is not meant to be made with boiling hot water, and by holding the cup body you can feel the warmth of the tea. People tend to have their own *yunomi* to use every day. I remember my grandmother and my parents had green tea (*sencha*) after their breakfast every day. As a child, I didn't drink much green tea, but my children love cold *mugi-cha* (barley tea) in the hot summer season. My mother was always making a big jug of *mugi-cha* to chill in the fridge for us.

'Now, as an adult living outside Japan, sharing green tea with Japanese friends brings with it all sorts of fond memories. *Matcha* was certainly not an everyday drink in our household, and I would think the majority of Japanese households would have *matcha* only on special occasions, or in their desserts, like cakes with *matcha* powder or sweetened *matcha* powder sprinkled on top of shredded ice in the summer.

'Not everybody practices *chanoyu* in Japan; it's a bit like having British traditional afternoon tea at the Ritz! Sometimes you can go to an old-style cafe that serves *matcha*, but on the whole *matcha* is special. The tea ceremony in the old days was for men, the rich and the Samurai to keep them focused before war. It morphed into something based on etiquette for ladies, but nowadays it is individual, based on your motivation for practising it.

'My *yunomi* take a relatively traditional Japanese shape. We have all sorts of different shapes for *yunomi*: straight, tapered, rounded, with a waist. I like the *yunomi* with a bit of waist, so your hand fits comfortably to enjoy the warmth of the tea. My *yunomi* are thrown on a wheel, but look hand-built because I alter the surface of the thrown pots when the clay is a little drier. I use a wire-slicer to shave the surface (called 'faceting') and finish the bottoms by hand rather than on a wheel (called 'turning'). This is to give the *yunomi* an individual look, and is also inspired by the Japanese *wabi-sabi* aesthetic. This philosophy was developed alongside the tea ceremony, mainly in the sixteenth century, and it is something very particular to Japanese culture. I like making shapes that look like a found object or something out of nature. I use the throwing technique to produce numbers, but hand-shaping the organic look feels more comfortable for me.'

south korea

Korea sits below China, and is separated from Japan by the Korea Strait and Sea of Japan. With such influential neighbours, it's no surprise that Korea's tea history is entwined with theirs, and that Buddhism again takes a central place.

It is said that tea first reached what is now North and South Korea back in 108 BC, when the country was known as Gojoseon. At this time the Han Chinese took over the country, influencing every aspect of indigenous culture, including the introduction of tea. Tea did not become fully established until the sixth or seventh centuries, in the middle of the Three Kingdoms Period, which corresponds with the Chinese Tang dynasty (618–907). At this time, Korea's monks and scholars were visiting the growing number of Chinese schools of Buddhism, where they were introduced to tea drinking traditions long established in China.

Various early monarchs took to tea, but it wasn't until 828, during the reign of King Heungdeok (826–836), that the order was given to bring tea seeds from China for cultivation. Although probably not the first to be planted in the country, they were sewn at the Ssanggye Temple of Jiri Mountain in Hadong County.

Tea culture thrived during the Goryeo (Koryeŏ) dynasty (918–1392) as rich aristocrats increased the popularity of tea drinking and Buddhist monasteries promoted the benefits of the rituals behind it. The development of mental discipline and the contemplation that came with this became highly valued. King Taejo, the first ruler of this period, gave gifts of tea (*uh-cha*) to worthy people such as Buddhist priests and monks and member of the military. Tea was also given as a reward for loyalty, or even in death or illness.

Tea became important to all classes of the population, unlike in China and Japan, and this reflected its use. Offering tea to the spirits of natural places or those of your ancestors became popular. These so-called *ch'a-rye*, ancestral commemorations, happened at New Year and during the full harvest moon. Less formal offerings were made to statues of Buddha in temples. Tea also began to be placed with the dead as part of funeral ceremonies. The growing demand meant that teaware production also developed, resulting in the start of celadon (greenware) pottery. Tea also became an intrinsic part of poetry, song, art and drama, and some of the oldest poems involved tea.

The popularity of tea stopped with the Joseon dynasty (1392–1897) and the seizing of power by the Yi family. They implemented a change from Buddhism to a variant of Chinese Confucianism, resulting in an end to Buddhist ceremonies and the destruction of many monasteries. The association of drinking tea with Buddhism led to a hefty government tax on the plant, the destruction of many tea fields and the widespread replacement of tea by wine as the formal drink. The purge was so severe that some accounts indicate that tea disappeared completely from the ruling classes at this time. Certainly the first great Korean written text on tea, the *Ch'aBu* or 'Rhapsody to Tea' by Yi Mok in 1490, did not even mention Korean tea, but focused on Chinese tea entirely. Again, it was Buddhist monks who ensured tea culture was kept alive through this time, although, oddly, there may also have been a Royal department responsible for tea.

The situation was only to get worse, as the few tea fields left in the Southern provinces were destroyed in the Seven Year War with Japan (1592–8), along with the massive destruction of Korea's settlements and farmland. To rub further salt in the wound, many of the skilled craftspeople and potters were exiled to Japan after the war. Korea's loss was Japan's gain as this surge in knowledge was absorbed and utilized.

There was a slight resurgence in the late 1800s thanks to a returning interest in Buddhist ways, but sadly this growth was again set to be disturbed. The Japanese occupation (1910–45), World War II and the Korean War (1950–3) all inflicted further destruction on an already fragile industry. However, from then until now there have not been any significant hurdles preventing the rebuilding of Korea's tea culture. By the 1960s, when tea agriculture had begun to grow again, farmers were growing tea as a business rather than for religious purposes. This marked a distinct change.

One man, Ch'oi Pom-sul (later the Venerable Hyo Dang), was a driving force in this restoration. Head monk of the Dasol-Sa Temple in the Jiri mountains, he wrote the first comprehensive modern study of tea in Korea, *Hangukui Chado* ('The Korean Way of Tea') in 1973. He founded the 'Korean Association for the Way of Tea' to promote the understanding and study of all aspects of his country's tea. Hyo Dang is known for a particular green-tea processing method still used to produce *panyaro* or 'The Dew of Enlightening Wisdom'. Unsurprisingly, he also had a part to play in the teaching of all the modern tea masters who are continuing his work on the revival of Korean tea.

Above all, Hyo Dang insisted that tea was to be 'drunk quite naturally, in the course of daily life, and should not be made the subject of unnecessary constraints'. We have already mentioned the complex rituals of the Japanese and Chinese tea ceremonies, with their exacting focus on the meaning of gestures and movements. In Korea this is not the case and a greater importance is placed on remaining natural while drinking tea with others.

The Venerable Hyo Dang died in 1979, but his cause of revitalizing the tea industry did not. One of his longstanding pupils, Chae Won Hwa, is considered as his successor and has continued in the promotion of the 'Way of Tea'. Every leading master of tea in Korea has been instructed by her since she took over the mantle. After his death the growth of the industry continued, helped by a period of economic growth that gave a welcome boost.

Compared with the rest of Asia, Korea produces a very small amount of tea per year, and a limited amount is exported. Although tea is grown in North Korea, it is South Korea that produces the majority, mostly towards its southern tip. From the 1980s onwards, tea production grew steadily to around 1,500 tonnes a year in 2005–6, then declined for a few years due to a surplus of green tea and the beginning of imports. Production grew to an estimated 2,500–3,000 tonnes per year in 2016. Today, Korean tea production can be split into industrial-size farms and small-scale farmers. The average tea farm size is less than 1 hectare, but in areas such as Boseong and Jeju Island larger farms exist, the biggest being over 500 hectares. The smaller family-run farms are mostly found in the Jiri mountain area.

Korea has four major tea-growing regions: Mount Jiri, Boseong, Jeonnam and Jeju Island. The first three are located on the mountain slopes near the ocean in the temperate south of the Korean peninsula, while the latter is a volcanic island off this coast. Boseong is the best-known area, making up of 40 percent of the total tea produced. Soosoo Choi, a tea farmer from Boseong, gave us a local perspective on the differences between the areas: 'the tea farms in Boseong continuously study customers' tastes and always adapt to accept new styles. It is important for the tea farms of Hadong (adjacent to Mount Jiri) to adhere to their traditional methods or to the personal styles they have invented. Jeju Island is a more special case. As it is a volcanic island, the soil differs from region to region and the flatland plantations mean that machines can be used. This area is also influenced by a large enterprise tea farm called O'Sullock from Amore Pacific. They harvest

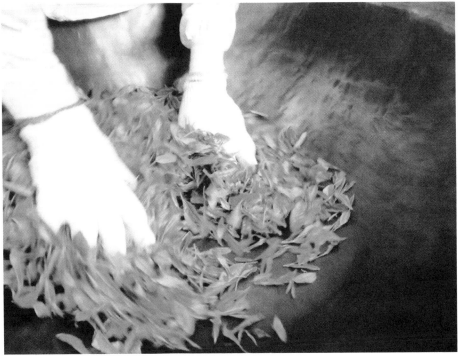

tea with machines and work with small, local tea farms.'

These areas produce mostly high-quality green tea or *nokcha*, which is often called *jaksul* when it is high-grade artisan tea. *Jaksul* translates as 'sparrow's tongue', because the picked leaf resembles the narrow point of a sparrow's tongue. Teas fall into four categories, depending on plucking time. These are governed by 24 seasonal dates according to the movement of the sun. The absolute first pick of the year and the most special grade is called *ujeon* and occurs before the first spring rain on April 20. *Sejak* ('small sparrow') is the second pick, occurring after the spring rain in early May. Then comes the *joongjak* ('medium sparrow'), which is picked in late May. Finally, *daejak* ('large sparrow') is made with mature leaves and plucked in late June.

There are also many oxidized teas made in Korea, known as 'fermented teas' there. In this case, unlike elsewhere, fermentation means the same thing as oxidation. These teas are often referred to as *balhyocha*, which covers all types of oxidized teas and extreme variation in the methods used by tea producers. This can be split up into further subcategories such as 'half oxidized' and 'partially oxidized', but even this does not seem to be consistent between farmers. Further to these is *hwangcha*, which can refer to a tea of any level of oxidation depending on the maker and may include yellow, oolong or even black tea. This can cause a little confusion to the western buyer, but seems not to in Korea itself.

Our South Korea

We first tried Korean tea when an enterprising garden sent some samples to our teahouse. We were blown away by the difference in flavour from our better-known Japanese and Chinese green teas and this chance tasting put Korea firmly on our list of countries to visit, the country we have explored most recently. One of the most surprising elements of the journey so far has been the tone of the conversations and connections we have made. In Korea, tea is about naturalness, comfort and connection, which is also a key theme for us at Comins, so this beautiful country, in which there is rising interest in the west, is the perfect way to end this chapter. This is our contribution to the spreading of knowledge about South Korean tea and tea culture, stories that demonstrate how South Korea is reaching out to the world to offer us a new and exciting tea experience that many of us in the west will never have tried. For us, the words of the Korean tea producers we profile here have an energy and spirit that is unique to South Korea, and we hope that these passionate tea ambassadors, who are at the forefront of the growing interest in Korean tea, ignite the same energy in you.

THE EXPORT EXPERT: JAEKWAN SHIM, HADONG

Michelle: In Korea I was fortunate to come across the extremely helpful and friendly Jaekwan Shim. Jaekwan is responsible for promoting exports from the Hadong area, a job that includes strawberries, persimmons, pears, fish and tea! He first truly appreciated Korean tea when he moved to Hadong.

Jaekwan Shim: 'The first time I drank tea here was a real surprise. The tea master made really good green tea – we infused the tea 9 times and the taste was amazing. I asked myself: "how is it possible to get the same amazing taste 9 times?" I never forgot this experience.' Jaekwan joined the Hadong County office in 2015 and now starts every day with his colleagues and a cup of Hadong tea, either green or fermented green tea. His daily work is all about helping farmers find a market for their exceptional tea: 'Tea farmers know how to grow the tea but they don't know how to export it. Export tea markets are growing, so we help the tea farmers achieve consistency in quality as well as with packaging and, of course, making connections with export customers. The main export from the Hadong area is green tea and green tea powder. *Ujeon*, the most premium tea, is very popular.' Jaekwan went on to explain how the area works: 'We work with small farmers – there are over 2,000 in Hadong. They are almost all Korean organic standard and most of the Hadong area is made up of a patchwork of 100-hectare farms. Hadong is the original place for green tea – production started here 1,200 years ago. Today there are 100 small tea companies making handmade green teas, and there are also larger companies with their own factories.'

He went on to explain the hand-making process in more detail. 'The freshly picked bright green leaves gradually go a dark green as you gently hand-toss them in a giant wok, wearing two layers of gloves to avoid your hands getting burned. Next, hand-roll and crush the leaves a few times, as if rolling tough pastry, before laying them out on a rack to dry. They then alternately get laid out in the sun and brought inside, and then they're ready for use. It's a laborious process, but worth it in the end for some of the finest tea available. Those leaves that are left in the sun longer start to ferment, producing longer-lasting black tea, while yellow tea is 50 percent fermented. The precious green tea is unfermented.

'The end result is distinctive in flavour, which is informed by the environment. The whole environment around Hadong is special, and clean – we have two national parks and of course we have the combination of three good mountains, rivers and the ocean. For the tea drinker, this environment produces a distinctively stronger cup than Japanese tea, which we produce continually from April to September. The best "bud" tea is produced in April.'

Like other tea-producing areas in the world, the main problems facing this area relate to labour. 'Many farmers don't want to continue with this life – there is more money to be made in the city and, of course, the city is more fun for the young. Our job is to try and encourage people to work in, and to drink more, tea. Our young people are increasingly turning to coffee and although more are drinking green tea, the majority is going into products such as tea noodles. We need to encourage consumption in the pure form.'

THE TRADITIONAL FAMILY FARMER: SEO JUNG MIN, HADONG

Michelle: So who runs these small tea companies in the Hadong area? I was intrigued to learn more about the families working hard to produce exceptional tea for Jaekwan to promote, and he introduced me to Seo Jun Min. Part of a younger generation of tea farmers, Seo Jun Min returned to his family farm in Hadong after a career in the city. He told me about his farm and his life, giving me a glimpse into traditional Korean tea farming in this incredible area.

Seo Jun Ming: 'My tea farm is two hectares in size and is called Youn Woo. My mother started making the tea when I was growing up. I left the countryside and went to work in the city for LG Electronics, but my mother was getting old so I moved back to Hadong County and started to make tea. You could say that I am a second-generation tea farmer.

'I remember that first day I returned to Hadong really clearly. It was snowing. I brought my young baby, my three-year-old daughter and my wife with me. My house is on the mountain just next to the tea farm, so you have to imagine that it is very hard to arrive at. However, the mountain location means the tea trees are strong compared to the low-lying areas. On that day the view was so impressive – all snow and no footprints – unforgettable.

'I make mostly green tea, but also some other teas including fermented tea. All of my tea is handmade and our farm has Korean organic certification. We hand pick the fresh green tea before withering, pan frying and rolling it. On a normal day we have 10 people working and in the busy time 20 people are involved in picking and making the tea.'

Like people in tea the world over, Seo Jun Min's experiences have left him keen to spread the word to others: 'I enjoy taking tea with my friends – for me green tea leaves me feeling clear in my mind. I want everybody to enjoy this feeling, so looking to the future my ambition is to make Korean green tea popular worldwide. Making delicious green tea has become my life aim!'

THE ENTREPRENEURIAL TEA MAKER: SOOSOO CHOI, BOSEONG

Michelle: The Boseong area has an interesting energy. My curiosity was sparked and I wanted to learn more about the tea landscape here. We were introduced to Soosoo Choi, whose story, feelings and optimism towards Korean tea mark the perfect end to this chapter, leaving us with a sense of the entrepreneurial energy that will see Korean tea make its mark on the world stage.

Soosoo Choi: 'I run a tea farm called Dachae in Boseong. Our farm is located at an altitude of 230 metres and is 9 hectares in total, with 2.9 hectares dedicated to tea fields. Three people work regularly on the farm, all of whom are family members, and we use extra people only temporarily when we make tea or manage the farm.

'We started our brand in 2010, focusing on the values of colour, diversity, harmony, and the beauty of Mother Nature. The name Dachae literally means "various colours", but also can be interpreted as "colour of tea" or "house of tea". We gave our name a lot of thought as we wanted it to convey something to the tea drinker before they experience the tea. Our collection of teas includes "pure" masters tea, herbal infusions and blends. We blend tea with seasonal plants in our farm, so it is always experimental.

'I first started out in tea farming because of an interest in plants, but later I fell in love with the dramatic changes of tea leaves that were influenced by human hands. I think the environment of Boseong also influenced me. The saying is that I did not choose to farm the tea, but I was chosen. I am a natural-born follower before I am a pioneer of the land.

'The original form of the Dachae Teahouse was SsiNal Farm, which dates back to 1998. Hoping to make a botanic garden resembling the colourful, harmonious beauty of nature, we started creating a peaceful landscape. Displaying aligning tea bushes was one way we did this. We then started to learn to make teas, and became professional tea manufacturers afterwards. Of all the plants, tea leaves always ensure us endless possibilities.

'Since tea farming is based on plant materials, the pattern of work is repeated once a year rather than once a day. Because our tea farm is small, the whole process of delivering a cup of tea to consumers, from soil, cultivation, processing and packaging to marketing and sales, is in our hands, and these activities follow a pattern and rhythm throughout the year.'

Soosoo and her team mainly produce green teas, which are more suited to the terroir of Boseong, but she explained the growing trend for other tea products, including green tea powder for use as an ingredient, and fermented tea. 'We are constantly evolving by following customers' requirements and tastes. For example, we also produce a traditional *byeongcha cheongtaejeon*, a coin-shaped, post-fermented tea based on Jangheung right next to Boseong. We are also working on a special brand called Korean Breakfast. It is a blend of products from 12 tea farms in the Boseong area. The tea master from Australia and all 12 tea farms evaluated the taste and scent, determined the ratio and completed it. Many people are expressing curiosity about this brand. We also plan to introduce the 12 individual tea farms step by step. We feel that if we keep developing this, it will strengthen the weaker points of Korean teas – production scale and production cost – and enhance Korean tea's competitiveness in the world market.'

Soosoo believes that the main challenge for Korean tea is to develop distinctive cultivars that are both suitable for the cultivation environment in Korea and have stand-out qualities when processed. She explained: 'this takes a lot of time and effort, so it's not easy for the producers to try on their own. Now, the National Institute of Agriculture Technology in Junnnam Province [JARES] has developed several kinds of green tea and used them in a few tea farms for test cultivation. If we have our own cultivars, we can finally have our own tea, making it much easier to introduce our Korean tea to the world market. In the short term, we continue to maintain a strong focus on building trust with customers. All the farmland in Boseong has been changed to organic cultivation. Our quality standards are in line with the guidelines set by the United States, Europe, and Japan, so we are entitled to sell with the Organic Certification Mark attached in these countries. As Korean green tea is not yet traded actively on the international market, there are huge opportunities to present this fresh new product to consumers!'

As we leave, I ask Soosoo what she believes makes the difference between good and great Korean tea. Her reply has really stuck with me because it is completely in line with my thoughts and feelings on tea. The enjoyment and ceremony of tea has never been a formal affair for me, rather a journey of discovery that excites me; if I allow my mind to be quiet, it takes me by the hand and helps me to become increasingly open to the world and to other people. Soosoo's words are the perfect end to this section.

'Nearly everything is important in producing a great tea. Choosing an appropriate cultivar, sensitivity in the handling of the tea and having a fine control of the details of a tea-processing process. All of these elements must be carefully considered, so you can start to see how much hard work sits behind making a great tea. Despite these endless efforts we understand that there has to be an exception. Each of us all have our own private history, a weight of life, context and drama. So when we make tea we already know in our hearts that our personal best may not suit others; these results may not immediately be seen as a great tea for everyone because each person has their own preference for tea, that is, personal history, so they can have different assessments.

'So I do not impose my personal taste on others. Some people would definitely dislike the robust, bitter taste of our tea – it doesn't matter whether you have lots of experience or not. We must respect each others' preferences and aim to leave a memorable scene in the tea drinker's mind, rather than preparing a formal ostentation. Tea makers should not force anyone who does not like the bitter taste to enjoy it. It is important to let people enjoy tea comfortably instead of making them "learn" the way to drink tea. All of this will leave good memories about tea and help tea drinkers to choose great tea by constant effort, and to see and appreciate how tea changes over time.

'Central to the approach I have described is the relationship between the makers of tea and the people who enjoy them. We must work hard as ambassadors of tea to engage tea drinkers and maintain their interest and curiosity.'

THE PREPARATION AND ENJOYMENT OF KOREAN TEA

For us at Comins, it is still early in our Korean tea journey. As our interest in Korean tea has grown, we have started to research and learn about ceramics and teaware. Very occasionally you come across something really rather special with someone equally special behind it. Thanks to an image of a beautiful teapot we met Seong Il, one of the most wonderfully open people we have ever met. Through him we have gained a real-life view of Korean tea culture and tea preparation. Rather than looking at formal ceremonies, in this section we aim to give you a taste of the sentiment behind tea preparation here.

THE CREATIVE CONNECTOR: SEONG IL HONG, POTTER, BOSEONG

Seong Il: 'My passion is Onggi – traditional Korean earthenware pottery that dates back to 4000–5000 BC, and is used for storage jars for things like kimchi, soy sauces and hot sauces that you want to ferment over time. Onggi clay is rich in iron materials, which means it has a lot of air in it, which in turn is good for the storage of foods that you want to ferment.

'Learning traditional Onggi pottery was the most important turning point in my pottery life. I left Seoul in 2000 and moved to Jeollanam-do Boseong, where I met my wife, who also came to study earthenware. Since moving here I have been making teaware. Tea culture is thriving in this area, along with Jeju Island and Hadong. Today, I run a teaware gallery, tea house and pottery studio. From this space I communicate with tea people and teaware lovers. I simply spend my days drinking tea with them and making pottery. People come to this place from all over the world, as far afield as Singapore, Switzerland, France and America. I find that westerners have a lot of interest in Asian culture, but there aren't many ways for them to access it. My space allows me to share my knowledge.

'I love to work at the wheel. The work I do on the wheel while the clay is wet is all about maximizing the properties of the clay. I like to be part of the change in the formation of the clay. I use clay from South Korea. The east–north line of the peninsula has a lot of white porcelain, and eastern Korea is famous for white porcelain wares. The west–south line of the peninsula has a lot of iron clay. This is darker and better for making the traditional Onggi. Onggi clay is the most interesting part of my work, but pure porcelain is also used to satisfy customer preferences and certain design elements. Porcelain clay is good for detail and the animals and carvings that are popular on the top of pots. In Korea, every year has an animal – 2018 is the year of the yellow dog (yellow meaning 'gold'). If the dog is represented on the items you own you will be happier this year.'

Seong Il showed me four types of teapots using different clay. One in particular used iron clay with white slip and clear glaze. This seemed an unusual combination, but Seong Il explained: 'In this area all the people want to show the iron clay like the white pottery. They put the white slip on it and put on the clear glaze – it is felt that this combination represents the history of the Korean ceramics.'

Seong Il gains inspiration for his wares from the long history of ceramics in Korea. He told me that 'we find a lot of inspiration in museums, and over time I have found that I prefer the variability of stoneware. Porcelain never changes, it stays white. When I make my pieces I choose the clay carefully, taking into consideration how the clay and ingredients will affect the taste of the tea. Porcelain is a very pure material – when fired it is not porous, and it has a very "tight" finish like glass. This is the type of teaware we use for green tea, as it does not affect the character of the tea. In contrast, stoneware has a relationship with the tea and affects the taste. This is the type of teaware we use for Korean *hwangcha* and *balhyocha*. At my studio we make different types of stoneware and experiment with different types to get the right stability and profile for each pot. Since the pot will become part of the experience of the tea, we always taste the tea in the pots we make to see how the clay affects the flavour. Some combinations are good: this is not "hard" data, but is based on our experience. I use around 30 percent of the iron clay from my local area along with clay from different areas to make a perfect combination. Some people like stoneware and some people don't; these pots are a very personal choice.'

Back at home, tea plays a central role in life, but as Seong Il explained, this is focused more on comfort than ceremony. 'At home I tend to drink my favourite tea, which I call half-fermented tea – I especially enjoy Korean yellow tea. I don't drink *puer* unless it is at least 20 years old. When we drink tea at home the focus is on comfort, the smell and the taste.

'Frankly speaking, tea culture in Korea hasn't been strictly established, compared to the tea cultures of China or Japan. Since the Korean War, it hasn't been connected directly to health or food matters, and still remains one of many choices of pastime. In day-to-day life this means, at least for me, that there is no fixed sequence like in Japan or China: tea culture in our country is more about the comfort and mental healing than the tea ceremony itself. I personally feel a lot of mental healing and security through the tea ceremony and the teaware that is used. Fresh Boseong green tea is enjoyed in our local schools, hot or cold depending on the season, but we don't teach or learn the tradition.' As in many other cultures in the world, Seong Il notes how in recent years coffee culture has surpassed tea, but he does see how in Korea, just as we see in the West, interest in the slower and more considered lifestyle surrounding tea is starting to gain people's interest.

'Our diet in Korea is very low in oils: we eat a lot of vegetables, rice and fruits. We can digest our food well, so have not felt the need to drink tea to aid digestion or for health, which is a big driver for consumption in other parts of the world. Secondly, we are a small country and our tea production is low relative to other markets. Our history of tea culture reminds us that it is related to healing, comfort and wealthy people rather than something to enjoy everyday. Lastly, in our busy modern lives we need coffee to help us work late into the night. You need more time to enjoy tea and people feel they don't have time – therefore tea is not perceived to be good for work.'

'Having said this, I have noticed that young tea lovers are becoming more interested in tea culture. Many individual, characterful tea places are opening in the commercial district. Koreans' preference in teas are not restricted to the boundaries of Korea. Korea's tea culture still has lots of opportunity to develop into a world-wide blue ocean in terms of expandability.' I love the optimism of Seong-Il and I have to say that, having tasted their teas from his beautiful pots, I quite agree.

This all sounds incredibly positive – but for us back home in the west, why should we buy and drink Korean tea and use Korean teaware? Back to Seong-Il to sell them to us: 'To me Korean teas are more tender and delicate compared to Chinese, Taiwanese, Japanese and other teas from the rest of the world. Chinese and Taiwanese teas have extraordinary scents, Japanese tea has a great colour, but Korean tea concentrates on the tea itself, so it has a more soothing taste and scent. Also, the quality is worth mentioning.

Soft, tender tea leaves are hand-picked and produced with numerous processes, and the results are consistently at a premium level. Small tea producers stick to small production and do not increase the amount, therefore maintaining quality. Last but not least, Korean teaware has adopted both the technological advantage of Chinese and the elegant beauty of Japanese teaware. Fancy, but also functional. Efficient Korean teaware has a proper structure to allow the enjoyment of different kinds of teas, so I am sure that they will gradually achieve their true value as the time passes.'

taiwan

Located just off the coast of China, Taiwan is a small mountainous island with a big presence in tea. It has a rich and varied past that didn't have any European contact until the Portuguese travelled there in 1590, naming it Ilha Formosa ('beautiful island'). It was, however, the Dutch, who occupied the country from 1624–62, who were the first to develop the tea trade in the area, mostly using it as a transfer post to meet the demand for Chinese tea from Europe.

A report by the governor of the Dutch East India Company in 1645 mentions that two wild tea subspecies (the so-called Taiwan Mountain Tea and Red Sprout Mountain Tea) had been found growing in the central mountain region of Taiwan. The presence of an indigenous species is backed up by a recent scientific paper that labels these plants as a separate species of the Camellia plant, naming it *Camellia formosensis*, significantly different in DNA structure from *Camellia assamica* and *sinensis*, which indicates that it evolved separately. Today, there are small pockets of this species around the island, such as in the Sun Moon Lake and High Mountain areas, all with different flavour profiles, but sadly they are in decline due to human disturbance. The plant itself has never been exploited commercially as it has thin, brittle leaves and a distinctly bitter taste, but when crossed with a Burmese *assamica* the result is the cultivar TTES #18 Hong Yu, which is extremely popular for making black teas today.

EAST CHINA SEA

TAIPEI
TAIPEI DISTRICT

HSINCHU DISTRICT

MIAOLI DISTRICT

YILAN DISTRICT

LISHAN MOUNTAIN

TAICHUNG DISTRICT

SUN MOON LAKE

NANTOU DISTRICT

DONGDING MOUNTAIN

LUGU

ALISHAN MOUNTAIN

SHANLINXI MOUNTAIN

CHIAYI DISTRICT

TAIWAN

SOUTH CHINA SEA

The first tea exported from Taiwan was from the wild *formosensis* species, as recorded in the Dutch Register of shipments. The Dutch are likely to have grown it on a small scale, but most tea consumed locally was imported from China. The Dutch were expelled from Taiwan in 1662, but it wasn't until 1683 that Taiwan came under Chinese control, at which time it became a prefecture of Qing-dynasty China. At this time, large numbers of immigrants from China's Fujian province came to settle in Taiwan, bringing tea seedlings and expertise as well as their tea culture. However, most tea was still imported and was used extensively for its medicinal properties as well as a beverage.

Northern Taiwan, around what is now the capital Taipei, proved to be a perfect place for this initial planting. Trading from these estates did not really start until the end of the 1700s, but by 1866 it had really taken off. In 1865 a British merchant named John Dodd had discovered the Taiwanese tea market on a trip to investigate the camphor industry. He saw the potential and started exporting to Europe and America, developing the reputation of Taiwan's tea and creating international interest. Dodd also imported seeds from Anxi province in China and offered loans to local farmers to grow tea, in particular Formosan oolong tea. Tea exports grew from 180,000 pounds in 1865 to more than 16 million pounds in 1885. By the end of the nineteenth century, tea was Taiwan's primary export. Dodd's legacy still exists to this day, as trading is still focussed in the north, despite most tea coming from the south. Nantou has the biggest yield and diversity on the whole island, but the big buyers don't tend to come south, and instead just visit the big trading houses in the north.

The period from 1894 to April 1895 saw the first Sino-Japanese War, fought between Qing-dynasty China and Meiji Japan, primarily for control over Korea. During the war, Japan occupied the Penghu islands off the west coast of Taiwan, thereby cutting off Taiwan from the mainland, an act that ultimately forced China to give control of Taiwan to Japan. This was resisted by Taiwanese forces, who declared Taiwan an independent republic, but the Japanese defeated the Republican forces and took control. The era that followed was to shape the tea industry dramatically, putting it firmly on the map.

The Japanese increased production of black tea to meet the demand in Europe, bringing in *assamica* plants to compete directly with the British tea-growing colonies. By growing black tea and continuing exports of oolong they also ensured they were not competing with their own green tea market. Japan also established a structure within the tea industry, promoted it at world fairs and developed further markets internationally. In 1926 the Tea Research Institute of Taiwan was founded, with the aim of developing methods to increase yield and variety of tea crops. This included the development of cultivars especially for Taiwan, many of which are used extensively to this day, and more scientific studies of where tea should be grown.

Japanese occupation ended in 1945. Taiwan returned to China, and the tea focus soon switched to green tea made the Chinese way. This was to be the main export tea for the next 30 years, with oolong mainly being made for the domestic market. Taiwan even began exporting to Japan in 1965, but by the mid 1970s the market for green tea declined. Competition from China and a limited demand from Japan meant that Taiwan turned its focus to developing its domestic market, something that still forms the bedrock of the industry. Tea is now produced for the local market, which, combined with a long-established tea culture and a focus on tea research, has maintained the industry. There was a marked rise in tea consumption in the 1980s, which mirrored the growing economy. This was also the time when the most famous teas of Taiwan accelerated in growth, with high mountain oolongs such as Ali Shan, Li Shan and Dong Ding gaining impressive reputations. However, these teas had only existed for a short period of time, as tea was not grown in the high mountains before 1969. This date marks the first successful crop sown on Li mountain at a height of around 2,700 metres. As we have seen elsewhere, high mountain teas and the areas in which they are grown are not without their problems (see pages 28–9).

Today, the combination of high mountains and sub-tropical lowlands create the perfect conditions for a wide variety of teas. Most famous for its oolong teas, but also producing excellent black, green and white teas, Taiwan is ranked 22nd in world tea-producing countries – not bad for a country about a seventh the size of the UK.

Our Taiwan

We first visited Taiwan in October 2013 for a whistle-stop tour of the most famous tea regions, travelling from Taipei down the east coast to, among others, Alishan mountains. The picturesque tea gardens, welcoming, passionate people and varied topography reminded us of Sri Lanka, but with oolong instead of black tea. We were blown away by wonderful oolongs, which spanned a huge range of flavours, and the skilful farmers creating them.

Rob: When I returned in 2017, I fell further in love with Taiwan on a trip that allowed me to explore more deeply an industry that was far more complex than I had realized. My first stop on this trip was Miaoli, the home of Oriental Beauty, an incredible tea (see page 120) that exists in this area because it's the perfect habitat for a particular small insect. I then moved on to near Mingjian in Nantou County, to spend time with a tea producer, a tea baker and some select farmers.

Agriculture in Taiwan is performed in small lots. There are no huge gardens, like in Sri Lanka, Indonesia, Africa and India. The vertically integrated system (where the farmer will grow, process and sell their own tea from their garden or estate) does exist in Taiwan, but it is not the norm. During our travels across the country we encountered a complex system in which the grower will often not process the tea, nor will they or the producer necessarily be involved in finishing the tea. Tea-making is a highly networked and collaborative effort in Taiwan and, as you can imagine, no matter where you are in the network, building a reputation based on quality and expertise is the key to success.

THE COMPLETE FAMILY FARM: JOJO, MIAOLI

Rob: Jojo comes from a family with four generations of tea farmers who operate an example of the vertically integrated system. They own and farm the land, process the leaves in their small factory and sell the final product direct. The farm today produces Oriental Beauty, a tea whose unique taste is dependent on the leaves of the tea bushes being bitten by a small insect, the green leaf hopper. When the bug sucks the leaf sap the plant produces a chemical to repel it. This combined with the bite, which starts oxidation, results in a unique 'honeyed' taste when the leaves are processed. This bug is prevalent in the Miaoli and Hshin Chu counties, so this is where the producers are.

Jojo: 'I have been around tea since I was tiny. My sister, brother and I used to go up to the same tea fields you see today to help. It was my sister who started me in my work in tea. She is a certified tea master and has been learning about tea from a very early age. She told me I should sell the tea she had decided to make: Oriental Beauty. This is what I do and love today – selling the tea my sister makes, finding trading partners and meeting customers.

'Our farm covers 4 hectares, which are mostly focused on Oriental Beauty, so we grow mostly the cultivar Chin Shin Dah Pan, but we also have Four Seasons oolong, Ruby 18 and Jin Xuan TTES12. For the Oriental Beauty we only pick one big bud and two leaves that have been bitten by the green leaf hopper; we leave the other ones. There are two harvests every year in winter, at the end of October, and in summer in July.

'My grandfather decided to make Oriental Beauty when it started to become more popular around 20 years ago. Our land and plants are good for it and it has a good history in the area. The altitude of around 200–400 metres means there are many hoppers, so it is natural to use them. In Miaoli it is the skill of tea masters that makes the biggest difference. We have a unique climate and environment, which makes it the perfect place for hoppers to live, but the flavours come from the process. Apart from our neighbour Hsinchu, the conditions are not the same anywhere else in Taiwan. We have more flowery, red fruit and honey layers in the tea, mostly honey flavours.

'Producing Oriental Beauty is not easy, though – managing the land is the hardest bit. We are organic, which means there is a lot of work to do. To keep the quality of the plants we use organic fertilizer, which we make ourselves and which costs lots of money, so we have to hope the crop is good. We cannot use any chemicals as this would kill the hoppers, so no pesticides or herbicides. We also have to weed by hand. If the fields are not kept in a good condition the hoppers will leave and go to another garden. They live there all year long, so there is no break. They like wet, but not too hot, conditions, and that is why our garden has lots of trees around it.

'After harvest we prune the bushes so that they will grow well again for the next season. The cuttings are put on the ground to help fertilize it. We have to do half-way pruning every 4–6 years when the bushes get older and have grown too big.'

Oriental Beauty commands high prices, but production output is lower than other teas. Not every leaf is bitten and the bitten leaves are stunted in growth. Carefully sorting and processing is key, especially for teas that will be entered into the annual Miaoli Oriental Beauty competition. This competition is a way for the market to control prices and promote quality. Teas are entered in 10-*jin* boxes containing 40 tins; a *jin* is equal to 600 grams. Judging is done anonymously by three judges who are Tea Research Institute leaders. Grades range from 1, 2 or 3 plum flowers, up to third, second and first prizes, and the grand prize. Plum flowers are used because it is Taiwan's national flower. Gaining a grading increases the value of a producer's tea, sometimes by a considerable amount. This can often attract businesses who buy tea from a farmer to enter the competition with the hope of being placed, gaining a reputation and building on their investment.

Jojo's family sets themselves the personal challenge of winning the grand prize every year. There are many hurdles along the way: 'The biggest challenge is finding enough pickers. The average age of our pickers is 80 years old. They love to work as they are otherwise not doing much and they like the money, but we need to start training up new pickers. The older pickers won't stop until they have to, so in order not to offend them we'll probably have two picking teams for the moment.'

Jojo is positive about the future of Miaoli Oriental Beauty; she feels that its uniqueness will mean it always has a market, both at home and abroad. The competitions are seen as the main way to access these markets and the county promotes her brand to the media, but Jojo must find more business partners to expand, as she can't find customers on her own. We are sure she will succeed because she is so passionate about what she sells.

'Tea is my best friend for the whole day. If I don't drink it I feel lost. For me, every single tea has a time. The weather, time, mood and feeling all make my choice. Usually I have my favourite, Oriental Beauty, in the morning because it makes me happy; after lunch I have high mountain oolong because it is light and clean and easy to drink. If it's raining I like to drink Oriental Beauty or black tea and when it's hot, white tea or oolong.'

What advice does Jojo have for us tea drinkers? 'Taiwanese tea is fresh and tastes amazing, but to get more enjoyment your customers should try to understand the drinking culture and appreciate that tea is made with both hands and heart. Tea is also far better when enjoyed with friends.'

THE PIONEERING PRODUCER: MR YU, MINGJIAN, NANTOU COUNTY

Rob: On our tea trips we visit producers or farmers we already have connections with and buy from, as well as those we think might be good partners for the future. Mr Yu fits the first category. I visited in 2017 to learn more about the GABA tea he produces (see page 48). This relatively new style of tea is getting a lot of interest in the tea world and we wanted to discover what drives a producer to embrace new techniques.

Mr Yu is an imposing figure, in an energizing, welcoming way. When I met him at his home and factory I found myself looking at his bare feet; I had been told before our visit that he never wears shoes. That provides a clue to the character of this pioneering man.

Mr Yu: 'I have been in the tea business 35 years. I never wanted to be in tea, but I had to return to look after my parents, who were not in the tea business. My father talked to me about rice, but I had realized tea was easier and would make more money. At that time, oolong tea was very popular and the government were giving courses on how to make this tea. From going to these courses I soon became passionate.'

Today, Mr Yu produces a huge range of teas, all EU compliant. His own piece of land is small, but it is diverse with many rarer cultivars. With only a small amount of his own leaf, Mr Yu also buys in leaf from the numerous contacts that he has built up. Producers like Mr Yu and larger factories are normally contracted to make the tea with the client involved in every step, from supplying the leaf to specifying and managing the production. Mr Yu, however, mainly makes batches of teas of his own choice and then personally sells them on; he is only occasionally contracted by others. To have operated successfully in this way and built his own market shows how respected Mr Yu is. Indeed, he is often hired by the government to attend seminars.

Mr Yu is the man behind the Mi Xian GABA that we sell at Comins. He started making GABA tea around 10 years ago after a seminar by the Tea Research and Extension Station. Mr Yu was told he would not be able to do it himself, so of course he did. The key piece of equipment for this is a metal tank which has the air pumped out of it, creating a vacuum. Mr Yu made the tank he currently uses, which is his second. His first one imploded because it wasn't strong enough.

Our conversation moved briskly on. Mr Yu is a busy man, but enjoys talking about his tea. Even through a translator I could sense his passion and energy. The talk turns to the some of the problems Taiwanese tea faces, such as poor soil management and the use of chemical fertilizers and pesticides. It seems that these are often used without a true understanding of when and where it should be done, an all-too-common issue around the world. Pesticides are often used as prevention rather than a solution to a problem, meaning they may well be unnecessary. Finding partners such as Mr Yu, who set high standards for transparency on leaf quality and are prepared to test their teas to demonstrate that they meet EU regulations, is key to our business.

Despite this situation, but unsurprisingly, Mr Yu is positive about the future. 'When Chiang Kai-shek came over in 1949 with the military there was a very short-term perspective on agriculture, and in the 1950s and 60s there was heavy use of chemicals in farming. Today some of the most wealthy people are the pesticide and fertilizer sellers. However, we have no GMO crops, no massive corporations and we have small stakeholders. This model means that if we want it and if we make it, change can happen.' If anyone disagrees, this will simply spur Mr Yu on. His unique take on tea, along with his attendance at TRES seminars, makes him an exciting prospect. As if to demonstrate this, while I was at his factory he brought out some tea cakes made from his tea, which he had found someone to press. They will be aged, which will add value, he hopes. I have no doubt they will.

THE MASTER BAKER: YUWEN, MINGJIAN, NANTOU COUNTY

Rob: My time in Taiwan was to end with Yuwen and her family, who live in
Mingjian, western Nantou County. This area has the highest concentration
of tea producers in Taiwan. Despite this, one third of the crops grown are
not tea; pineapple, dragon fruit, ginger, bananas and a large variety of local
vegetables create a diversity made possible by the small plot system. This is
not only necessary for the survival of many farmers, but is also helpful in pest
control, as natural barriers are created to stop the spread of disease.

You might think that this would be the perfect place to live and work in tea,
but in reality farmers in this area cannot demand the prices achieved in
other more famous areas, such as the high mountains of Dong Ding, Ali
Shan and Li Shan.

Yuwen's specialism is baking, which I have been fascinated by since I
witnessed the process on my first trip to Taiwan. We look at the intricacies
of tea baking elsewhere (see pages 37–8). Alongside baking, Yuwen and her
husband also buy fresh leaf to finish, buy finished teas from other producers
to export or bake and even manage fields themselves. This combination of
skills means they are well connected in the tea world, and also demonstrates
how necessary diversification is to make a good living in this part of Taiwan.

Yuwen: 'I first started in tea when I went to my father's tea factory in China
at the age of 21 or 22. When I arrived I knew very little about tea, but he
needed extra tea bakers, so I was put in charge of baking. I worked there for
four years, living and working at the factory. As the boss's daughter I could
not admit that I didn't know anything – I just had to learn from the workers,
what they asked and their comments. My father encouraged me, telling me
that making tea is a job that you enjoy, sitting down with your customers and
serving them. He was very patient in tea, and this was also his attitude to
business. He influenced my career greatly, as he told me I should work in the
international market. So I worked with a trading company to see how to do
it. I returned to Taiwan and worked for other people, then with my brother,
before starting my own business.

'Working in tea is never boring. It is changing all the time, so I am always
learning. I particularly enjoy the baking of tea, which I have been doing
for 20 years, and I learn new things every time I bake. The hardest part of
producing tea is that once you are baking, there can be no break until it is
finished. This is why I bake in the evening, so there can be no interruption
from my two boys. Being able to arrange the business around the children is
the best part, but we find ourselves working all the time!'

Sitting with Yuwen, drinking their amazing teas and chatting about
the industry, I get an insight that changes my understanding of Taiwan
dramatically. Yuwen and her husband have spent years building up their
network: they have made clear the standards they expect, provided feedback
on which teas sell well, and now finally find themselves in a position where
farmers come to them with fresh leaf of the required quality, or approach
them when they have made a specific style, type or unique tea. In a land of
enormous variety and with trading going on in all directions, this network is
invaluable. In reality it means that during picking times they may be woken

up at 2 a.m. by a farmer who has fresh leaves to sell. It's a cash business and if a buyer is not found then it's a true disaster for a farmer, especially if they are a high-mountain one. Conversely, if Yuwen doesn't wake up they could miss out on the best leaf!

A multitude of these tea networks exist across Taiwan, making this a country with a highly connected tea industry. In order for the system to work, the whole process must be carefully managed, something that would seem an impossible task, but to those in the industry it's quite straightforward, as it always is when you know how. At the centre are the pickers, who need to be at the right gardens at the right time. This requires management, and those in charge of choreographing this movement are rewarded with an intricate knowledge of who is picking, who has the best leaf, and so on. This knowledge is shared with those further down the chain involved in processing and finishing, and who are waiting to purchase. My contacts told me that prices are pretty much fixed; of course, there's always the possibility of buyers paying more for good leaf if they choose, but sellers cannot put the price up. This approach allows transparency and if anyone behaves in an unfair way they'll be found out, which will affect their reputation and put their business at risk. This makes it easy to do good business if you are trusted and know the network, but harder if you are an outsider with no connections. Due to the separated nature of each stage of the tea production in Taiwan, a new buyer may fail to find anyone to buy from if they go about it the wrong way. For Yuwen and her husband, the network is continually shifting and strengthening and is critical to their business, as it is to ours. Enlivened and keen to continue learning about this complex country's tea, I left feeling in awe of the dedication that is needed to farm, produce, finish and procure high-quality Taiwanese teas.

india

When the British think of tea we often romanticize about the tea hill stations of Darjeeling and the lush plains of Assam – it seems for us, that tea and India are intimately entwined. However, India's tea-drinking history is short compared with China's, despite being one of the birthplaces of the tea tree. Wild, indigenous tea trees are thought to have been growing in Assam, northern India, for as long as those found in China. But it was not until 4,500 years after Shennong had his realization about the tea tree in China that the drinking of Indian-grown tea became widespread.

The leaves from the Indian tea tree were first used over 900 years ago by the Singpho and Khamti tribes in the northeastern part of the Brahmaputra Valley. Rows of tea bushes were found growing close together in lines in this area, indicating early cultivation. Use would have been medicinal with occasional inclusions in cooking, but there is no record of its use as a beverage; this came much later when tea leaves were added to the traditional spiced infusion, now called *masala chai*, that had been around for thousands of years. There is revived interest in Singpho tea, which is still produced in the traditional kitchen gardens of Singpho villages. These teas are traditionally heated in metal pans before being sun-dried and tightly packed into bamboo tubes and smoked over fire. The result is a hardened tea that can be stored for up to ten years; small circular pieces are simply cut off and boiled when required. Hopefully, by the time you read this, you will be able to try some at Comins.

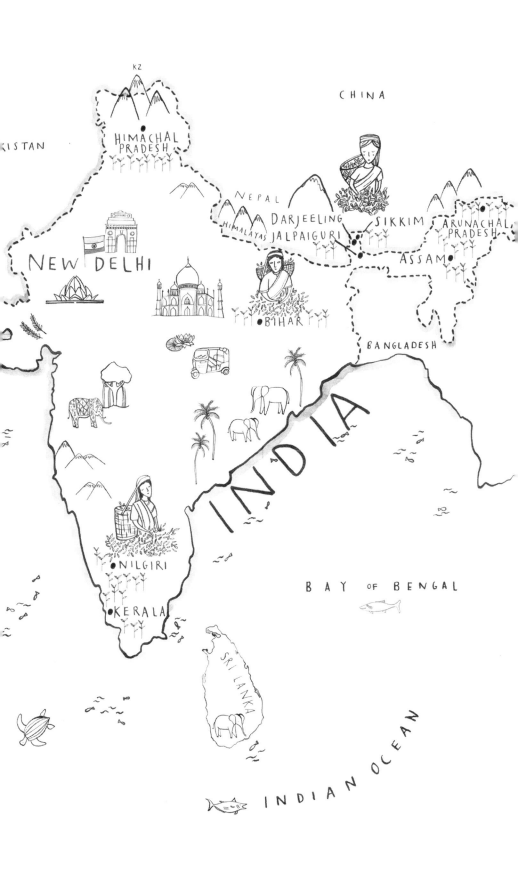

It was the British who propelled tea from low-level use into the beverage that has become such an intrinsic part of daily life. Interest began in 1788, when the English naturalist Sir Joseph Banks suggested that the climate of Assam would be ideal for the cultivation of tea, not knowing that it was already growing there naturally. The British had been drinking Chinese tea for nearly 200 years by this point, so he had some idea of what might be required. However, Banks' idea was dismissed thanks to China's monopoly on the production of tea. A move to grow tea elsewhere would have broken this monopoly and jeopardized the lucrative illicit opium trade that supported it.

In the 1820s, though, discussions resumed as to Assam's suitability, resulting in an expedition by the Scottish trader and explorer Robert Bruce in 1823. He met a local merchant named Maniram Dewan, who introduced him to the Singpho tribe chief, Bisa Gaum. Bruce found that the tribe were drinking something distinctly similar to tea, made from the new leaves of a wild plant, which were dried in the sun, then placed in a bamboo tube and smoked. After sampling the brew, Bruce was sure it was tea, so he took samples to be analysed. Sadly, he died before he could follow up on his discovery, but thankfully his samples were passed on to his brother, Charles Alexander Bruce. Charles didn't pursue his brother's discovery until 1830, when he sent some of the samples for testing at the Calcutta Botanical Garden, also planting seeds in a nursery in Sadiya, northwest Assam. However, the Superintendent of Calcutta Botanical Garden did not acknowledge the samples as tea. The leaves were much larger and more robust than the Chinese tea plants he was used to, so they were dismissed. But the story did not end here.

At the same time, and with no knowledge of these discoveries, the powerful British East India Company had started experimenting with growing tea within the British colonies. They had the monopoly on tea trade from China while also controlling the sale of Indian opium to China. Their endeavours to grow tea elsewhere used smuggled Chinese seeds, which struggled in the heat and tropical conditions of areas like north India and Sri Lanka. Their appetite for non-Chinese tea was linked to distinct signs that their monopoly on the tea trade was about to end.

Sure enough, in 1833 the British Parliament abolished the monopoly. Without this in place, the race was on to end the Chinese stranglehold on the tea trade. The very same year a special Tea Committee was set up, and sent a party to Upper Assam area to collect indigenous plants. These new samples forced the aforementioned Calcutta Botanical Garden to reconsider its opinion, leading to the organization of a proper expedition in 1835. After meeting the Singpho tribe, it was confirmed that the plant they used was indeed tea, albeit a different variety they named *assamica* (from Assam). Sadly, the Bruce brothers were never given proper credit for their part in this discovery, even though Charles had started a tea plantation in Assam a year earlier. However, it was his plants that made up the first consignment of Assam-grown tea delivered to England. Only eight of the 46 chests he shipped were saleable on delivery, but these were sold at auction in 1839 and approved by the Tea Committee in London.

Assam had proven itself a legitimate source of tea, but to be a success the tea's quality had to be comparable with the Chinese competition, which it wasn't yet. Development was needed, something the British did very well. In 1839 the first-ever tea company, the Assam Tea Company, was founded. Of the 10,000 shares, 8,000 were offered in England and 2,000 in India. The company soon merged with another new one, the Bengal Tea Association, and performed so well that Queen Victoria instructed court to favour Assam teas over Chinese. Indian-grown tea had started on its path to becoming a world power.

This amazing period in tea also saw advances in the quest to grow the Chinese tea plant in India, which was still seen as the best location. In 1834 the first Chinese expedition took place. The secretary of the Tea Committee, a Mr G. J. Gordan, travelled to China and managed to obtain 80,000 seeds. Of these, 20,000 were planted in Calcutta and the rest were shared among Darjeeling, Kumaon and Assam in northern India and Ooty in southern India. It was to end in disaster, as the majority of the seeds failed to grow in the heat of Calcutta, Assam and the south. This exposed the biggest issue that the British faced, that of knowledge, which would hinder production for many years.

It wasn't until 1839 that Chinese seeds were planted with any success. Archibald Campbell, the first Superintendent of what was then a new British-controlled region called Darjeeling, planted a few experimental seeds at his house. His reason was not to further the cause, but to attract settlers to this remote area because he felt lonely. The seeds flourished and growing had begun.

A major leap forward came in 1843 with another Scot named Robert Fortune. Fortune was an excellent botanist and traveller who spoke fluent Chinese thanks to an earlier trip sponsored by the Horticultural Society of London. On this expedition he had also gained a great deal of knowledge about the mysterious tea plant. He was the first westerner to discover that green and black teas came from the same plant, something which is still a surprise to many people. His superior knowledge attracted the East India Company, who saw him as the ideal man for a daring spying mission. He was tasked to infiltrate the tea gardens of China to collect plants and, most importantly, knowledge about growing and manufacturing. In an expedition full of drama and intrigue, Fortune was able to obtain 20,000 plants of the best green teas, which he preserved during travel in then state-of-the-art Wardian cases. These hermetically sealed, portable mini-greenhouses kept the plants in pristine condition during their journey to Britain and, more importantly, India. This remarkable achievement was backed up by a huge wealth of knowledge. Sadly, a very small fraction of the plants survived to the planting nursery in India.

His second trip proved more fruitful, however. Having learned from the first trip, he dispatched cases containing planted seeds rather than mature plants. These germinated on the journey and proved more resistant to its rigours. A large proportion survived and were planted succesfully. Fortune also used his contacts to employ eight Chinese tea masters to travel to India and oversee the growing period. They also brought all the equipment needed for the processing of the tea leaves, thus ensuring the success of the project. Thanks to Fortune's trials, the first official tea nursery in Darjeeling was established in 1847, with the first commercial plantation, the Tukvar Tea Estate, set up just three years later in 1850. By 1962, 100 tea gardens were flourishing there. Thanks to many intrepid travellers, combined with a good dose of British colonialism, Indian tea was able to compete with Chinese in quality, and the monopoly had been broken.

The British laid the foundations for commercial tea production in India, but even when they left in 1947 the industry continued to grow. India is now the world's second-largest producer of tea, creating over 1.239 million tonnes in 2016. Today, according to the Tea Board of India, there are 43,293 tea gardens across the whole of Assam, 62,213 in the Nilgiris and 85 in Darjeeling. In order to ensure the supply of genuine tea from each area, a compulsory system to certify the authenticity of exported tea was incorporated into the Tea Act of 1953 and registered under the Geographical Indications of Goods Act of 1999. This means that only tea produced at these specific locations and using the correct methods can be called Darjeeling, Assam or Nilgiri.

The current Indian market is still very much geared towards export; much of the tea is too expensive for local consumption. However, milky tea and *masala chai* (spiced tea), containing the traditional spices, milk and sweetener combined with strong black tea, is consumed widely. Each family, community and region make their own chai variants, with roadside chaiwallas serving hundreds of steaming cups to all sectors of society. Specialist stores that serve and sell fine teas are pushing the domestic market forward, which means that more and more is staying in the country. From shaky beginnings, India now produces some of the finest teas in the world.

Our India

We have had a long love affair with India. It's where our company was born, and Darjeeling is the cup of tea that wakes us up every morning. From 2008 to the present day we have made frequent and varied trips to India, and it's hard to think of a country or a people that make you feel more alive. From the minute you step onto the streets of a big city like Kolkata or Mumbai you are met with a contagious mix of life, colour and culture that extends to every corner of the country. From eating steaming momos with a light, fragrant Darjeeling tea in the hills to breakfasting on black rice porridge in rural Assam, if you, like us, seek adventure, human connection and are relaxed enough to take the journey as it comes, then India is the country for you!

As we journey from Assam to Darjeeling and down to the Nilgiris, the tea producers' stories will take you from smallholdings of 5 acres to larger family-run gardens that offer a unique glimpse into what it takes to produce sustainable, quality tea of all types. In a market still dominated by the large plantation-style gardens, modern pioneers are working hard to transform the tea industry against a backdrop of multiple environmental, economic and human challenges. The enthusiasm, knowledge and thirst for innovation we have encountered in India is infectious. Standing next to the withering beds late at night with Parveez, the tea maker at Glenburn Tea in Darjeeling, whose excellent teas are described later, listening to his deep affection and respect for the tea plant and appetite for continued learning, sent shivers down my spine. Our hope is that by promoting an understanding and appreciation of their stories of dedication, we in the west can start to develop a new relationship with this tea giant, one that helps us appreciate quality Indian teas and seek a more modern and transparent partnership with the Indian tea growers.

THE SMALL-SCALE ORGANIC FARMER: PALLAB NATH, KANOKA FARM, ASSAM

Michelle: Situated in northern India on either side of the Brahmaputra River, Assam is one of the birthplaces of tea. Initially an area of thick jungle that had to be cleared to create tea fields, it is now the world's largest tea-growing region. More than half of India's tea is grown here, and it is a beautiful place. To date, the climate and soil have been perfect for growing, with high humidity and daytime temperatures, a combination that delivers the malty flavour the region is famous for. However, in a story common to tea, warmer temperatures and changing rain patterns are affecting both production and quality here. Stagnant tea prices, rising production costs, stiff competition and oversupplies of cheap black commodity tea are all contributing to difficult times. We believe it's time to find a new appreciation for the quality this region has to offer, and be prepared to pay more for it, moving away from faceless, low-quality teas to those rich in flavour, quality and provenance. Let's meet a few of the people producing quality Assam teas, which will definitely have you setting aside the milk and sugar.

It became a running joke that every journey we undertook in Assam took 5 hours, and so, after stopping off to view rhinos at Kazaranga and buy tea from roadside stalls, our driver, Chandan, followed our escort and host, Pallab Nath, down a dusty track to his home. Pallab, his father and his wife Pompee didn't seem at all fazed to welcome three women into their home and offer us a bed for the night. The small operation here is a family affair and is a sign of grassroots change in the Indian tea industry. Perched in their cosy living room, we made our introductions over tea and soon the story of this entrepreneurial family started to emerge. It all started when Pallab decided to return home to Assam after studying small industry management in Delhi and started a small business with his brother, Pranab.

Pallab: 'My grandfather owned a house in Assam and we had seen the tea gardens, but no-one in our area was focusing on organic cultivation so we decided that would be a good route to follow. We came across an abandoned paddy field which had seen no cultivation for 5–6 years due to its highland position, so we bought it – 3 hectares in total. The only problem was that we knew very little about tea. In 2008 we tried to grow from cloned tea plants and lost 50,000 rupees in the tea nursery. After that we decided to establish our nursery from seed, since clones were too difficult. It took a year to go from seed to plant and 3 years before we could start to pluck. In 2012 we started to pluck small amounts and made green and orthodox black teas.

I spent time visiting other gardens and learning from other makers. In 2013 I made 70 kilograms of green tea and sent a sample to my brother. The feedback wasn't good and I had to throw it away.

'The local tea pluckers use their hands to make tea in their homes, so I decided to ask them. They use large baskets to collect the green leaf, which allows air to pass easily – this is helpful for the oxidation process involved in black tea manufacture. The pickers use an instrument called a *theki* to break the leaves and then pan-fry them. They traditionally used wood, but I decided to smoulder the leaves with LPG gas because we did not want any smoke in the flavour of the tea. Quality improved and I decided to move away from green tea and focus on orthodox black tea. On our small plot, one other person and I roll the tea, producing around 1,000 kilograms annually. We apply organic principles, using smoke, chilli ginger spray and black pepper water to treat insects. The land is fertilized with the dung from our seven cows, and we sometimes place dung in cow horns which, when buried, creates a bacteria that you can spray. My belief is that after 4 years of following a pattern of farming you have reset a cycle. Keeping environmental harmony is the most important factor in long-term organic farming.

'We start to pluck the leaves in April, when six women come to the garden to pluck. You'll often see them wearing the traditional *japi* hat. The leaf is then withered on my bamboo racks for 20 hours, before being rolled for 4 minutes. If it has been raining I will often leave the leaves for 3–4 hours in the basket. In the manufacture of black tea, oxidation is very important. During the rainy season temperatures are low and we keep the leaves in the basket so that oxidation starts early and to make sure that the leaves don't catch moisture. I have a small dryer and dry the tea for 2 hours at 50°C; I only know when it's ready by touch. That's the approach for just for one tray in the dryer – if there are more it takes longer and I must rotate them. All of this takes place inside the small factory I built myself – I made the walls with mud and bamboo. It took just a month to build.

'Our first flush is lighter in the cup and we pluck from April until June. The second flush is from July and the plucking standard is always two leaves and a bud. This year has been challenging; the heavy rains have delayed production and overall yield will be down. However, the nature of our teas – organic, hand-plucked, hand-rolled tea and made using minimal machinery (only a dryer) – means they always stand out from machine-made teas. We enjoy our own teas here at Kanoka in the early morning and evening time after work, perfect with or without milk and always served with a small snack.'

The snacks at Kanoka were really quite legendary. Pallab's wife Pompee is a wonderful woman and makes the most amazing *gulab jamon*, a milk-based south Asian sweet, and black rice porridge, perfect with a bowl of Kanoka Assam. The team here are also supporting other local enterprises, such as cotton tea bags hand-stitched by a self-help group in Assam run by a family member, Aunt Daisy, and her friend. And with Pallab and his family now building a small homestay, I know I can't wait to return.

THE FAMILY-RUN ESTATE: DIWAKAR THAPLIYAL, KHONGEA TEA ESTATE, ASSAM

Michelle: I first discovered the smooth and distinctly moreish Khongea Assam while living in Belgium. I had never really thought of Assam as a tea I could enjoy without milk, but this tea changed all that. Khongea is located in the upper reaches of the Assam region, on the south bank of the Brahmaputra River. Established in the late nineteenth century, it passed into the Prakash family over 50 years ago and under their management has set standards for many other large estates in the area. In 2017 I finally got the chance to visit and stay at this garden under the care of Diwakar Thapliyal, the wonderfully kind garden manager.

The first evening was one I won't forget. The house is located just yards from the factory, and as night fell the lights turned on and the hum of the fans filled the air. This was tea heaven. Diwakar has a long history in the Indian tea industry, having grown up in Mussoorie, an Indian hill station where he had seen tea growing and gained his basic knowledge. Two topics dominated our discussions: people and quality. Diwakar explained how an estate like Khongea, which covers 470 hectares and has three factories, is a democracy of over 2,000 people working together towards a common goal. Tea is a people-dominated industry, not an automated one, upon which thousands of people across large estates in India are reliant. For this system to work this requires a relationship based on partnership and mutual respect. Diwakar put it like this: 'Tea is like family, and a manager is like a priest and a counsellor and everything in between. Everything from birth to death is the responsibility of the management'. Not all estates think or work like this, which is why you need to know where your tea comes from and support those, like Khongea, that do.

Introductions over, we jumped in the jeep and headed out into the gardens. The skilled pickers were out, so we tried to stick to the well-trodden channels between the sections of tea garden. These were in fact drainage channels – tea plants do not do well in standing water – and walking along them we could clearly see the path of the tree roots, which run to around 1 metre deep. Looking up across the tea fields, we could clearly see the established 'table' or height of the bushes, which here was 15–20 centimetres above the ground. This is the mark the pluckers stick to, and the ideal is to keep the bushes 'heavy' so that they produce better-quality leaves.

At Khongea they follow a seven-day round of plucking, six if conditions are very good, which means the pluckers move around the garden in a pattern, visiting each area every seven days and plucking for eight hours a day. As we walked we talked about the importance of respect for nature in tea farming. Diwakar observed that 'everything with tea is about balance, and there is a human element to all of it. In fact, it is more than human: tea plants are more sensitive than humans, if you don't see them often enough they don't behave well.'

As our time at Khongea came to an end we stood and tasted tea with Diwakar and his team in a space at the heart of the factory, something the team do at least twice a day. As with all the people we visit and work with, quality is key.

Early samples are tasted to see if any improvements can be made and packing samples are tasted to ensure quality before the teas are packed to ship.

The top-quality teas from Assam will come from May onwards until mid July. Which producer makes the best tea is always a question of who has harnessed the best quality through the multiple steps of harvesting, handling and processing. Success will be ultimately be determined by the market reaction. For larger producers such as Khongea, a small proportion of high-grade teas will be sold directly to people like us, but the majority will go to the auction in Kolkata, where brokers will assess their quality before the market decides their price.

THE TRADITIONAL AGRICULTURALIST: MURALI SUBRAMANIAN, NILGIRI HILLS

Michelle: Of the 1,200 million kilograms of tea produced in India annually, south India accounts for 20 percent of production. Most of the tea farming here is geared towards CTC (cut-tear-curl) tea consumed locally with milk or in chai. This high-volume, low-price commodity industry results in low pay for farmers and their workers, but there is appetite for change. The Indian Tea Board is encouraging small gardens to improve leaf quality and move towards orthodox or speciality tea, and consumer preferences are changing.

Until a few years ago, for most Indians tea meant only tea with milk or masala chai. Nowadays, green tea consumption has skyrocketed and, although limited, there is also growing awareness about various speciality leaf-grade teas. Some small-garden pioneers are venturing into orthodox tea production on their own. Murali Subramanian is one such grower, and his story offers a fascinating glimpse into the world of traditional Indian agriculture and small-scale tea manufacturing

Murali: 'The summers are hot and humid in the plains of Coimbatore in the southern Indian state of Tamil Nadu, but the local town, Nilgiri, is a paradise with its cool temperatures and rolling mountains covered in greenery. We wanted to buy a small cottage as a summer getaway but ended up buying a 5-acre tea garden. We had no idea how deep we would get into the tea business at that time. The garden was naturally maintained and the general practice in this tea-growing region is to pick the leaves and send them to the nearby factory where they mass-produce CTC-grade black tea to be used in Indian *chai*. My brother, who lives in the USA, saw another future for us. Given our high-mountain location at over 2,000 metres, he told us we could produce leaf-grade green, black and oolong teas; his only stipulation was that it should be done organically.

'Over the next couple of years we built a small cottage at the garden, assembled a dedicated team and imported 2 rollers, a dryer and a withering machine from China. Although the machines are Chinese, the agricultural practice is unmistakably Indian. Agriculture in India is at least 12,000 years old. With its deep emphasis on respect for the soil and all the animals, it continues to sustain a huge population to this day. A small

Indian farmer with few acres of land and a couple of cows can keep the farming self-sustainable. We want to tap into this farming lineage and keep our tea garden on a self-sustainable model. The plants are grown under abundant shade from 500 cypress trees and are cultivated using traditional Indian *panchagavya* techniques. This Sanskrit word refers to a traditional concoction of five cow products. In addition to warding off pests and diseases, the use of *panchagavya* is said to impart a fruitier, earthier aspect to tea leaves. The tea leaves are hand-picked and processed carefully by the team to produce the finest leaf teas that Nilgiri has to offer.'

Like small businesses the world over, Murali Subramanian's farm is reliant on a regular and skilled team. Attrition rates are extremely high at tea gardens, and labour shortages are a big issue. In the booming Indian economy, many sectors, especially construction, have created many opportunities and pay higher daily wages: 'With a labour shortage, it becomes difficult to maintain tea gardens and there is a risk of people just leaving the garden unattended and eventually selling it to real estate, resorts or vegetable growers,' he explained. 'Many of the younger generation go to the cities to study and settle down there. This breaks the family farming continuity and eventually the garden gets sold.'

The fact that his workers have been with him and his wife for years is testimony to how they treat them and care for their wellbeing. There are nine people employed at the garden: Gautham, who operates the tea machines, a native of West Bengal and now settled in the Nilgiris, whose family has been at the garden for two years; Sonali, Gautham's wife, who helps in tea machine operation, sorting fresh leaves and also leaf picking; expert leaf pickers Lokamma, Gowri, Chitra, Navamani, Jyothimani and Jayalakshmi; and Sekar, an expert in managing tea bushes.

Murali and his wife Kameswari provide year-round employment, pay their workers above the market wages and give them yearly Diwali festival bonuses and advances to help them however they can. On the days when the leaves are ready and available, the team follow a regular pattern of work. If leaves are not ready the workers are given cleaning, weeding and pruning tasks. No matter what the day holds, Murali is sustained by at least three cups of fresh black tea and three cups of green or oolong tea from his own garden. 'My personal favourite is Nilgiri black leaf tea,' he says. 'With its smooth taste and fruity aroma, it's in a class of its own.'

As we leave, Murali shares his hopes for the future. Like all the small farmers we continue to meet in India, he tells us that small investments can make a big difference. Supporting small tea gardens that show promise can offer a big boost to this sector. If one small garden succeeds, others are likely to follow and soon there will be many small gardens producing quality leaves in successful regions. In the meantime, he and his small team will continue to be fixated on quality and 100 percent organic methods, and committed to creating an organic tea garden society including nearby organic tea farmers, enabling him to impart his knowledge and experience to them. 'When multiple gardens in our area start producing good-quality tea, this would in turn attract more buyers and everybody will benefit.'

THE VOICE OF SMALL FARMERS: BHAWESH NIROULA, DARJEELING

Darjeeling, that mystical, magical land, produces some of the world's finest teas, often with a romantic vision of tea pickers on the sides of the tea packets on supermarket shelves. Situated at over 2,000 metres above sea level, Darjeeling is the former British outpost where the tea industry began to flourish. Often referred to as the 'Champagne of teas', Darjeeling is famous for delicate hand-plucked teas that reflect their distinctive Himalayan terroir.

Look a little closer, however, and all is not quite as it's presented to us; a delicate ecosystem lies behind our deliciously fragrant cup of fine tea. The steep slopes of Darjeeling are increasingly prone to landslides; we have seen the aftermath of many on our trips here. Changeable weather patterns bring long, dry spells when there was once rain. Unpredictable summer monsoons wash away the precious, nutrient-rich topsoil, exposing soils depleted from overuse of pesticides and fertilizers and therefore incapable of holding the volumes of water that pass over them.

Hand-plucked teas also require dedicated workers, and the majority of the workforce in Darjeeling is made up of the Himalayan Gorkha community. As you drive through the hills of Darjeeling, Kalimpong, Kurseong and other hilly districts you will often see signs demanding an independent Gorkhaland for the Nepali-speaking people who live and work here. The history of the Gorkha movement is decades old. In short, the Gorkhas captured most parts of northeast India in 1780, but it was surrendered after defeat to the British in 1816, at which point Darjeeling was given back to Sikkim before being leased back in 1835. After partition in 1947, Darjeeling was merged with West Bengal, bringing together two completely different cultures and languages. The movement for a separate state began in 1949 with large protests in the late 1980s and ongoing disputes in more recent years. In July 2017, unrest between the West Bengal government and the Himalayan Gorkha community saw an unprecedented closure of the region at the peak of the harvest season. Consequently, very little 2017 second flush Darjeeling was produced. The details are beyond the scope of this book, but there is no doubt that the ongoing disputes affect price, availability and quality of Darjeeling tea in the UK market. The impact is far more serious for the growers and workers, who have to deal with huge losses in revenue in a region where the tea industry is the largest source of employment.

But there is light in the hills. Ethically run family gardens like Glenburn tea, great ecological pioneers and a new generation uplifting the small tea growers in Darjeeling are thinking and doing things differently. Supporting them and others like them can help change the trajectory of Darjeeling. Let's meet a few, and through the decisions we make about where to buy our tea, support a positive future for this region.

Michelle: In July 2017, due to the ongoing closure of Darjeeling, we diverted to Jalpaiguri to spend some time with the small grower association there. It turned into one of the most bizarre days of my life in tea, which culminated in an appearance in the *Times of India* (I'll tell you over a cup of tea one day) and a press conference organized just for us! At the back I noticed two very well-presented and humble men. I was told that they'd come from Darjeeling, which seemed impossible as the roads in and out were closed. I felt humbled that they would make such efforts, and felt sure they must have a story to tell – the most interesting people do the craziest things.

The man standing in front of me was Bhawesh, who, it turned out, ran a small independent family tea farm in a small hamlet called Chota Poobong, 10 km from Ghoom railway station in Darjeeling. His story reflects a new generation working hard to provide new opportunities for the small tea growers in Darjeeling, a group for whom the current system often results in them selling their fresh leaves at under market prices to larger, leased tea gardens in large cities like Kolkata and New Delhi. In 2018 I returned to Darjeeling to visit him, his beautiful family and his tea farm.

Bhawesh: 'The story starts with my father, Bikram, a retired government employee who started planting tea in 1999 as an alternative crop because all the other conventional farming was not successful due to the local wildlife destroying it. He was selling his green tea leaves to big traditional tea gardens through a society. This process continued for a decade because we (small tea growers) didn't have any other options for making or selling our teas. The big tea gardens always had a high-handedness over us, dictating their own terms and prices. At this time I was working in Bangalore as a software engineer until, in 2014, my father got sick and had to go through dialysis, which is still happening today. I left my lucrative job and came back to Darjeeling. I did a lot of soul searching for almost a year – what was to be done? I had no idea about tea. Slowly I became interested in tea as my father took me on tours to the tea garden. I learned a lot during these times, including how to hand-roll tea, and started selling teas locally, with a lot of good feedback.

'My father has always talked about helping the poor small tea growers in Darjeeling, so we started thinking about how to make tea farming in our village a viable way of life again. After a year of research and the confidence of a bank in me, we started Darjeeling's first farming cooperative in 2015 and built our own manufacturing unit to support it. We now collect leaves from neighbouring farmers at a very good price (two to three times the average rate), a model that is encouraging new local plantations. People who may previously have given up on farming and left for more lucrative possibilities in the city are starting to see the opportunities that can come from cultivating tea, a crop that offers an eight-month harvest season and now, with Niroula's, a direct and more profitable route to market. Today, we still have our personal ancestral plantation area of 25 acres and collect green tea leaves from 180 small tea growers in and around Darjeeling. The total tea plantation area is 350 acres. For now we are staying focussed only on Darjeeling orthodox black tea, with a team of nine guys working in the factory and five in the field.'

THE SOIL PIONEER: SANJAY BANSAL, AMBOOTIA, DARJEELING

Michelle: My first taste of Ambootia Darjeeling marked the start of a new addiction. Our customers agreed: the Rainbow Darjeeling from Ambootia, Kurseong and the Gold Mist Assam from Jamguri, Golaghat, Assam (which is part of the same group of gardens) stand out from the crowd and have gained a firm following at our teahouses. Our sourcing trips to India in 2017 and 2018 included a visit to the tasting room at Ambootia HQ in Kolkata and the garden itself. In both cases a team had stayed late to welcome us, and the tasting table at the HQ was a visual reminder of just how diverse the teas from Darjeeling and Assam can be, which was also confirmed by the tasting. The story that accompanies these gardens is no less extraordinary, and shows how respect for the land and for the people who work in this fragile environment can deliver benefits for all.

In 1948 Darjeeling, post-independence adjustments were being made to the way things were run and a Mr S.P. Bansal Snr moved to the northeast of India. From 1954 he managed Ambootia TE until 1968 and after this stint he undertook the responsibility of turning around other sick and ailing tea estates in the region. He was a much sought-after planter of his time and a champion in turning around sick tea estates. In the absence of his leadership, Ambootia Tea Estate could not be managed aptly by the owners and it became sick. The garden was put up for sale during 1984 and 1985, but without a buyer. Several big companies who had purchased other ailing estates in Darjeeling would not consider the purchase of Ambootia, partly due to the catastrophic landslides, the political turmoil in the district and deteriorating industrial relations at the estate. This, combined with huge outstanding liabilities, wage arrears, statutory and welfare issues with the workers and a large encroachment in the tea area, resulted in the garden being locked down between 1981 and 1986, and a complete breakdown of management. In August 1986 the Head Clerk of the Estate was murdered in the garden office by the workers and the garden was put in a 'lockout' situation, in which the gates are locked with no work and therefore no pay for the workers.

On 1 January 1987, at the request of the workers, Mr Bansal Snr took over the tea estate to protect the future of the 923 estate workers and successfully revive it to what we know today: a successful and profitable garden making exceptional teas. An important step on that journey has been the introduction of organic and biodynamic agriculture introduced in 1994 by Sanjay Bansal, Mr Bansal Snr's son. Across the garden, other initiatives are in place to ensure that the whole system is self sustaining, socially responsible and economically viable. The Income Augmentation Programme in Workers' Homesteads provides each worker with a rent-free house and a plot of land to cultivate, then identities uses for the land which will deliver good returns, such as organic ginger for the export market and organic turmeric, oranges and honey for domestic use. Support is provided to grow these organically and biodynamically in the workers' homesteads.

The power supply from the fossil-fuel powered West Bengal grid can be incredibly erratic. Tea estate facilities and residents often fall back on the use of diesel generators and coal or wood to cover the power shortfall. Recognizing the potential of the natural water resources and small and medium-sized rivers that flow through the estate, the team at Ambootia are working to harness them for small hydroelectric plants. Creating energy in this way is much more in line with the garden's philosophy, enjoys active participation from tea estate workers and generates local employment.

The work in this fragile tea area will always be ongoing. The landslide of 1968, the largest in Asia at that time, affected the entire viability of the tea estate. There were no human casualties – the villagers became alarmed due to incessant rainfall and fortunately moved away from the area in time. However, that did not save the nearly 300 houses and the complete village that was wiped out in a whisper. Tea bushes had to be uprooted to make way for new houses and, in the last few years, soil binding grasses and trees have been planted in and around the landslide. More than 5,000 kilograms of palletized seeds have also been sown in the landslide area, which have taken root and successfully bound the soil. This area is now home to 100,000 trees, showing that, in time and with care, these lands can heal, become productive again and continue to produce the great-tasting Darjeeling teas we know and love.

A POWERFUL WOMAN: SONIA JABBAR, NUXALBARI, DOOARS

Michelle: Assam and Darjeeling are probably names we're familiar with. But what of the other regions we know less well? What happens to the tea produced there? After we appeared in the *Times of India* I received an email inviting us to visit the Nuxalbari tea estate. I love serendipity, and this needed following up. Returning in 2018 we uncovered the incredible story of a remarkable woman, Sonia Jabbar, and her fight to continue her family's legacy in tea after the untimely death of her mother, who ran the estate for 30 years. As Sonia told us, 'since then I have slogged to try and make magic'. This story highlights the beautiful connection that can exist between tea grower and land, and shows just what is needed to make a success of large independent gardens in the less well-known areas of India. It is a struggle few of us are aware of; after all their efforts, the tea from gardens like this will often be blended, their identity lost. Sonia's story makes a strong case for supporting larger gardens with a positive and sustainable vision for the future – they represent hope. It also highlights the need for more transparency in tea, so that work like this and the teas it produces can be understood and celebrated.

Sonia: 'My brother Iqbal and I are fifth-generation planters. Our garden, in Darjeeling district, is very close to the high Himalayan range, which gives Nuxalbari teas a high-grown flavour. We are not classified as Darjeeling because we do not have the altitude to be included in the geographical indication, and as a result our teas are often sought to be blended with the best of Darjeeling. Our garden produces high-quality black teas, both CTC (cut-tear-curl) and orthodox, and green tea, over 1,200 acres, with 12 acres certified organic. We have plans to convert another 370 acres to organic over the next five years.

'At times, making a success of a garden like this is a really difficult task. The cost of our inputs has gone up and our selling price has remained static or even declined. We have sold at auctions for the past 100 years and in 2016 the price the top buyers paid dropped, and this year their average is below our cost of production. At the same time, the buyers have increased their margins and retail prices. Small tea growers don't have the same statutory labour laws that we do. They can simply close down over the dormant period in winter, whereas we have to employ a permanent labour force. Sometimes it feels like we are just trying to survive – but I want Nuxalbari to thrive.'

In order to open up new markets and opportunities for Nuxalbari tea, Sonia is making brave decisions – see page 17 for more on her soil and cultivar innovations. She explained: 'My market is wherever there are people who want excellent quality, ethically sourced teas with aroma and flavour. Everyone is madly trying to increase yields because they believe that only when you produce millions of kilos annually can you bring down the cost of production and beat the small growers. But I don't want to play that game – it's a dead end. People don't realize that it's living soil, and you can't keep increasing yield without exhausting the land. So I am doing the absolute opposite. I'm not sure it's going to work, but I know the other model is definitely not going to work. I am honouring the soil, honouring my tea bushes and trees, honouring the people who work for me, while trying to make good-quality teas. I can only hope that all the little steps made in the right direction will add up!' One exciting step has been realized in 2018: when we visited in May, Sonia had just been informed that she will be awarded the label of 'elephant-friendly tea' for the work she and her team have done to provide elephant corridors through the tea gardens. Nature and tea living and working respectfully together.

sri lanka 1839

Sri Lanka is an island nation south of India in the Indian Ocean. Its diverse landscapes range from rainforest to highlands and dry plains to sandy beaches. Tea from Sri Lanka is often referred to as Ceylon tea, as this was the island's name when it was a colony under British rule, when tea was first planted and the industry began just over 150 years ago.

Tea seeds initially arrived on the island in 1839 when the Superintendent of Calcutta Botanical Garden, Dr Nathaniel Wallich, sent seeds sourced from an expedition into Assam (see page 130) to the Peradeniya Botanical Gardens near Kandy in Sri Lanka. It was thought that these would grow well on the island, but not much happened initially. Seeds were also sent in 1842 and planted in the much higher Nuwara Eliya area, with some success, but not on any scale. At this point coffee was the key crop in Sri Lanka. By 1960, Sri Lanka was in the top three coffee producers in the world, along with Brazil and Indonesia.

BAY
OF
BENGAL

SRI LANKA

●DIMBULLA

●KANDY

●UDA PUSSELLAWA

●NUWARA ELIYA

●UVA

COLOMBO

●RUHUNA

INDIAN OCEAN

The first commercial attempt at growing tea in Sri Lanka was in 1841 when the Austrian Worms brothers began to cultivate the Chinese tea plant on two of their estates. Due to the high costs, the project was abandoned. It was to be a young Scottish planter named James Taylor who would establish the first tea bushes in 1866 on the Loolecondera Coffee Estate near Kandy, where he worked. Initially, he obtained Assamese seeds from the Peradeniya Gardens and planted them along the roads into the estate. A year later, when these had grown well, Taylor was instructed to plant 19 acres of the new bushes in a new clearing on the estate. Growing progressed well, leading to the building of a factory and the first sale of tea in 1872.

This proved to be the perfect timing, because in the late 1860s and early 1870s a massive fungal epidemic or 'coffee blight' devastated most of the coffee plantations. Tea was the logical replacement and spread rapidly, replacing almost all the coffee estates by the early 1900s. One famous Scottish grocer named Sir Thomas Lipton spotted the potential of Ceylon tea and in 1890 purchased five failing coffee estates, converting them to tea production. This allowed him to sell directly to the British consumer, something which has made his brand famous to this day.

By 1965, the now-independent Ceylon had grown to be the biggest tea exporter in the world. In 1972 Ceylon became the Republic of Sri Lanka, leading to the nationalization of the tea industry and a Land Reform Act. Through this, the Sri Lankan government ensured that no single company could own more than 50 acres of tea-producing land. Many of the foreign-owned estates were therefore taken back.

The next major development came in 1976, when the export of Sri Lankan tea pre-packaged in teabags began, which enabled Sri Lankan companies to add value to their crop themselves. Ceylon tea's strong, robust flavour makes it ideal for blended English Breakfast-style tea that had become popular, and this move further strengthened the country's position. Soon after this, in 1983, the highly mechanized CTC process was introduced, which is mostly used in tea bag production.

Today, Sri Lanka is the fourth largest tea producer in the world, with orthodox black tea accounting for 95 percent of tea production. In 2017 almost three quarters of Ceylon tea was produced by smallholders, a result of the Land Reform Act. Tea is grown and picked all year long due to the favourable climate. Famed for its bright and invigorating black teas, the flavour characteristics are defined by the altitude at which it is grown. Low-grown tea is from sea level up to around 600 metres. Mid-grown tea grows from 600–1,200 metres and high-grown tea is above this up to about 2,000 metres. As the altitude increases, the tea becomes more delicate as the growth rate slows, bringing out lighter flavours.

Mr Rajaratnam, the manager of Idulgashinna Garden (see page 153), described the main types for us.

NUWARA ELIYA: DELICATELY FRAGRANT
Nuwara Eliya is unique and so is its tea: the fragrance of cypress trees, wild mint and eucalyptus floats through the air and contributes to the tea's characteristic flavour. It has been said that Nuwara Eliya, at 1,900 metres above sea level, is to Ceylon tea what champagne is to French wine. Brewed light, it makes for a very smooth cup of tea that can also be iced for a refreshing difference.

UDA PUSSELLAWA: EXQUISITELY TANGY
Located east of Nuwara Eliya, the tea grown on the Uda Pussellawa mountain range experiences two periods of superior quality. The traditional season from July to September is the peak, but the dry, cold conditions of the first quarter of the year yield a range of rosy teas. Medium-bodied and subtle, these teas produce a majestic flavour.

DIMBULLA: REFRESHING AND MELLOW
One of the earliest areas to be planted, Dimbulla is perhaps the most famous region associated with Ceylon tea. The plantations, located at 1,100–1,700 metres above sea level, cover the western slopes of the district. The monsoon rain and cold, dry weather produce a range of teas, from full-bodied to light and delicate.

UVA: EXOTICALLY AROMATIC
Grown at an elevation between 1,100–1,700 metres above sea level, on the eastern slopes of Sri Lanka's central mountains, Uva teas have a truly unique flavour. They are commonly used in blends but, with their distinctive characteristics, they can also be enjoyed on their own.

KANDY: INTENSELY FULL-BODIED
The ancient capital of Ceylon, Kandy is the first place where tea was grown in Sri Lanka. These mid-country teas, grown on plantations at 600–1,200 metres, produce a full-bodied tea, ideal for those who like theirs strong and bursting with flavour.

RUHUNA: DISTINCTIVELY UNIQUE
These teas' uniqueness begins with the low elevations of its plantations. The southern part of Sri Lanka, though not traditionally known for its tea, does produce exceptional leaves. Grown up to 600 metres above sea level, the condition of the soil gives the leaves blackness and imparts a strong and distinctive taste. A perfect cup for those who like their tea thick and sweet, with or without milk.

Our Sri Lanka

Rob: Our introduction to Sri Lankan tea occurred right at the beginning of our tea life, predominantly due to the kindness of one man: Merrill Fernando. Now let's be clear, Merrill is a big deal in the tea world. He launched his company, Dilmah Tea, in 1988, which was the first producer-owned tea brand, offering tea 'picked, perfected and packed' at origin. Even back in 2010, it was considered one of the top ten tea brands in the world, and Merrill is a highly respected businessman and philanthropist.

We were nervous about meeting him, and once again we had that feeling of being way out of our depth, but somehow we continued to go deeper. Merrill shook our hands warmly and proceeded to chat to us for an hour and a half. He talked at length about which sorts of teas he recommended and the estates we could get them from. He explained how tea moves through an auction system in Sri Lanka, and that he could help us to understand and navigate the system. In addition to this practical help, he talked about his commitment to the quality and authenticity of what he calls 'real tea'. This ethical approach sees the tea business as a key to building communities and supporting ecosystems, rather than being purely commercially driven.

Of all the advice and information he gave us, one thing stuck with us above all: 'Don't overvalue your tea, but don't undervalue it either'. In other words, pay and charge a fair price for good-quality tea, but don't become greedy and lose sight of your values. This has certainly been a constant rule in our business since then. That initial meeting in London has been fundamental in shaping us and showed us how accessible the tea world is if you approach all new contacts and opportunities with an open and humble mind, always making time to listen and learn. For us, Imboolpitiya Ceylon offers a constant reminder of the kindness and help he gave us, and that no matter how much we have on our plate, we can always make time for others.

Michelle: Colourful, vibrant, rich in culture and with fabulous food, Sri Lanka was an instant love affair. It's one of the most accessible places to learn about tea, as tea estates line the roads that lead to Nuwara Eliya. It's not surprising, therefore, that a lot of customers have visited factories or gardens in Sri Lanka. Orange pekoe is often requested, and people are almost always referring to the orange pekoe (OP) grade of Sri Lankan tea they have enjoyed on their travels. This high-grade black tea requires no milk, and is a flavour revelation to those who have previously only enjoyed the standard British cup of black tea.

Tea is celebrated in Sri Lanka, and although many people choose to take it milky with sugar, a quality cup, which can and should be enjoyed black, can be found in many places across the island. We mostly enjoy Sri Lankan black teas in the morning, and as a result of making breakfast a ritual on our travels, we were introduced to the delights of the Sri Lankan egg hopper, a crêpe-like 'bowl' made from coconut milk and rice flour which, when cooked in a special hopper pan, forms an edible bowl in which eggs are cooked. These street food snacks, when combined with a bowl of fine Sri Lankan tea, make an amazing combination. On our return to the UK we knew that hoppers had to become part of our lives and our business.

Finally, to the tea estates themselves, and the people working in them. Both of the estates here were firsts for us. Imboolpitiya was one of the first teas we ever stocked, and Indulgashinna was our first hands-on experience of biodynamic tea farming (see page 26), something we had learned about at Makaibari on our very first trip. These two estates also perfectly illustrate an important factor in determining the final profile in the Ceylon cup: altitude. Imboolpitiya is located in the mid country around Kandy. Indulgashinna is located in the high country. Their stories offer insight into what makes Ceylon tea so unique, while highlighting the present-day opportunities and challenges.

Alongside estates like these, there is a large number of smallholders, where the majority of the tea in Sri Lanka is grown. There are over 400,000 such smallholdings, of which around 80 percent are below half a hectare in size. Most are very small plots, following multi-crop models that are the primary source of income for families, making up around 2 million people in total. They either feed the green leaf directly into a factory or, more commonly, sell to a tea dealer or collector who then sells to a factory.

The relationship between smallholder and estate is not as simple as just the exchange of leaf for cash, but involves the larger estates sharing best practice and incentivizing growers to farm in a certain way. This is certainly the case with Idulgashinna. This estate has plans in place to support the smallholders surrounding them, benefitting their productivity while ensuring they do not impact on Idulgashinna's status as biodynamic and organic.

THE HIGH-ALTITUDE GARDEN: IDULGASHINNA ESTATE

Rob: When I first visited Idulgashinna in 2016 I arrived slightly late to a full welcome committee who presented me with flower garlands and a traditional paint dot on my forehead. I was then shown around the biodynamic area of the garden, the medical centre, the Fairtrade department and the staff accommodation. Thoroughly impressed, I was told we'd be catching a train to the factory as the drive was long and bumpy, whereas the train went straight. But somehow we missed the train, so the long, windy drive they had tried to spare me was the only option. Halfway, our car overheated on the steep, muddy road, so a tuk-tuk was summoned. This fared better, until the road became so shattered that we were unceremoniously ushered out to walk by the driver. He bounced on until the road became flat enough for us to retake our seats, and we continued at a crawl to the factory. This sort of journey is not unusual, but sticks with me because of the sheer beauty of the surroundings, which prevented any feelings of stress or anxiety. It was very much a part of the experience, and of course makes for a great story.

Idulgashinna Garden is situated just below the famous Horton Plains in the Uva province in southeast Sri Lanka. This beautiful biodynamic garden is 1,000–2,000 metres in altitude. The garden is made up of 274 hectares producing around 200 tonnes per year of some of the finest tea in Sri Lanka, plus 10 hectares producing 500 kilograms of coffee.

We choose to buy tea from Idulgashinna because of two factors: the character of the tea it grows, due to its high altitude, which brings out lighter,

more complex flavours; and how the garden grows its tea. It's biodynamic
and therefore organic with an enormous focus on soil, something which we
are very passionate about.

Mr Gnanasekaran Rajaratnam is the garden's manager and is in charge
of agriculture, manufacturing and social development. He is in charge
of the 450 workers and 65 staff. He told us why the garden is so special:
'Idulgashinna started life as a tea garden in 1984 and it soon became one of
the pioneers of organic tea farming, becoming certified organic in 1989 and
then biodynamic in 1999. The biodynamic agriculture practices were started
because of buyers' requests, and we've found it's very useful for controlling
pest and insects, and quality has improved. Idulgashinna now offers
comprehensive advisory and consultancy services for plantation and farms
that want to implement the methods of biodynamic agriculture.'

One of the main focuses of biodynamic tea growing is on soil quality,
but before you start to care for your soil it is important to be growing in
the optimal area. Mr Rajaratnam explained: 'The lands selected must be
undulating terrains, well drained and with a good soil depth and un-eroded.
It is advisable to avoid eroded lands with slab rock, concentrated boulders,
surface rocks and gravel. In Sri Lanka the ideal conditions for tea cultivation
are well-drained lands with less than 70 percent slope and mid elevations of
55 percent, with more than 60 centimetres of soil depth, less than 20 percent
surface rockiness and less than 50 percent gravel in the top layer of soil. Flat
lands adjoining paddy fields, water or boggy areas are best avoided due to
poor drainage and soil aeration. Idulgashinna matches all these criteria.'

I was shown the incredible biodynamic production area, where everything
that maintains and balances the soil is prepared, including the cow pat
preparation hut and the liquid manure hut. When it comes to the soil,
'incorporation of well-made compost is vital for maintaining and sustaining
the humus content, microbiological life and and earthworm activity.
Compost has two uses: as an immediate source of nutrients for a crop, and
as a soil conditioner. When compost is applied there is an active and quick
initial breakdown of protein, with temperatures of 60–70°C, that lasts
for about six weeks. The second stage is slower, forming the humus and
promoting worm activity.'

As well as compost, considerable quantities of green manure are obtained
from well-managed medium-sized trees and crops inter-planted with
the tea. Lopping and spreading of these provides organic matter in large
quantities, which improves the soil's physical properties and provides
nitrogen and other mineral nutrients. Cover crops are planted between the
tea bushes to reduce surface run-off, increase the rate of infiltration, prevent
soil erosion, retain soil moisture during dry periods, provide nutrients and
reduce weed growth. These factors, combined with the unique properties of
the garden, create a high-grown tea rich in flavour and goodness.

Another attraction for us is that social responsibility is also a high priority:
'The organization takes great pride in declaring to the world that the welfare
requirements of the workers are met. They have a social development
team chosen from the youth of the community and led by experienced

coordinators. The living conditions of the families improved when it was decided to implement an integrated social development programme, rather than organizing a few welfare and relief activities, for the steady development of physical health care, mental wellbeing, economical progress and the spiritual stability of the community. Every cup of tea is hygienically, naturally produced in a happy and healthy working environment.'

THE MID-COUNTRY GARDEN: IMBOOLPITIYA ESTATE

Rob: Imboolpitiya Estate is located in the Kandy district in the Central Province of Sri Lanka. The estate covers just over 180 hectares and ranges from 478–758 metres in altitude. When we first launched our tea business online in November 2011, Imboolpitiya was one of five teas we stocked. The tea we buy is graded BOP, which stands for Broken Orange Pekoe. This grade gives a good, strong flavour and astringency and is similar to the traditional breakfast-style tea that's so popular in the UK, making it a great choice for a launch tea. Imboolpitiya was recommended by Merrill Fernando as an estate that would be perfect for our needs. How right he was: seven years on, it's still a core tea in our range. It is often this tea that shows someone new to loose-leaf tea that black teas can be pleasantly rather than harshly strong and have a range of flavours as well as bitterness.

Our last trip there was just over two years ago, just before the current estate manager, Mr E.M.D. Rajasekara, joined. Under his management, the estate has won multiple international and local awards. Each plucking brings slightly different characters to the tea, but there is never a dip in quality. We enjoy these minor changes because they create a greater connection and understanding of tea as a plant that is subject to annual variations. Mr Rajasekara explained the key aspects of his job: 'It's all about about planning for continuous improvement, implementing good agricultural and manufacturing practices, and monitoring, delegating to people, supervising and looking after people's welfare.' This, combined with the consistency in quality, also highlights one of the key strengths in Sri Lankan tea production: the effectiveness of the infrastructure. Introduced initially by the British, these systems and methods, such as plucking standards, grading, recording and so on, still form part of the basis of estate management. Many of the tea-processing machines are still the original British-made ones, with the occasional addition of an automated Japanese tea sorter – and, of course, there has been evolution and change over time as the industry has changed.

Mr Rajasekara reminded us that underpinning these lush and romantic landscapes is the very real threat of a changing climate, a reminder that our tea choices matter. 'Our teas are enjoyed by tea-lovers all over the world, and I am proud to be a part of that. We aim to produce tea for the niche market that caters to the customer demand for quality and allows the real value of Ceylon tea to be realized. This in turn benefits the people who work here and those involved by association. My biggest fear for the future is climate change, as extreme weather and prolonged drought are becoming more of a problem. We also can suffer from a worker shortage, as fewer people want to pick tea. This is a big challenge and will get bigger over time.'

nepal

Nepal sits in an enviable physical position in the middle of the
Himalayas, between the two giants of tea production, China and
India. Nepal's tea history started towards the end of the nineteenth
century. Some accounts tell of a gift of seeds from the Chinese
emperor to Prime Minister of Nepal Jung Bahadur Rana in 1863.
They say the planting was implemented by the Prime Minister's
son-in-law, Colonel Gajraj Singh Thapa. Other sources describe
how the same man, Colonel Thapa, was on a tour of the East India
Company promoted estates of Darjeeling in 1873 when he was
impressed by tea growing there and decided to grow this magical
plant in his home country. Either way, the first Nepalese plantation
was the Ilam Tea Estate in the hills of Ilam district, east Nepal. This
produced orthodox tea, while another plantation, the Soktim Tea
Estate in the Jhapa district, grew tea destined for the CTC (cut-
tear-curl) process. At this time all leaf was sold to Darjeeling
factories. Tea production was very much under government rule
for more than 100 years, and this is perhaps why it did not progress
enormously until recent times. The early Rana dynasty was a time
of political turmoil and poor economic growth, so while neighbour
Darjeeling flourished, Nepal could not grow enough even to meet
domestic consumption.

The first private sector estate was the Bhudhakaran Tea Estate, established in 1959. This was followed in 1966 by the formation of a government body to aid tea development, the Nepal Tea Development Corporation (NTDC). In 1978 the first tea processing factory was built in Ilam, which, combined with the NTDC's encouragement of small farmers to see tea as a cash crop, meant that by the 1990s the industry was starting to become fully commercial. The next step came in 1993 when the profit-orientated NTDC was privatized and its role was handed over to the non-profit making National Tea and Coffee Development Board under the Agricultural Ministry. More processing factories were built and demand increased.

Today, fine, aromatic teas are being produced in the blossoming estates on the plains and in the high mountains. Nepal is now the twenty-first largest producer in the world. With altitudes of 900–2,000 metres above sea level, which provide similar growing conditions to its close neighbour, Darjeeling, teas can be made that have similar characteristics, but with a distinctive sweetness and darker infusion colour. Despite the strict geographical indicator system in place in Darjeeling (which certifies that Darjeeling tea must come from a designated area and meet certain standards) and the standalone quality of Nepalese teas, a large proportion of them still end up being blended with or sold as Darjeeling to support the increasing demand there, and because prices are often higher. The second flush season of 2017 in Darjeeling was heavily disrupted by striking workers demanding a separate homeland for the majority Nepali-speaking Gorkhas. This meant that very little second-flush tea was made, leaving a gap in the market which it is reported was often filled by Nepalese tea. These circumstances may provide the Nepalese tea areas with a much-needed boost in demand, but do little to improve consumer knowledge of their standalone quality.

The future of this small tea nation looks good, however. It benefits from the smallholder system promoted at the end of the last century. Individual farmers who own and farm their own land have more control, and this model seems to result in more care and attention in tea production. However, challenges do exist. A dependence on Kolkata in India as a port, the devastation of infrastructure by the earthquake in 2015 and consequent lack of structure in the industry all create a strain. However, as knowledge spreads there are more and more people willing to support Nepal and its beautiful teas.

Our Nepal

Michelle: My first trip to the tea-producing areas of Nepal was in June 2017 and I returned again a year later. Leaving Jalpaiguri in India in the early hours on that first trip, we headed for the border at Kakarbhitta, a small town and the most easterly crossing point between India and Nepal. I love the energy at border crossings like this. It does require a little patience, but after a few trips back and forth across the bridge to get the appropriate stamps and permissions, we were finally in Nepal. Our time here was spent in the Ilam region, in the hilly region of the Mechi Zone in the Eastern Development

Region of Nepal. We were here to find great tea and gain more knowledge about the growing speciality sector of the tea industry in Nepal. It was misty and wet, but when the cloud cleared we had tantalizing glimpses of this beautiful tea country.

One of the people we spent time with was our good friend Chandra Bhushan Subba, owner of Sandapkhu and CEO of the Himalayan Orthodox Tea Producers Association (HOTPA). Bhushan provided an invaluable layer of local knowledge. 'Large tea producers sell around 4.5 million kilograms to India, but around 20–30 percent of the "quality" segment is now exported. This new segment started in 2009 and there are now just over 100 units producing all kinds of speciality tea. Most small tea producers are experimenting, so it is an innovative time in the speciality sector.

'In the long run, our hope is to sell overseas directly as a Nepali brand – but it's early days and this will take time. In order to differentiate the Nepali tea industry and build interest, we need to focus on what is different about Nepali tea. Part of this is displaying our logo on all Nepali tea products. Our logo stands for respect for people, respect for nature, transparency in the production process and commitment to quality. I strongly believe that people should be able to visit and witness the tea being made.'

Bushan explained Nepal's great natural biodiversity: 'From the north to the south, the tea-growing areas cover a distance of only 98 kilometres but within that space there are 136 different ecosystems. Understanding these can help differentiate Nepali tea because each ecosystem has its own specific climactic variation that affects the tea. Nepali tea is different from other types because of the latitude, virgin soil and the raw material. The combination of soil type, elevation and planting material in Nepal deliver a highly 'tippy' tea rich in shining leaf buds or tips, as the tea bushes are young. This boosts the complexities and delicate notes in the finished tea. The original bushes were planted in 1862 from Chinese seeds; most of the new plantations are derived from those planted in Darjeeling, so they are all tried-and-tested varietals. Tea in Nepal is not a monoculture; farmers grow their teas among fruit trees and vegetables in areas dedicated to agriculture, far from the city.'

Here is an introduction to the world of Nepali tea through the words of three of the extremely generous people we have met, who also work within three different tea-farming models. Their stories offer us a first-hand insight into what makes Nepali tea so unique, and highlight the contemporary opportunities and challenges.

SINGLE COOPERATIVE FARMING: CHANDRA BHUSHAN SUBBA, SANDAKPHU TEA PLANTATION, JASIBREY VILLAGE

Chandra is a one-man force for change in the Nepali tea industry, and his passion for tea started many years ago. He explained: 'I had a real craze for tea drinking when I was young. Later, I found an opportunity to specialize in tea from Assam, and then did my postgraduate studies on green tea from Japan. Tea was therefore a natural choice for me. I found myself as the only tea expert in the country.'

Sandakphu tea plantation and production unit is located in the foothills of Sandakphu Peak in Jasbirey village, Maipokhari, Ilam, an area around 2,000 metres above sea level. This cooperative of 46 farmers, some as high as 2,400 metres, organically farms an area of 100 hectares, hand-picking the leaves to a standard ranging from one leaf and one bud to two leaves and one bud. I took the bumpy road to this beautiful place in 2018, and the factory and the team they have created here is special; I could have stayed for weeks. As we chatted with the co-operative members perching on the edge of the withering beds upstairs in the small factory, I felt their desire to spread the word about Nepali tea. I also understood why the tea from this particular area, cooperative and people is so special.

Sandakphu is reputedly recognized as a place for monks to meditate. It is the highest habitable point in the district of Ilam, which adjoins the Sikkim and Darjeeling hills. It is also claimed by Darjeeling because the eastern slope of Sandakphu peak falls in India. This unique area of high biodiversity stands alongside the Mai Pokhari Ramsar site, a Nepalese world heritage site for wetlands, which houses many endangered species of wild flora and fauna. In Chandra's opinion: 'Tea crafted in this tranquil environment and at such high elevations within the 26° North latitude provides flavours and character that have no comparison. We pick across all four seasons and each delivers unique characteristics in the cup.'

Initiated in 1990, the tea plantation at Sandakphu produces high-quality tea varieties planted locally by farmers who migrated from other villages in the district. The plantation is nearing maturity, and the quality of tea is therefore highly rated as compared with many other tea areas of Nepal. Each farmer in the cooperative owns their own land. The farmers and Chandra share a belief that this model is key to quality tea: 'Ownership and quality are intrinsically linked. High-quality leaves mean high-quality teas, and these will enhance the reputation and of the cooperative and the price that can be achieved.' Sandakphu also stands out because it is headed by a woman, Bimala Mukhia, a fact that has not always been very well received. In 2015, Chandra and his wife Twistina had to close the factory as the result of a dispute over female management. They stuck to their principles and suffered a substantial financial loss before finally buying out their shareholders and reopening in the late summer. Three years on, two highly skilled women hold the positions of production and finance manager and a new project has emerged to support the schooling of the children of workers at Sandakphu. The fear of having to close the factory highlighted the fragility of the children's education as, fearing for her job, one worker removed her child from the school. Chandra intervened and committed to pay for the child irrespective of the factory closure and job situation, something he is now developing into a charitable idea.

Michelle: The life that Chandra and Twistina have chosen to follow is undoubtably challenging. Sitting in his Kathmandu tea room in 2017, he told me that 'the weather pattern and green leaf quality are always at the front of my mind. I decide which tea to make according to the weather conditions.

'My day starts with calling the factory (if I am away in our head office in

Kathmandu) and enquiring about the leaf arrival, their quality and condition and the weather, then deciding on what to produce. After calling the factory I go to my tea room, where I carry out tea tastings and evaluate orders.

'I spend a lot of time checking and keeping records on when particular teas were manufactured, recalling the leaf condition, season and weather patterns, so as to work out how to repeat the production of similar teas. All of this takes place against the backdrop of the usual issues of electricity failure and bad road conditions, which are a constant phenomenon at the moment. I am working on a permanent solution to these problems for the factory and farmers' fields.'

The range of speciality teas he produces across the seasons in Nepal no doubt make his day run more smoothly. 'I probably drink 10–12 cups of black tea a day. I switch from Ruby to Himalayan Gold in the morning and after dinner. During the day, I prefer our hand-rolled White Orange. Autumn calls for Green Peony, and Spring urges me to our Spring Whites. The monsoon absorbs me with Green Pearls and oolongs.'

Chandra has an infectious enthusiasm, but there is no doubt that he means business. He knows that for Nepali tea to succeed it needs to be recognized and asked for by name. As more smaller factories produce quality teas, markets need to be developed for them to sell into. As I gave Chandra and Twistina a goodbye hug in their tea room in Kathmandu, he shared his final thoughts on how Nepal will achieve this, and the part that Sandakphu can play: 'I feel strongly that quality is the key to getting recognized overseas. Quality lies with the farmer – bringing them on board, working as a partnership. When we started Sandapkhu our idea was to go to a remote area, make a small factory and start producing quality teas. In the end, our aim is to be able to help the farmers buy the factory back, and own and run it themselves. It's an idea we have shared widely with the small tea growers and small factories across Nepal who come to us for training.'

THE FARM AND FACTORY MODEL: REGGIE GOODWIN, KANYAM TEA ESTATE

Michelle: It was a misty afternoon when we finally arrived at the Kanyam Hill Gardens. Located 1,560 metres above sea level, with the factory at the highest point, we could only imagine how beautiful the scene would be when the clouds lifted. We were late, very late, which is quite a common theme with tea travels. We need not have worried, as we were greeted by the hugely charismatic Reggie, the man in charge at Kanyam, with an impressive family history in tea. His father was the son of a British SAS operative who was based in Japan and fought along with the allied forces. His mother came from royal stock in Burma and was the princess of the Shaan state of Toungee. They had to flee to India after his grandfather was killed during World War II in Myanmar, ending up in Nepal, where his father started the first tea nursery in 1966. From there the Nepali tea industry was born.

Reggie: 'My father was on a garden called Chillingkot. I remember the fun when, as small kids on winter vacation, we used to come back home and try to earn some extra cash working in the nursery. Of course, being the Burra

Sahib's (chief officer's) kids had its benefits and more fun was had than work being done. The plants from the nursery were used to supplement the small area that had been planted out in Soktim and Ilam way back in 1857 by the erstwhile Rajah. Dad was instrumental in getting the Soktim factory built, as well as putting the Ilam factory in order. Even today, Ilam and Soktim retain the sections that were planted out in 1857 with the original Chinese hybrid clone that gives both gardens their distinctive flavour. Sadly, the Soktim factory has been closed after privatization.'

Our time at Kanyam was to be enlightening. This garden is quite unique in Nepal in that there is an 'owned' garden alongside a factory, rather than a group of smallholders feeding into a cooperative. This has its advantages in the consistent approach towards maintaining quality; 60 percent of the teas produced here are sold to the internal market, while 40 percent are exported to Kolkata. Reggie focuses on making black teas with a greenish tinge. They produce a light cup which, to me, is unique to Nepali tea. Reggie explained: 'We achieve this by going for a hard wither 20 centimetres deep, then a hard roll to get the green tinge. Very little oxidization is allowed to retain the freshness of the brew. We try to pluck most of the areas on a strict seven-day round, but due to a scarcity of workers (a common theme in Nepal), we have to leave out some areas, which are plucked on extended rounds. At the moment, the 125 people in the 299-hectare garden are operating on a 13-day plucking round. Of course, the teas are manufactured separately and packed and sold as secondary teas.' As the rain pelted the glass of the tasting room we enjoyed the teas with Reggie, Rajnish, the manager of Kanyam and Jitman, and the factory assistant manager.

As we tasted we talked about the image of Nepali tea, which is often seen as the poor cousin of Darjeeling, sent to be blended, lost and unappreciated as a single-garden offering. We also spoke about the labour shortages here; I had seen very few people plucking in the gardens, in stark contrast to what we had seen over the border in Assam. Reggie explained that the optimal land-to-person ratio here is 2.5 workers per hectare, but they were operating at 0.8, a highly challenging situation that is leading many large-scale gardens to move to machine plucking. In Reggie's experience, this labour shortage was due to a lack of interest among the young to get their hands dirty working in a larger garden like this. He knows the impact that moving to machine plucking often has on quality, so at Kanyam the majority of tea is still hand plucked, with some minimal use of hand shears. We also discussed the changeable weather – last year there was no rain from October to April. Reggie explained the impact of this: 'Due to a prolonged drought and then heavy showers, the bushes are highly stressed. This may be hard to understand, but they behave differently in terms of yield and also quality. A continued cycle of this type of weather has also brought about changes in Assam and Darjeeling.'

From Kanyam we headed up to Ilam Tea Estate to see the oldest tea garden in Nepal, which is located in the centre of the town. This smaller garden is 48 hectares, originally planted in 1857 as 4 hectares. Here, Reggie and his small team of 3 workers focus simply on green tea. The plucking standard is two leaves and one bud, all hand picked with no withering. At 12 p.m. and 3.30 p.m. the leaves come in and the team cool them down, then place them in the enzymer, a machine in which the tea simply runs through at 125°C in order to 'kill-green' or halt the oxidation of the leaf. The leaves are then rolled before being dried for 24 minutes at 120°C. They then leave the tea overnight to develop the flavour and get an even bloom before sorting.

As our time together came to an end, talk moved on to more general topics. Our short time together had clearly shown that Reggie has adventure in his blood, and it was interesting to learn that his motivations for a life in tea are similar to those of many people we have met in tea: an underlying desire to do something good for an industry on which many people rely. 'I have always loved the outdoors and refuse to live in a city. In the beginning, tea offered me a nice lifestyle, but I started in 1983 and I'm still at it. I love the thrill of seeing something grow and mature and then become a source of livelihood for many people and a source of joy to millions around the world. I left my job in Assam to come back to Nepal, where I saw my first tea bush. This will probably be my last formal job as a planter; then I want to stay in Nepal and help the smaller farmers get better so that one day an industry that my father helped start can take its place as a quality source of tea.'

For Reggie, love of the land is at the heart of this positive future for the tea industry in Nepal, and when not at work he is riding around the hills on his motorbike, Mustang Sally. 'Nepal is a land of sheer joy if you have the right attitude. Fruit grows so easily here, along with many spices and rare herbs. There are opportunities galore in a place as gorgeous and fertile as this, provided that you love the land.'

ORGANIC MULTI-COOPERATIVE FARMING: UDAYA CHAPAGAIN, GORKHA TEA ESTATE, SUNDERPANI

Michelle: On our 2017 visit, our final stop in Ilam was the rolling hills of the small village of Sunderpani. We were there to visit the team at the Gorkha Tea Estate to learn more about their organic practices. Gorkha sits at 1,676 metres above sea level, with an owned land size of 30 hectares. As well as its own 30 hectares, Gorkha works with four other tea cooperatives that include 278 small tea growers. The man in charge is Udaya Chapagain, a Nepali who came into tea by chance on a trip to Germany.

Udaya: 'When I was a young chap I got an opportunity to visit Germany and Britain. Back in Nepal, I remembered that when I was in Europe, Darjeeling tea was popular. Since I lived in the eastern part of Nepal I knew little about tea – at that time we had only two gardens that belonged to the government, one in Ilam and another in Kanyam. But I thought, why not start a tea business? I went to Germany in 1984, taking some samples along with me, visited Hamburg and invited a man who seemed interested to visit Nepal. He came in 1984, when there were no vehicles in the Terai area, so I found an elephant to travel around the tea gardens, then visited Kanyam and Ilam. He stayed for a week, tasted the tea and decided to buy some. That was my start-up business and I have been in tea ever since, establishing the first private-sector factory in Fikkal Ilam.

'In 2000 I started my own organic tea factory, Gorkha Tea Estate. I chose Sunderpani for its virgin land, high hills and fertile soil. In the beginning I planted the tea seedlings in the barren land and visited more than 300 farmers to try to convince them to go organic. It was very hard work, but I eventually successfully convinced them and started construction of the factory. Manufacturing started in 2009 and we gained all the relevant certifications in 2011, including for all the farmers involved.'

If you consider the number of farmers involved, this was no easy task. The certificates are displayed proudly in the factory, evidence of the underlying ethos at Gorkha: 'to stop the use of synthetic agro-chemicals and increase the soil fertility through sustainable organic farming, maintain biodiversity, create an eco-friendly environment and share organic concepts and ideology with small tea growers. We provide all sorts of support free of charge, from technical support to biogas facilities. We also strengthen cooperatives by giving them financial support. Organic cultivation is hard work and it is also challenging to ensure the farmers stay organic. We are also supporting them by paying the maximum leaf prices.'

The day we visited Gorka was extremely misty. Horses were coming and going from the main entrance of the factory, led by smallholder farmers bringing in the leaf. These are the images you never forget – for us in the west, a vision of a romantic existence, but in reality, a wet day heaving tea leaves down the mountain. Nevertheless, the farmers were sociable and gracious in their work. As the light faded, the factory lit up and we were led by the team into a small office, where we learned more about their approach. There they explained that 'the farmers bring 10–60 kilograms, depending on the size of their garden. They are contracted with their respective cooperatives and the cooperatives makes an agreement with the Gorkha Tea Estate to supply us the green leaves. The estate and the cooperatives decide the price of the green leaves, and the estate has established a new model to pay a price that doesn't vary according to the seasons.'

Michelle: Walking through the co-operative closest to the factory on a return visit in 2018, we stopped for tea in a farmer's house. Through casual conversation, our hosts revealed real enthusiasm and plenty of new ideas for the future of the sector here – clear evidence of the optimism about the future of Nepali tea.

As we came to leave, Udaya shared his belief that it is the combination of the unique environment, the hand-plucked tea leaves, the new seedlings and the cooperative model that make his teas stand out. 'Our focus, now and always, is on quality, not quantity. We are hopeful for the future of speciality Nepali black tea, and plan to access tea connoisseurs through the international market. Nepal is a natural country with beautiful high mountains. The tea gardens are spread through the lap of the Himalayas. Quality organic production and gaining international recognition for Nepali teas are our main concerns, hence the collective Nepal tea logo "Nepal tea – quality from the Himalayas". Underpinning this is a need to upgrade small tea growers to growing and plucking quality leaves, and to make sure this ethos spreads to our factories, ensuring quality in the consumer's cup.'

malawi 1878

Malawi is a landlocked east African country around half the size of the UK. Currently in the top ten world tea exporters, it was one of the first African countries to market its tea and has been growing commercially since the early 1890s. Tea was first brought to Malawi (formerly Nyasaland) by the gardener to the Blantyre Mission of the Church of Scotland in 1878. These initial attempts failed, but in 1886 seeds sourced from Kew Gardens were successfully germinated, confirming that growing tea in Malawi was possible. It was not until 1891 that the first commercial plantings took place, however. Henry Brown, a Ceylon (now Sri Lanka) coffee planter who came to Malawi after the failure of coffee on the island due to disease, was responsible for this expansion, the first commercial planting in the whole of Africa. Later plantations were established at Mulanje and Thyolo in the Shire Highlands.

Tea failed to flourish when it was experimented with in other areas. A hindrance to development was the difficulty in transportation of tea for export, which around 1903 was only possible by river steamer down the Shire River to the sea, a costly and intensive business. However, in 1909 the Shire Highlands railroad was completed, cutting costs and time dramatically. A further development came in 1911 when the Lauderdale Estate in Mulanje built a factory powered by hydroelectricity. This stimulated the local tea economy and more factories were built to support the small estates who could not afford the cost of specialist machinery, sowing the first seeds of the smallholder model in Malawi. In the 1920s and 3os the decline in the tobacco industry lead to a growth in tea estates, and this growth has continued at a steady rate until this day.

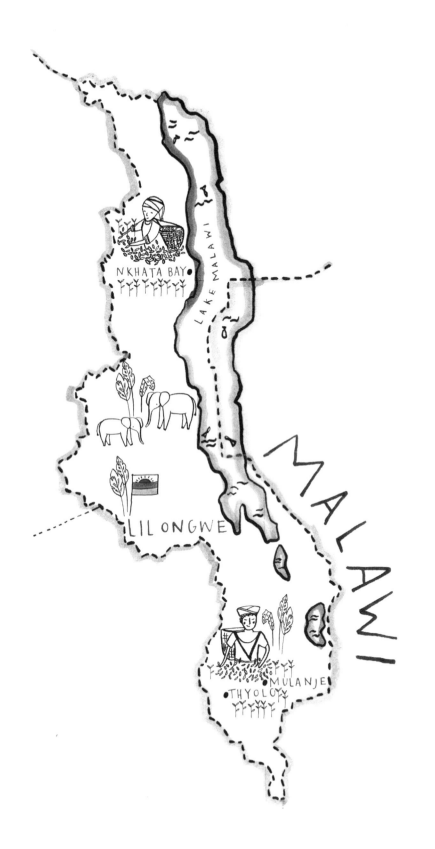

In 1923 the Satemwa Tea Estate was established in the Shire Highlands. Today, as more and more private companies are acquired by huge companies looking to produce high-volume, low-price tea for the commodity market, Satemwa is one of the last family-owned tea estates in the region. They work closely with the extensive smallholder network in Malawi to procure fresh leaf, following a model that was first introduced in the 1960s. This smallholder model has seen turbulent times. Established in 1964 in the three districts of Nkhata Bay, Mulanje and Thyolo, the Tea Authority provided extensive support for smallholders to set themselves up and enter a government-run system under which they received prompt payment for their leaf. This model prospered until the 1990s when a change in government saw sweeping changes across the tea sector, resulting in privatization, factory closures and a loss of security for small farmers.

In Malawi, just as in other tea-producing countries, smallholders facing such challenges had little opportunity or expertise to independently improve their position. With the price of their leaves determined by large organizations and their expertise in growing rather than marketing, they needed the system to change if they were to survive. Gradually, this started to happen with private tea companies such as Satemwa establishing new partnerships, which guaranteed the purchase of their leaves and ensured a fair price.

What you may not know as you read this is just how important Malawian tea is to your daily cup of tea, because Malawian tea is a key origin in many British blends. Known to blenders for its brisk flavour and quick colouring, Malawian tea gives a reddish tone to your cup and is ideal for drinking with milk – you would certainly notice if it was taken out! The lack of transparency in cheaper commodity teas means most of us are ignorant of the contribution of Malawian tea and tea growers to our daily tea break, but people may be aware of the work that organizations like Fairtrade have been doing to try and secure a better future for growers here, and more widely in Africa.

Malawi is one of the poorest countries in the world, its economy heavily reliant on tea export, and the livelihood of its often marginalized tea communities is at the mercy of a multitude of factors, not least the changing global climate. January 2015 saw the worst floods in a lifetime, the deaths of many growers and the destruction of the tea and other crops. People's hopes and dreams vary, but many of us would say that we want to care and provide for our families and give them the best opportunities for a happy and healthy future. When Fairtrade asked the tea farmers in Malawi this question, the desire to provide for their families was part of all their replies.

Our Malawi

At Comins we don't deal in bulk commodity teas – we predominantly deal with small gardens that produce high-quality orthodox teas. We only trade directly, and in Malawi we deal only with Satemwa. The wider reality, however, is that tea bags will have played an important part in many readers' lives. Although it's not the focus of this book, it seems appropriate to raise the issues that organizations like Fairtrade are trying to tackle in countries such as Malawi. At Comins we believe that to build a fair and sustainable future for the tea industry and the millions who depend on it. Those involved in the tea industry should aim to understand each others' work, try to find ways to collaborate and ultimately work towards building a set of shared values in the way tea is sourced, purchased and sold.

Emma Mullins works in the Tea Team at the Fairtrade Foundation, so we asked her to give us a quick education about their work. Around 75–85 percent of all globally traded Fairtrade tea comes into the UK. Fairtrade works with small-producer organizations (cooperatives), single-estate organizations and multistate organizations. Certified producer organizations have access to tailored support from Fairtrade's staff on the ground, including training on critical factors such as financial literacy, workers' rights and child labour.

'However, the biggest difference comes when the purchaser agrees to buy the tea on Fairtrade terms. This means that they pay the Fairtrade minimum price and the Fairtrade Premium, which for non-organic CTC is 0.5$ per kilogram'. The Fairtrade Premium is an extra sum of money, paid on top of the selling price, that farmers or workers invest in projects of their choice, such as improving their farming, businesses, or health and education in their community. 'A lot of the Premium in cooperatives is spent on the local community, such as on maternal health and access to medicine, which brings huge benefits to tea communities. If purchasers choose not to buy on Fairtrade terms, they cannot put the Fairtrade mark on their product but, more importantly, the producers do not derive any value from the work they have undertaken to gain certification.'

At the time of writing there were 5 Fairtrade-certified gardens in Malawi, but only a fraction of tea grown in Malawi is actually sold on Fairtrade terms. 'The global average for tea sold on Fairtrade terms is just 5 percent of the eligible Fairtrade crop, which means that many purchasers buy teas for their blends from Fairtrade gardens, but choose not to buy these on Fairtrade terms,' Emma explained.

Whether or not you agree with the approach that Fairtrade takes to tackling these important issues, it is clear that change cannot be expected only at the grower and supplier end. Consumers need to be encouraged to look more closely at their purchasing decisions and be prepared to pay more for their tea. Again, the need for transparency comes to the fore, and while this is easier in the premium market there is no reason why greater transparency could not be also be applied in the commodity market. It's something we, as tea drinkers, can all demand – and some people in Malawi are already working successfully on making it a reality.

MODERN PIONEERS: ALEXANDER KAY, SATEMWA TEA ESTATE, SHIRE HIGHLANDS, MALAWI

Rob: Fairtrade growers in markets like Malawi are not just sitting around and waiting for things to get better: modern pioneers are reviving the tea industry, making brave decisions and taking risks to bring us truly great teas. Alexander Kay is a third-generation tea farmer at Satemwa Tea Estate. We have worked with the team at Satemwa for a few years now, and their hand-rolled Zomba Pearls are incredibly popular at our teahouses. We have discovered a talented team prepared to have open and honest conversations around the shape and direction of the tea market. Their story is one of optimism, innovation and great-tasting teas.

The family-owned Satemwa estate sits at an altitude of 1,000–1,200 metres on the slopes of Thyolo Mountain in the Shire Highlands in Malawi. The micro-climate of this area in the Southern Hemisphere sees one main rainy season from December until April, a cold, dry season with showers from May/June until July, and a hot, dry season from August until November, mirroring those areas such as Assam in the Northern Hemisphere. Their First Spring Flush is therefore produced in September/October. The soil here is acidic red soil (*terra rossa*) derived from a dark grey dolerite rock, which provides a nutrient-rich environment for the 900 hectares of tea, 52 hectares of micro-lot speciality coffee and 400 hectares of sustainable wood used to dry the tea.

Wouter Verelst from Satemwa told me that about the strong sector-funded Tea Research Foundation in Malawi, which has overseen the development of the cultivars here: 'It has worked hard since the 1960s to develop some endemic Malawian cultivars adapted to the unique terroir and specific climate and also high in theanine and catechins. They did, and are still doing, a lot of research on climate change-resistant varieties.' From these cultivars Satemwa produces a range of high-quality pesticide-free teas and is certified by Fairtrade, Rainforest Alliance and UTZ. Wouter went on to explain that 'around 90 percent (2,500 tons) of the tea produced at Satemwa each year is black CTC tea bound for the bulk commodity market, so the estate and all the smallholders dependent on it are subject to the challenges of the low-value, high-volume market.' Where Satemwa differs is that over the last 10 years it has worked hard to revive the production of orthodox speciality teas (white, green, oolong, black and dark tea) for a high-value, low-volume market. 'I say "revive",' Wouter explained, 'because orthodox production was actually the standard production method on Satemwa in the 1930s. Alexander decided to revive the production of the orthodox teas in 2006 and what you see today is the result of hours of experimenting and tasting by Alexander and the Satemwa Speciality Team informed by trips to Sri Lanka, China, India and Japan to look at different techniques and production methods. We never wanted to simply replicate teas from elsewhere – the aim has always been to create a Satemwa style, with our own character and signature.'

This approach is incredibly forward-thinking and shows that successful diversification is possible in markets predominantly known for commodity black tea. Satemwa is the only estate in Malawi producing orthodox teas at the moment. 'We are constantly innovating, constantly learning more about seasonality and cultivars. We have some limited-volume orthodox lines and some we scale up for larger volumes. Across all of our teas we aim to offer the tea drinker a distinctive Satemwa signature, a quality unique to Malawian tea and informed by the unique and Shire Highland terroir and climate. We also place a high value on traceability: each batch is monitored throughout the entire production process. Tasters approve each batch and then the teas are packed and marked with a unique code so that customers know every detail of each tea, which allows us to celebrate and recognize our growers.'

The approach is working. Teas from Satemwa are directly traded, served and sold all over the world. They have found their way into high-end tea places in New York, Paris and Tokyo, and of course to us at Comins. The success of their model, based on quality, transparency and traceability, has enabled them to take the Malawian smallholder model to a new level, and it's a principle that could offer a far brighter future for Malawian tea. 'We selected a number of small holders tea farmers around the estate to work more closely with, partnering with them to diversify their crops by planting herbs and flowers that can be blended with our speciality teas, and also helping them improve their plucking standards,' Wouter told me. 'We pay the smallholder a higher premium for this higher-quality plucked green leaf. When we sell the tea we can give the buyer full transparency down to farmer level, which demands a higher price, the profits of which we share with the smallholder.' One such farmer is Jonas Makata, one of the 198 independent small farmers around Satemwa who follows a 7-day plucking rounds at his 1-hectare plot of land. At 77 years old, he still has a passion for tea and two of his five children are still dependent on him, so the profit share from speciality teas makes a real difference. 'For each kilogram of speciality tea green leaf Jonas delivers he gets a premium higher than the normal CTC green leaf he sells us. Satemwa turns his better-quality green leaf into an OP1 (orange pekoe, referring to a black tea mostly made up of complete leaves) black tea and we share part of the profit with Jonas when we are able to sell his tea.' This is a situation in which everyone wins: the smallholder, the estate, the buyer and the tea drinker.

'The key to long-term success at Satemwa has been establishing a reputation for Malawian orthodox teas based on craftsmanship, knowledge and experience, the details of which are shared and celebrated with partners like us. Our Zomba Pearls consist of leaves that are hand plucked, withered, hand rolled and dried in a sustainable wood-fuelled micro drier. This gives a delightful full bodied, buttery and mellow flavour. The Bvumbwe Handmade Treasure is also hand plucked from a specific variety, withered, rolled in an orthodox roller, oxidized and hand turned all the time, then dried.'

As I got ready to leave I had the sense that this was only the beginning. 'Nowadays we are also making Satemwa Dark Tea, for which we start with green, light, semi-oxidized tea before we pile-ferment the tea for 3–4 weeks at a constant temperature in a dark and humid place. We use a specific fungus to keep quality and taste stable before stopping the process with a minimum of 3 drying cycles. Experimentation will continue as we learn more about this type of tea.' Watch this space!

kenya

Kenya was one of the first countries in Africa to grow tea. The first bushes were introduced in 1903 by the Briton G.W.L. Caine and planted near Limuru in the Kiambu district, but were only for ornamental purposes. Commercial production started in 1924 by Brooke Bond, later to become the biggest tea company in the world, on colonist-occupied farms. In 1931 the Kenya Tea Growers' Association (KTGA) was formed to promote tea growers' interests. In 1960, the Ministry of Agriculture realized the potential of smallholders and formed another body which, after independence in 1963, became the Kenya Tea Development Authority (KTDA). This was later privatized on the recommendation of the World Bank and became an agency instead.

The country's location on the Equator means that there are few fluctuations in the weather, and tea grows all year round at altitudes of between 1,300–2,300 metres. Another benefit, according to the KALRO-Tea research institute, is that no pesticides need to be used on Kenyan tea bushes. High levels of polythenols, a type of antioxidant, create a bitter taste in the leaf and act as an insect repellent.

SOUTH SUDAN
ETHIOPIA
KENYA
LAKE TURKANA
UGANDA
SOMALIA
NANDI
MERU
KERICHO
NYERI
NYAMIRA
KIRINYAGA
SOTIK
MARAGUA
KISSII
BOMET
THIKA
KIAMBU
VICTORIA
NAIROBI
MOUNT KILIMANJARO
TANZANIA
INDIAN OCEAN

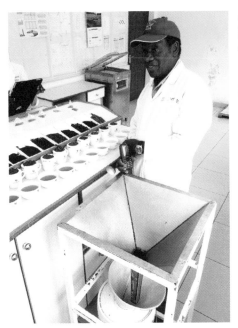

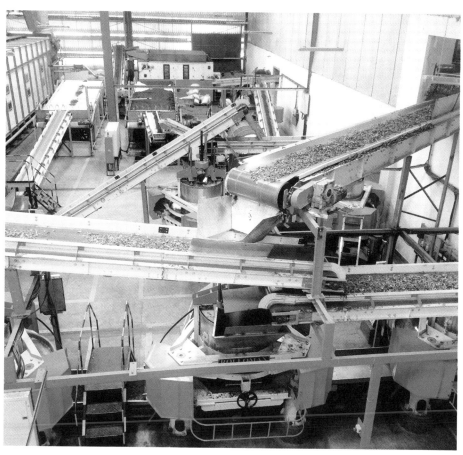

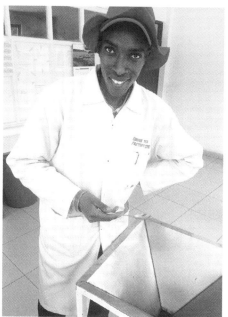

Despite tea-growing still being relatively new, Kenya has become the world's third biggest producer, making 474,808 tonnes in 2016, with the majority exported for use in commodity tea around the world. In fact, nameless Kenyan teas make up a large proportion of most tea bags, valued for their strong flavour, aroma and bright liquor colour, all of which are highly desirable. It is considered by many to be superior in quality to other similar-style teas around the world, which is why it has consistently been bought to be blended. The combination with cheaper teas reduces the cost per tea bag but maintains a good flavour and colour. The effect of this is that most tea produced in Kenya is CTC (cut-tear-curl) tea, the process used to make very small and uniform tea particles, which are mostly used as part of the blend in breakfast-style tea bags.

In Kenya, around 60 percent of the tea is produced by small-scale farmers, who sell their freshly picked green leaf to the KTDA. They have 68 tea factories where the tea is processed and then mostly sold through the world's largest tea auctions in Mombasa, although some is sold directly. Until a few years ago, these factories were all CTC producers, but now there are three orthodox factories. The remaining 40 percent is produced by large farms owned by companies like Unilever, Finlay, Eastern Kenyan Produce and Williamson, which also sell through the Mombasa auction. Again, this is mostly CTC production, with various speciality orthodox teas being produced to order. There are a small number of independent producers who form a very small sub sector. These are estates and farms with their own tea factory, mostly producing CTC, only a couple making orthodox tea. However, falling prices due to a worldwide surplus of commodity tea means that adding value has become more important. A move towards larger loose-leaf specialist tea has begun, which should unlock the incredible potential of Kenyan teas and see the strong flavour, aroma and bright liquor colour appreciated in orthodox offerings and requested by name. Increased demand for speciality loose-leaf teas globally has led a few East Africa producers to add orthodox black, green and white varieties to their range. In 2017, purple tea, green tea and orthodox tea lots featured in the Mombasa weekly auctions for the first time – a sure sign of change.

Our Kenya

We often find serendipity in our lives in tea, and this is how our story starts in Kenya. On a summer's day a friendly lady wandered into our Bath teahouse and enquired about our range of Kenyan teas. When we explained that we only buy from growers or gardens we have visited or have direct relations with, she told us that her relative owned a tea estate in Kenya and asked if we would like to be connected. Our answer is always YES! It's only by saying yes on pretty much a daily basis that Comins Tea is what it is today.

We were introduced to Nick Kirui and Sharon Kimeto, who would host and guide us on our first trip to the Kenyan tea fields, introducing us to the challenges being faced by farmers in Kenya and also to potential farms to source tea. Nick is incredibly experienced in the Kenyan tea industry, having started with Brooke Bond Kenya as a management trainee and risen through the ranks before retiring as the National Health and Safety Manager responsible for all tea plantations and factories in Unilever East Africa. His time in the industry has bred a passion for small tea farmers in Kenya: 'The smallholder farmer is at the bottom of the tea chain and always gets a raw deal, especially when it comes to take-home pay,' he told us. He is making efforts to link farmers directly to credible markets that are interested in improving tea farmers' lives and rewarding their efforts in the production of tea. Sharon's motivations align with Nick's. Her company Sav-Nordica has the main aim of helping Kenyan farmers find a direct trade link, in turn, ensuring that 'Kenyan tea farmers get a fair price for their products in Western markets.' She sees a clear path forward for Kenyan black tea: 'Action is needed in three areas. Firstly, we need to work with the farmers and educate them on the importance of sustainable farming practices and the shape of the premium tea market. This will contribute to the production of high-quality products for the international market.' At the other end, she explained: 'We need to educate the end customer on the supply chain as it looks now, showing the benefit of buying directly from the farmers who will get a fair price for their produce.' In countries like Kenya a small change in income can make an amazing difference in the rural areas where most farmers are based. 'Finally,' Karen said, 'we need people on the ground, key voices who can speak directly to farmers at the grassroot level, making it easier to incorporate and spearhead change.'

For us, as tea merchants focussed on single-garden teas, the growth in orthodox production and independent producers in Kenya is exciting. As producers move from CTC to orthodox tea they move from a model that emphasizes volume and consistency of flavour profile to one that centres on bringing out the best possible flavours from the individual characteristics of the leaf. We don't get asked about Kenyan tea by name as we do about teas from other countries, mostly because it is hidden away in tea bags. Our trip was the first step to try and change this, at least in our own teahouses. Driven by a belief that wonderful teas can originate from right across the tea world, Rob set off to find passionate people with the right approach, and expertise and raw materials to match.

The trip certainly showed us that change was beginning, but also highlighted how complex that widespread change will be. The stories we share here highlight the hurdles presented by the current system, but also an appetite for change, and the people we met inspired us with their entrepreneurial endeavours and ambitions for the future.

THE ORTHODOX FACTORY: ROBERT AND EMILY KETER, EMROK TEA, RIFT VALLEY

Rob: Emrok Tea is owned and operated by Robert and Emily Keter at an altitude of 2,000 metres in Nandi County in Kenya's Rift Valley region. It consists of a new factory surrounded by its own estate in Ogirgir. The estate originates from 1960 and was aquired by the Keters in 2002; they built their new factory in 2012. The factory is also fed by approximately 3,500 smallholders in the surrounding area, giving it a total area of around 330 hectares. All tea can be traced back to the estate or the smallholders.

The tea is grown organically (although is not yet certified so at the time of writing), is pesticide free and Rainforest Alliance certified, and the factory is also part of the Ethical Tea Partnership (ETP), a non-profit membership organization that aims to improve the sustainability of tea production, the lives of tea workers and the environment in which tea is produced. The tea is all hand plucked by pickers who are trained to select only the best two leaves and a bud, or even one leaf and a bud for some teas. Leaf is purchased from the smallholders at an agreed price higher than the standard rate, but they may get more if the tea sells well. Workers also have access to many social programmes to improve the lives of their community.

Emrok is an inspirational estate with quality at its heart, and an orthodox speciality tea line has been built in the last year. Designed by Emrok's speciality tea technical consultant, Anand Varma, it is one of the most high-tech, efficient systems I have seen on my tea travels, and one of only a few in Africa. The team can process between 16,000–20,000 kilograms of fresh leaf in a day and clearly understand the vital role that their workers play in the success of their company, and that high standards, sustainability and profitability must go hand in hand with providing a better life for the tea community here. I observed an environment of highly motivated individuals during my time here, a great example being Jeremiah Kosgei, a production assistant on the Emrok tea orthodox line. Jeremiah explained: 'When I report to work I am always jovial and focussed, as this is a job all about passion. You must have a goal and work hard to achieve it. I start work at 6 a.m. at the factory and finish when I have achieved what I wanted. The best part of the job is experimentation – I am really interested in diversifying to look at new products and really believe that we need to improve the manufacture of orthodox teas in Kenya.'

I left Emrok excited that high-quality orthodox tea was being produced on such a scale and in such state-of-the art facilities. This model clearly works, but also requires a high financial input. What if that is not available? My next visit took me to a place which, when it is finished, could be the blueprint for the Kenyan tea industry of the future.

THE ENTREPRENEUR: CHAI'S FACTORY PROJECT, KERICHO

Rob: Chai is a Kenyan with Indian heritage. He represents an exciting future for Kenyan tea: he is passionate about it as well as resolute about how people should be treated. I met him in the shell of the factory he is slowly building during an incredible downpour on the roof that created a deafening roar.

Chai: 'We have been in tea for quite some time – our family has been here since the turn of the century, when my great grandfather came to work on the railway. In 1896 he started living in Londiani, not far away. When the tea was beginning to grow in this area, Londiani declined as a town and my grandfather told my father to move to this area, which he did in 1956. He chose to focus on tractors. What we have today is built on the work we have done with tractors.'

Chai was encouraged into the tea world by his mother and he was taken under the wing of a number of people, including the massive tea company Brooke Bond. Recognizing his mechanical background and understanding the need for better mechanization in the industry, the company encouraged

him to do whatever he could. Soon he was taken on by Unilever in their research and development department to bring their factories up to standard, then did the same at Finlays. This huge amount of experience in the field, rather than in an office, shows. In recent times his focus has switched to speciality tea and he has started to build a factory, designed by him, to contain machines made by him. The aim is to support and benefit the local area by empowering the local women and employing locals who may not otherwise be employed. The plan is to feed all profits back into the factory and community. This has not been without its problems, but that does not bother Chai too much.

'Speciality tea was not within the norms of the tea industry in Kenya. We were the first people to get licensed, after a lot of push and pull. What we wanted to do was within the rules and regulations of speciality tea but they did not want to licence us. When we started to build it took us three years to get licenced. However, we did not complain and that's the way we want to keep it. I have been given lots of challenges in life but I just love being part of this community. My strong sense of who I am comes from the elders of the local community, who have blessed me and made sure I have enough stamina and enough blood in my veins to continue. To put it in a nutshell, look at Rudyard Kipling's poem *If* – that is me.'

I recognized this feeling, and it's something we see in many tea producers. Tea has to be a passion first, then a business. It supports or makes a community, depending on where you are in the process. It was fantastic to meet such a positive person, who despite many challenges keeps the focus on the benefit, rather than the problems. 'We want to see farmers with small holdings of 5 acres or 10 acres doing their own small cottage factory at home.'

One of Chai's final observations shows that in a country whose staple is tea with milk, habit changes can take place, and here the health benefits shine through: 'I have drunk black tea with milk all my life, but since the beginning of this year I have been drinking yellow and green teas. At my time in life, aged over 50, I feel blessed to be able to drink these types of teas, which I drink in the morning, at lunch and after dinner. I've been a vegetarian for over 30 years, and it's not easy to find a balance while still being nourished. I find that the teas offer me the nourishment I need.'

THE FUTURE: THE KENYA AGRICULTURAL LIVESTOCK AND RESEARCH ORGANIZATION (KALRO-TEA)

Rob: At the KALRO-Tea research institute I talked to a very passionate scientist, Lilian Kerio, and her colleagues, whose work puts them at the cutting edge of Kenyan tea. They are relied upon by companies and the KDTA for information on topics like cultivars, disease and future trends in tea. This last one is the most interesting for us. Currently, Kenyan tea is mostly black CTC (cut-tear-curl), sold at the Mombasa auction, then shipped to unknown areas around the world and blended without reference to its origin. There is a glut of this sort of tea made worldwide, which has led to stagnant auction values. The industry must change.

Lilian: 'Diversification has only started in the last five years, which is why the Kenyan Tea Board and the tea industry are encouraging the cottage tea industry. You cannot have large production of orthodox teas – you produce small amounts that are more highly valued and can be sold into direct markets. This is in its infancy and there is a lot of scepticism based on the theory that if there is a market for CTC, why would we move to orthodox? The emphasis to change and diversify has come from the Tea Directorate, as they have seen other countries moving in the direction of orthodox. We as Kenyans have to impress, we have to change, we cannot rely on the one product and expect things to change. Kenyan tea has a distinctive flavour, which is why it is used in blending, and this is the strength which we should be exploiting, but there is much more to Kenyan tea.' Here, Lilian was referring to health benefits. The team at the KALRO-Tea research institute believe that this health message should be a big part of promoting Kenyan tea, and the jewel in their crown is Purple Tea, a particular strain of the tea plant developed by them over 25 years that is high in anthocyanins, making the leaves purple and also increasing its antioxidant level, thus benefiting health (see page 184). Another health positive is that good-quality Kenyan orthodox black tea does not need milk or sugar. 'These compromise the health benefits of tea by complexing (or combining, in simple terms) with the tea polyphenols,' Lilian explained. Domestically, this is a hard sell; the British introduced tea, but it was the Indians who introduced the style of consumption based on their own chai, which is tea boiled with milk.

Kenya certainly has the resourcefulness to change and the raw materials to excite the premium tea market, but its future depends heavily on the upper echelons of the tea industry to stimulate change. Lilian summed up the simple truth: 'There is a bright future if we can find more foreign markets and increase our domestic consumption. We have a population of 48 million, yet only 5 percent of our tea is consumed here. We want to encourage our population to drink more tea, to generate more income, which will stabilize the market so that if external markets are not favourable we can still survive.'

tea *and* health

A query we often receive at the teahouses is of global interest, and one of the reasons that many people choose to work in tea: its health benefits. From the first leaves that 'saved' Shennong's life all those years ago to modern-day medicine, tea has always been known for its health-giving properties. Chinese medicine has always recognized the usefulness of the tea plant, but its qualities have not been proven in science until relatively recent times. There are now a great many scientific papers on the subject, as well as all sorts of more spurious benefits used as marketing tools.

At Comins we focus on the experience, ceremony and taste of taking tea rather than on drinking tea for health, but we are of course interested in the properties of the plant itself. The main benefits that have a scientific basis behind them are listed below, and we encourage you to take them as an introduction to further reading and research. One often overlooked aspect is the mental health benefits of the process of taking tea, whether it's as simple as putting a tea bag in a mug or as complex as a full *gongfu* infusion. The time taken to relax, to rejuvenate, to think or indeed not think, if taken regularly, is as important as any physical boost the tea will give you. We see the results in our teahouses every day.

Antioxidants

Antioxidants have been linked to the possible prevention of things like cardiovascular disease, cancer, blood pressure, as well as delaying the ageing process and increasing vitality. They do this by countering the harmful effects of 'free radicals', naturally occurring unstable molecules that, if present in large amounts, can damage cells in our bodies. Antioxidants are contained in flavanoids, a category of polyphenol that makes up a large proportion of a tea leaf. The most common type of flavanoid are called flavanols, which encompass catechins. These are especially plentiful in green tea. Of these, epigallocatechin gallate (EGCG) is the focus of most studies, as it may have cancer-fighting properties. EGCG is also fairly simple to extract and use for pharmaceutical purposes and is continually being researched and refined.

The flavanoid group also contain anthocyanins, found in Kenyan Purple Tea (see page 183). Black tea contains more complex varieties of flavanoids called thearubigins and theaflavins.

Vitamins and minerals

There are plenty of these found naturally in the tea plant. Most teas are a very good source of vitamin C, a potent antioxidant. Vitamins B1, B6 and also carotene, which is converted into vitamin A in the body, are also present. These all have antioxidant qualities. Minerals such as manganese, potassium and fluoride can also be found. Manganese is key for bone growth, potassium aids the heart and fluoride the teeth.

Caffeine
Despite its usually negative reputation, caffeine does have benefits. It promotes digestion, promotes cardiac function and can be known to help weight loss by promoting digestion.

L-theanine
L-theanine is an amino acid that increases relaxation by stimulating alpha-wave production in the brain. It also slows down the release of caffeine into the body. The short-term effect of this is to create a feeling of controlled stimulation that can last for a long period of time. It is this feeling that first drew monks to tea, who found it useful during long meditation sessions. Longer term, it is said to reduce psychological stress, improve the memory and aid against viral infection by improving the immune system.

Aromatic substances
There are hundreds of aromatic substances in tea, which we notice mainly in the flavour and aroma of the tea. However, they can have a deeper impact as painkillers with anti-bacterial and anti-inflammatory affects. They can also promote relaxation through their soothing nature.

The health benefits of different tea types
Every tea contains different levels of the compounds mentioned above, and certain types are linked with certain health properties. Processing brings out, decreases or changes these properties.

White tea, being the least processed and containing more antioxidant-rich leaf buds than other types of tea, has a high concentration of antioxidants, making it great in fighting illness. It is also calming in nature. Green tea has a similar amount of antioxidants to white tea, as well as a wider range of polyphenols, which are especially good at countering the effects of free radicals and therefore reducing the risk of cancer. It has also been shown to lower blood pressure and reduce levels of harmful cholesterol, thus protecting against heart disease.

Oolong tea is known to aid digestion because its properties stimulate the metabolizing of lipids. This is why oolong tea is often irresponsibly touted as a 'slimming tea'. As with all health claims, it must form part of a suitable health programme. Black teas have been shown to lower blood pressure and protect against heart disease due to their higher levels of theaflavins. Finally, dark teas have a history of being used to aid digestion, particularly by the nomadic tribes of Asia whose diet involved the rich meat of yaks. They also are known to reduce harmful cholesterol and raise levels of good cholesterol in the body.

The variations within each type of tea are enormous, so health benefits can only ever be generalized. Add to this the variation in biology of each tea drinker, and how this controls the absorption or effect of each compound, and it is obvious why tea and health is such a tricky subject. Certainly there is much to gain from tea but, as with many aspects of tea, these beneifts are still not fully understood.

CAFFEINE

All true teas (in other words, those made from the *Camellia sinensis* plant)
contain caffeine. Caffeine is a naturally occurring stimulant that is soluble
in water and extracted when brewed. It's a methylxanthine, a bitter-tasting
compound produced naturally by plants to discourage the nibbling of new
buds or the damaging of shoots. It's not possible to generalize about caffeine
levels in tea, but here are some pointers that will allow more informed
decisions to be made. The caffeine level in any particular tea depends on
a wide variety of factors.

The plant

In general, *Camellia sinenses* var. *sinensis* plants are lower in caffeine than
var. *assamica* ones. So, for example, African teas that are mainly *assamica*
are higher in caffeine than Chinese ones. Plants also adapt to suit their
environment, and those that adapt best thrive, whether this occurs naturally
or deliberately. A favourable adaptation may be a resistance to insects caused
by a higher level of caffeine. Another controlling factor is altitude: the higher
the growing environment the lower the caffeine levels, presumably due
to there being fewer insects. Variation in insect numbers may also be why
growing season is a factor: the faster growing seasons of spring and summer
produce higher caffeine levels because there are more insects around.

The final element is how the plant is grown. If it comes from clonal vegetive
propagation (a cutting fixed to root stock) rather than planted as a seedling,
caffeine levels can be 100 percent higher. A real-life comparison is between
new planting in Africa and old seedling planting in Asia. Older leaf, China-
type seedling bushes, under fertilized in the autumn season have low caffeine
levels of 1–1.5 percent. Well-fertilized, fast-growing young tips in African
clonal plants yield caffeine levels of between 5–6 percent.

Human impact

When a plant is given a lot of nitrogen fertilizer, caffeine is higher. This is
common practice in Japan. Leaf shading while the plant is growing has a
similar effect. Leaves for *gyokuro*, for example, can be shaded for around
20 days before picking. This increases caffeine but also an amino acid called
L-theanine, which moderates the release of caffeine, so the higher caffeine
level is released over a longer period of time, thus limiting the effect.

The part of the tea plant used is also important. A tea made from leaf buds
and tips has more caffeine than one using just leaf only. Young leaf buds have
the highest concentration, as this is the part that needs most protection from
insects. The higher the plucking standard, the higher the caffeine.

Once the leaf is picked, its caffeine content can still change; slow withering
at a moderate temperature results in the highest caffeine. A long wither also
means higher caffeine. Oxidation, another step in the processing of some
teas, reduces caffeine. Once the tea is in your cup, caffeine levels can still
change. The higher the water temperature, the more caffeine is extracted.

Decaffeinated tea

This is a wide-ranging subject, but there are three basic processes, all of which involve adding a solvent to strip the caffeine from the leaf. The first is methylene chloride, which is now banned in the United States because of health risks. The second is ethyl acetate, a solvent naturally found in tea, which is less effective and harder to remove afterwards, leaving a chemical taste. The third and best way is using carbon dioxide at a high pressure and temperature, which attracts the caffeine but does not significantly alter the leaf. None of the processes available completely rid the leaf of caffeine, and they can leave chemical residue behind, greatly reduce the flavour or make a cheap tea expensive. We think it's a better idea to explore the various caffeine-free infusions available.

In conclusion, without chemically measuring each spoon of tea leaf you use it is impossible to say how much caffeine there is in it. All you can hope to do is make a rough estimate, but for this you need to know where you tea is from, how it was grown, processed, picked and brewed. We aim to know all these things, and to provide this information to our customers. However, it can be hard to process, so the alternative is to experiment with how a tea affects you. Caffeine's effects are different for everyone, so this may be the only true way to know.

TEA AND MEDITATION

Michelle: The role that tea plays in my life continues to evolve every day. It is still at the centre of my activities, but in recent years, since having children, it has given me new opportunities to learn and grow. In January 2016 we were moving towards the opening of our new store in Bath, a period that involved Rob working day and night at the Bath store, and me being at home with the children and running the Dorset and online business. I saw an advert for meditation with the headline 'How to live well' and, as you can imagine, it was exactly what I needed. Since our first meeting, Camille and I have spent many hours sharing tea and learning about each others' lives. Her view on the role that tea can play in modern life gives a valuable insight into both meditation and tea.

Camille: 'I discovered meditation in my late twenties, when I was going through a particularly difficult period in my life. Desperately seeking some kind of solace, I turned up at my local Buddhist group for a meditation class. From that first evening I was hooked. Those moments of stillness brought me to a deep understanding of myself, and with that came healing and a renewed love of life. I've been meditating for more than 15 years now, and although I've moved away from my strict Zen training, my practice remains strong.

'Now I offer guidance to people who want to learn how to live mindfully. It seems essential to me in this fast-paced, high-pressure lifestyle we all face and in a world where we tend to think we can do it all. Messages from the media keep us believing that in order to be successful and happy we must make the most of every minute. Self-improvement and productivity have become the ultimate goal, while advances in technology mean we never switch off.

'We are starting to see much more discussion about the benefits of mindfulness, how slowing down and being deliberately aware of your activities can help to calm the mind and heal the body. What's great about mindfulness practice is that it can be incorporated into any daily activity, immediately making it a restful and restorative experience.

'Tea drinking is a perfect example. By slowing down and using our senses to fully connect to the experience of making and drinking tea, it is transformed into an enriching and enlightening ritual – a meditation of sorts. Tea meditation is simply the practice of drinking our tea carefully and mindfully. It can be a poignant way to mark the end of a work day, or a stretch of activities, a way of telling the mind and the body that it can rest and be still. It offers the opportunity to relax, and to enjoy the pleasure of simple things. There is a gentleness to the tea meditation that allows us space to be present and at peace. It becomes a gift we give to ourselves, a gift of time slowed down and of life expanded.

'As a student of Zen Buddhism, I was fortunate to experience the wonder of tea meditation on many occasions. During silent retreats we would take breaks from our sitting meditation practice (zazen) and drink tea mindfully on our own, in the stillness of the monastery. We would also take part in tea ceremonies, where tea would be made by the attendant and shared with the group. We would sit on our cushions in two rows facing each other, and as each person received their tea they would bow to the attendant, palms and forehead to the floor, and the attendant would bow in return. The tea became an offering, a symbol of humility and respect, and it was always a moving experience.

'I still use tea as a focal point in my classes, albeit in a more casual fashion. After a session of relaxation and meditation we all gather around a pot of tea to talk about the things that matter to us. It is a simple ritual that brings the group together, and it marks a period of reflection and sharing. Drinking tea mindfully together encourages each person to be fully present, and I've noticed that people are more connected and respectful towards each other as a result. They take time to really listen, and conversations are richer and more heartfelt.

'The best way to understand the benefits of tea meditation is to try it for yourself. It's such an uplifting and relaxing experience, and you'll find it offers a valuable moment of respite in an otherwise hectic day.'

Tea meditation: Camille Elizabeth

Once your tea is poured, take a moment to simply sit with your tea.
Appreciate the beauty of the bowl and the colour of the tea within.

Give thanks for the cup of tea in front of you. Acknowledge everything
that had to happen around the world in order for you to experience this
amazing cup of tea.

Hold the tea bowl in both hands and notice the temperature. Focus your
attention on the texture of the ceramic.

Notice the steam wafting up. Notice the aromas arising out of your cup.
Lift the bowl to your nose and breathe them in.

Sip slowly. Take your time, and really notice the taste. Is it earthy or grassy
or floral? How does the taste change with each pouring?

Give yourself completely to the process of drinking your tea.
If your attention wanders away from the act of drinking, gently return it
to the activity.

Once you have finished drinking your tea, spend a moment observing how
you feel. Give thanks again, as you did at the beginning.

This marks the end of the meditation.

*'Drink your tea slowly and reverently, as if it is the axis on which the world earth
revolves – slowly, evenly, without rushing towards the future. Live the actual
moment. Only this moment is life.'*
Thich Nhat Hanh, Zen Master

time *for* tea

Now that we have the ingredients for a great cup of tea – fine tea and fine teaware – let's make some tea! We don't believe in setting out 'right' and 'wrong' ways of doing things – that seems to detract from the pleasure of tea making. However, we do recognize that some guidelines are helpful. Once you've learned the traditional preparation techniques you'll no doubt find your own way, adjusting temperature, infusion times, amount of leaf. Your choice of teaware will also alter the brewing – for example, brewing a tea in a conventional teapot requires a different approach to brewing the same tea in the *gongfu* style. These variations are a beautiful part of the tea experience and a constant source of debate and learning.

PREPARING AND ENJOYING CHINESE TEA

Using a Chinese gaiwan

A *gaiwan* is a Chinese lidded bowl used for multiple infusions of tea leaves. Invented during the Ming dynasty (1368–1644), it consists of a bowl, a lid and a saucer. Although it can be used for all types of tea, the *gaiwan* is most suited to the more delicate ones, as it's especially good at bringing out subtle flavours. The lid of the *gaiwan* means that the brewed tea can be either drunk straight from the bowl, decanted into a jug for sharing among multiple cups or decanted into one cup. The lid retains the leaf, which is important as these teas can be infused multiple times.

> **You need:** *gaiwan*, *cha hai* (tea jug), cups.
> **Types of tea:** the *gaiwan* is typically used to brew delicate teas such as green and white teas because the porcelain it is made from absorbs the heat and therefore does not damage the leaf. Depending on the tea being infused, the rinsing or 'awakening' of the leaves (see opposite) may also be done with the *gaiwan*, and the lid offered to the tea drinker to appreciate the essence of the tea before drinking.
> **Example:** Long Jing, Hangzhou, Zhejiang Province, China. To make other teas using this method see the Tea Directory on pages 198-201.
>
> **Method:** Heat the *gaiwan* with hot water. Place approximately 1 heaped teaspoon (5 g) leaves tea in the *gaiwan*. Pour water at around 80°C over the leaves, ensuring they are all wet. Leave the tea to infuse for 1–2 minutes, or for as long as desired. Pour all of the liquid into a tea bowl, using the lid to hold back the leaves. Smell the inside of the lid to appreciate the delicate aromas. Taste your tea. Reinfuse by repeating the infusing steps above, shortening the later infusion times.

Chinese gongfu cha

Gongfu cha originated in Fujian Province around the early seventeenth century. The term translates basically as 'making tea with skill'. The characters denoting *gongfu* are the same as those used for the martial art, *kung fu*, which reflects the skill needed to master the process. The whole process is about the appreciation of the tea and is not a ceremony but a procedure. The rinsing or 'awakening' of the leaves not only prepares them by softening and ensures there is no tea dust, but awakens the drinker's senses with the introduction of the aroma. This attention to the experience of drinking is continued when the tea is is poured into the jug for the dual purposes of stopping the infusion and equalizing the flavours. This ensures the first and last drinker don't experience different strengths, ensuring that everyone has the best experience.

We often observe that people's reactions to the aroma of the leaf changes over time. For new tea drinkers it can seem quite odd at first. For more experienced tea drinkers you often see a change in their demeanour, a visible relaxation as their body prepares for a wonderful tea experience. Although on first sight the *gongfu cha* can seem quite a rigid process, there is plenty of space for the drinker to adapt it to meet their own specific tastes. Core to it is the idea of patience, concentration and attention on what you are doing. This focus leads to a very fine experience, in which tea is savoured and time is taken.

You need: Yixing teapot, a *cha hai* (tea jug), sipping cups, water tray.
Types of tea: *gongfu* cha is mainly used for brewing oolong teas, but is also used for *puer*.
Example: Zheng Yan Rou Gui, Wuyi Mountains, northwest Fujian, China. To make other teas using this method see the Tea Directory on pages 198-201.

Method: Heat the utensils with hot water, pouring the water from the teapot into the jug and sipping cups to warm them. Place 2 or 3 teaspoons (7–10 g) tea leaves in the teapot. Enjoy the aroma of the warmed dry leaf.

Rinse the leaves by pouring a small amount of hot water over them, then discard the water. Enjoy the aroma of the wet leaf.

Pour water at around 100°C over the leaves, ensuring the teapot overflows. Put the lid back on. Pour hot water over the top of the pot. Leave the tea to infuse for 5 seconds for the first to third infusions, then 15–30 seconds thereafter. Pour the liquid into the pre-warmed jug, ensuring no liquid is left behind and the infusion is stopped. Pour from the jug into the sipping cups and taste. Reinfuse by repeating the infusing steps above, lengthening the time of brewing if desired.

PREPARING AND ENJOYING KOREAN TEA

Korea's tea culture started in the era of the Qing dynasty, but after suffering greatly when the Joseon dynasty developed into a modern form of state and during the Korean War, it has lost its form and meaning. Today's tea-brewing procedures have evolved from the Goryeo and Joseon dynasties, and also the Japanese methods that arrived in the 1970s.

The preparation of the tea depends on the type. Green tea is brewed at 80°C, whereas fermented teas are regularly brewed at 100°C. For brewing, porcelain, celadon or buncheong-ware are used, and bigger teapots than those used in China (around 200 ml). However, there is a growing trend to use smaller teaware (around 100 ml).

> **You need**: teapot (*cha-ho*), pitcher (*suk-woo*), teacup (*chat-zan*), water-disposer (*toe-su-gi*), tea tray (*da-zi* or the larger *da-hae*). Seong Il (see page 110) explained the role of the water disposer: 'When I brew tea I pour the hot water on top of the teapot to maintain the temperature. When the tray beneath the teapot is full we pour the water into the disposer.'
> **Types of tea:** green tea, fermented tea.
> **Example:** Korean Sejak green tea; fermented tea.

> **Method:** For green tea, use 100 ml water for ½–1 heaped teaspoon (2–5 g) tea. Pour in water at around 80°C over the leaves and replace the lid. Make three infusions: the first for 30 seconds, decreasing to 15 and then 10 seconds for the last infusion.

> **Method:** For fermented tea, use 100 ml water for ½–1 heaped teaspoon (2–5 g) tea. Pour in water at around 100°C over the leaves and replace the lid. Make 5–10 infusions depending on the tea: the first for 30 seconds, decreasing to 15 and then 10 seconds. After the fifth infusion, increase the infusion time.

PREPARING AND ENJOYING JAPANESE TEA

Using a Japanese kyusu

The main vessel we use for brewing Japanese green tea is the *kyusu*. The design dates back to Song dynasty China, but used in its current form dates from the early 1700s when *sencha* first came into being. There are many ways of brewing using a *kyusu* depending on tea quantity, water temperature and brewing time. These vary between tea masters and definitely between drinkers. In our teahouses we recommend the following method to those new to Japanese green tea. Our more experienced drinkers often vary this approach using more leaf and variable temperatures and infusion times.

You need: *kyusu*, cup or tea bowl.
Types of tea: all Japanese green teas.
Example: *sencha*
Method: Fill the *kyusu* with hot water, then pour it away. Place 1–2 teaspoons (4–7 g) of the tea in the *kyusu*. Pour in water at around 80°C over the leaves and replace the lid. Leave to infuse for 1–2 minutes to your desired strength. Pour the tea directly from the *kyusu* to the cup, ensuring every last drop is poured. Enjoy immediately. Re-infuse the leaves up to three times – each time the flavour profile of the tea will change.

WATER TEMPERATURE

From our experience, water temperature is the key factor that affects customers' enjoyment of Japanese green tea. Although temperature-regulated kettles are becoming more common, not everyone has them. In Japan, temperature is adjusted by the use of, among other things *yuzamashi*, water coolers. On average, pouring water into one of these will drop its temperature by 10°C. Wait 30 seconds and it will drop another 10°C.

Another method is to pour cooler water into almost-boiling water. A little experimentation with a kitchen thermometer will allow you to work out how much needs to be added. With a little practice this will soon be done by eye.

Rob: On visiting a teahouse on Fukuoka on Kyushu Island while sourcing tea in 2017, my eyes were opened to the use of variable temperatures in Japanese tea service. The menu was entirely in Japanese, so I asked for a recommendation. I was served a Tsuyu-hikari *sencha* from Yame, Fukuoka Prefecture. Tsuyu-hikari is a hybrid of Asatsuyu and Shizu 7132 cultivars and gives an amazing taste, which was demonstrated incredibly by the proprietor, Hayakawa-san. I had come to Japan to learn, and I certainly did that day. Everything was prepared on a central kettle, which heated the water and had a serving area surrounding it. Initially, Yasuhiko showed me the leaf to smell, then heated the tea vessels, including a *hohin* (handle-less teapot), in preparation. My first cup was infused at 60°C for 3 minutes and accompanied by the word 'umami', and so it was – the best example anyone could ever have. The second was 80°C for 1 minute and described as 'bitter', which again redefined what bitter can be. Strong and full, but pleasant and flavousome. The third and last cup was infused at 90°C for 1 minute –'big' was again an accurate description of the flavour, but unfortunately not the bowl. I was entirely satisfied by the three infusions, which had shown the tea off perfectly. The tea was accompanied by a *matcha* sweet or *wagashi* that was also quite incredible. The use of variable temperatures in Japanese tea service is now one of our offerings at our teahouses.

Matcha

Matcha has been central to the Japanese *chanoya* or 'the way of tea' since it began in the twelfth century. This cultural practice today consists of hundreds of carefully choreographed steps according to rituals laid down over many centuries. The most elaborate expression of *chanoyu* can last for up to 3–4 hours, including a meal and meditation. This is called *chaji* and is an extremely rare occasion. A much shorter and more widespread version is named *chakai* and lasts around half an hour. There are many factors to these practices, and to do them justice is beyond the scope of this book. Indeed, it takes ten years to master *chanoyu* to a level where it can be performed in public.

There are two main types of *matcha*: *koicha* (thick tea) and *usucha* (thin tea). During a *chaji* guests are served koicha and usucha as part of the ritual. Guests at a *chakai* recieve *usucha*.

In our teahouses we serve *usucha*, which we whisk in front of our guests, ensuring we reference *chanoyu* in its structure and form, as well as its history. We believe this is important for furthering the understanding of this amazing art. Our time spent studying and talking with *matcha* producers in Japan has allowed us to practise a way of serving that is a balance between the formal practice and a practical way of enjoying *matcha* as a tea in the home.

> **You need:** *chawan* (tea bowl), *chasen* (tea whisk), *chashaku* (tea scoop), *matcha* powder, sifter.
>
> **Types of tea:** *matcha*. Matcha powder can be categorized from low grade to high grade depending on its quality. *Usucha* can be made with any grade of *matcha*, whereas *koicha* requires high-grade *matcha* to ensure an acceptable level of bitterness and astringency.
>
> **Example:** superior-grade *matcha* (*usucha*).

> **Method:** Before you start, warm the *chawan* and the *chasen* with hot water. Discard the water once the *chawan* is hot and carefully wipe the inside with a cloth.
>
> Sift the measured amount of freshly opened *matcha* using a fine sieve. For one bowl, 2 *chashaku* (1 level teaspoon) is required. This ensures there are no lumps, making the final froth smoother. Place the sifted powder in the *chawan*. Pour around 60ml of water at 70–75°C into the *chawan*. We use a *yuzamashi* water cooler to reduce the temperature of nearly boiling water. Using the *chasen*, whisk the tea in a 'W' action until a froth forms. Remove the whisk carefully from the foam, ensuring any larger bubbles are burst. Enjoy your tea.

Japanese sweets and tea

Michelle: Our first taste of Japanese sweets was back in March 2009 at the cultural centre in Kyoto, where we were having our first experience of *chanoyu*. In 2017 we had the pleasure of learning more from a third-generation, passionate *wagashi* (Japanese confection) maker, Mr Wake, who came to Bath to hold a workshop in our teahouse. Mr Wake was born, raised and still lives in Utsunomiya City in Tochigi Prefecture, Japan. He is the third generation of the *wagashi* confectionary business, Kourindo.

Mr Wake: 'For Japanese people *wagashi* usually means Japanese confectionery made from sticky rice or beans, especially a sweet bean paste made from azuki beans. There is a wide range of *wagashi*, from professionally made *nerikiri* to rice cakes or balls filled with red bean paste, which some people make at home. People throughout Japan have enjoyed *wagashi* for centuries; each region has a *wagashi* made with local products such as strawberries, yuzu or apples.'

There is a strong relationship between *wagashi* and tea, but there are no strict rules, except that *nerikiri* is usually served with *matcha* or strong green powdered tea as it was originally developed as a part of *chanoyu*. You will generally see people enjoying *wagashi* with a range of Japanese teas: green tea, *genmaicha*, *matcha* or *houjicha* (roasted green tea) The enjoyment of *wagashi* and tea can be seen as the equivalent of British tea and biscuits. Nowadays, Japanese people eat a lot of western sweets, but *wagashi* is still popular. Beautiful in both appearance and taste, I am passionate to spread the knowledge and enjoyment of *wagashi* to the West. Many *wagashi* shops face the issue of having no successor and I want to show that *wagashi* chefs can be cool!

Japanese cold-brewed powdered tea

Rob: While visiting Japan in 2017 and spending time with Mr Sakamoto and Toshiro Irie I learned about the growing trend for powdered green teas. I mainly saw and tasted *gyokuro* but there are 'generic-style' powdered green teas as well. Although many places across Japan produce powdered teas, it would seem that much of this is destined to be used as an ingredient in the growing ready-to-drink market, This is not the case for Mr Sakamoto's powdered *gyokuro*, which he gave to us in individual sachets ready to add to cold water and shake to mix. They create an 'instant' tea that is refreshing and functional. The drinker is also getting the full benefit of the health qualities of the tea, with the benefit of it being just tea, with nothing else added. I'm pretty addicted now. Who needs all the flavours and additives in many of the cold-brew offerings on the market when the pure leaf tastes this good?

PREPARING AND ENJOYING TEA IN A WESTERN-STYLE TEAPOT

When most of us think of tea, we tend to imagine a traditional western-style teapot. All the teas described in this book can be prepared in this kind of teapot (although for fine Japanese teas we recommend using a pot with a very fine mesh), but it may not extract the full range of flavours from certain teas. At our teahouses we use traditional teapots for our black Indian, Sri Lankan, Kenyan and Malawian teas, as well as some of the green teas.

Black tea is often considered to be the most 'standard' category of tea, the closest to our morning cup of tea. We hope we have managed to show you the incredibly diverse range of black teas available across the world. As we have taken this journey ourselves, one skill we've had to master is the art of tasting, and who better to equip us for a black tea exploration than our wonderful friend Nibir, who works with the team at Glenburn, the family that owns and runs Glenburn in Darjeeling and Khongea in Assam, India (see page 135). On the following page Nibir makes the case for black tea, and shares some helpful tips for tasting it.

Nibir: 'In my opinion, black tea has the most diverse and varied range of flavours, and that makes it the most interesting tea. Its diversity starts from the location it is produced in, the cultivars, the processing techniques and most of all, the fermentation that brings out different taste notes. The most popular black teas are from India, Sri Lanka and Kenya, but even China has its fair share, where it is known as red tea.

'When you taste tea you are looking at the colour of liquor, aroma, taste, mouthfeel, texture of the liquor, flavour profile and finish. In order to properly evaluate these you need to prepare yourself and the room for tasting. Strong natural white light is important for assessing the appearance – the ideal time of day is between 10 a.m. and 2 p.m. There also should be an overhead white neutral light bulb. The mouth should be rinsed with water. Thereafter, one can also rinse the mouth with the first cup of tea laid out for tasting in a batch. Rinsing the mouth with tea opens up the sensory nerves to perceive the tea taste.'

Although black tea is traditionally tasted straight from the tasting bowl, Nibir recommends using a tasting spoon 'because it ensures that the same quantity of tea sipped from each cup, which helps you compare the other factors in the taste, such as mouthfeel'. Differing brewing times (3–5 minutes) also bring out its ideal taste notes.

'Black tea liquor has layers of taste like top note, base and finish, which can be perceived by repeated tasting. Black teas can be woody, nutty, fruity or flowery, but not vegetal. Black teas from the same region but processed differently (for example, CTC and orthodox) can taste very different.

'Black teas tend to be bold and brisk, and are often described as astringent. The flavours of single-origin teas can be broadly described; different origins produce different flavour profiles due to their unique terroir. Classic single-origin flavour profiles include:

Assam black tea: bold, malty, brisk
Darjeeling black tea: delicate, fruity, floral, light
Nilgiri black tea: fragrant, floral
Ceylon black tea: varies by origin, but is generally bold, strong and rich, sometimes with notes of chocolate or spice
Keemun black tea: wine-like, fruity, floral, piney, tobacco-like
Yunnan black tea: chocolate, dark, malty, complex notes
Kenyan black tea: bold, astringent, clear.'

A brief history of the western teapot

Large western-style teapots have evolved over hundreds of years, but their exact time and place of origin is not clear. Many sources say that inspiration was drawn from Chinese teapots, whereas some say they grew out of ideas formed in the west.

One theory is that western teapots originated from Chinese wine-pots or *ewers*. These bulbous-based vessels with wide spouts would have been exported as interesting pieces for rich aristocrats and were often packed with tea to prevent them breaking during shipping. They weren't meant for brewing, but western merchants may well have jumped to the wrong conclusion. Another theory has the inspiration coming from the coffee pots being brought to English coffee houses via trade routes from the Middle East.

No matter what the origin was, at the beginning of the eighteenth century the East India Company was importing vast amounts of Chinese teaware along with the tea. They were also commissioning Chinese potters to make teapots according to designs sent from England, which matched the tastes of the time. It took many years for European potters to discover the Chinese methods for making stoneware and porcelain, but by the mid-eighteenth century the technique had made it to England and was widely used for teapots and teaware.

Further changes to design came with the advent of afternoon tea, which created an enormous demand for teapots. In the 1730s, the silver teapot started to become popular. In the late 1790s came a key discovery: while experimenting with the porcelain process, Josiah Spode invented bone china, a type of very strong porcelain, allowing much thinner forms to be made. This, combined with its ease of manufacture, made it the ideal material for the increased demand of the nineteenth century.

Over the last few hundred years in the UK teapots have grown in size as the cost of tea has become more affordable, mostly due to the invention of the tea bag. Tea bags have also led to the disappearance of the internal strainer, along with an overall decline in the use of teapots. Despite this, there are many modern-day teapots designed for use with loose-leaf tea with integral removable infusion baskets. The ability to remove the leaf to avoid over-brewing is vital, but unfortunately is still not demanded by many consumers. In our teahouses our customers are often surprised when we tell them that their tea has brewed and that we have removed the leaf. This seemingly simple step is a concept many people are not used to, which can only be blamed on suppliers and establishments.

Brewing in a western-style teapot

You need: teapot, cup or tea bowl.
Types of tea: all types of tea, but especially black teas.
Example: Assam Golden Tip black tea from Khongea Tea Estate, northern India.

Method: Heat the teapot with hot water and pour it away. Place 1 teaspoon (2 g) of tea per 200ml water into the strainer of the teapot, if it has one. Pour in water at around 100°C to fill the pot and replace the lid. Leave to infuse for 3–5 minutes to your desired strength. Remove the infuser to stop the infusion and discard the leaf. Pour the tea directly from the teapot to the cup. Enjoy immediately.

MODERNIZING WESTERN TEA PREPARATION: RACHEL DORMOR, POTTER, CAMBRIDGE

Michelle: Inspired by the simple bowls we have admired in teahouses around the world, we wanted to design a Comins tea bowl that suited the British market and with a teapot to match; something substantial for everyday use, but also elegant enough to make teatime special.

After a long search we met Rachel Dormor at Origin: The London Craft Fair and were instantly captivated by the combination of elegance and everyday functionality in her pieces. They matched our vision exactly. Rachel, an apprentice-trained potter based in Cambridge, works mainly with porcelain to create functional tableware, and has been our partner ever since. Every Comins tea bowl is carefully hand thrown from British porcelain, dried, fired once, glazed and re-fired to a high temperature to make it hard and glossy. A logo is applied by hand and the bowl is fired for a third time. Due to the many processes involved, slight variations occur in size and finish, which enhances the individuality and charm of each item. I can't imagine Comins without Rachel's bowls. We use them for black, green and white teas in combination with traditional teapots, also made by Rachel, kyusus and gaiwans. They put a distinctly British stamp on the modern enjoyment of fine tea, while also celebrating British craftsmanship.

Rachel: 'If you are making careful choices about the food and drink you consume, you should also consider how and where things are made and support local, sustainable and renewable options whenever you can. When you buy from a British maker all the money spent goes back into the local economy and supports our creative industries and heritage skills.'

We appreciate beautiful pieces made on far-off shores, but we can be much slower to praise our home-grown industries and the skill needed to produce individual items, a point reiterated by Rachel: 'Sometimes the actual throwing only takes a couple of minutes, but the preparation and the finishing are what takes the time. The plates and tea bowls are made on the wheel and the teapots are cast in a mould. It's a time consuming and extremely physical process and there is a connection between the maker and the piece every step of the way. The pieces have been made to be used and enjoyed every day. As they are made from porcelain and fired to a high temperature, they are incredibly durable.'

tea directory

WHITE TEAS

Mr Zheng's Silver Needle
◐ Xiamen Chan Village, Fuding, China
📋 April/May
Cultivar: Da Bai
Tea maker: Mr Zheng
Plucking standard: Top buds (leaf shoots)
Experience: Gentle, floral and high in antioxidants
Recommended preparation: *Gaiwan*

Mr Zheng's Bai Mu Dan
◐ Xiamen Chan Village, Fuding, China
📋 April/May
Cultivar: Da Bai
Tea maker: Mr Zheng
Plucking standard: One leaf shoot (unopened bud) and two newly sprouted leaves
Experience: Sweet like hay, calming, floral
Recommended preparation: *Gaiwan*

Mr Zheng's Shou Mei
◐ Xiamen Chan Village, Fuding, China
📋 April/May
Cultivar: Da Bai
Tea maker: Mr Zheng
Plucking standard: Upper leaf and tip
Experience: Fruity, rich and sweet
Recommended preparation: *Gaiwan*

Nilgiri White
◐ Nr Ooty, Tamil Nadu, southern India
📋 July
Cultivar: The plants are of 'China plant' variety. No known cultivar

name or number. With small, thin leaves, it is suitable for producing quality orthodox tea. It has adapted to the Nilgiri Mountains very well and developed its own distinct flavour.
Tea maker: Murali Subramanian
Plucking standard: One leaf and one bud or two leaves and one bud
Experience: Smooth, sweet and fresh
Recommended preparation: *Gaiwan*

Glenburn Silver Needle
◐ Near Singritan, Darjeeling, West Bengal
📋 June/July
Cultivar: A mix from all the cultivars, because the main parameter is picking the long, thick, succulent buds.
Tea maker: Glenburn
Plucking standard: Buds
Experience: Gentle, refreshing and floral
Recommended preparation: *Gaiwan*

Glenburn Moonshine
◐ Near Singritan, Darjeeling, West Bengal
📋 March
Cultivar: AV2
Tea maker: Parveez Ashad Hussain
Plucking standard: Two leaves and one bud
Experience: Bright, light with gentle citrusy notes
Recommended preparation: *Gaiwan*

Satemwa Zomba Pearls
◐ Satemwa, Shire Highlands, Malawi
📋 April/May–September/October
Cultivar: Zomba Cultivar: an endemic Malawian slow-oxidizing cultivar
Tea maker: Satemwa
Plucking standard: Two leaves and

one bud
Experience: Mellow, buttery and full-bodied
Recommended preparation: *Gaiwan*

YELLOW TEAS

Huoshan Huangya
◐ Gu Fu Tang, Huoshan, China
📋 Qing Ming (early spring) until the end of May
Cultivar: Huoshan Morning (or golden chicken)
Tea maker: Mr Zhang
Plucking standard: One bud and one leaf to one bud and three leaves
Experience: Mellow and refreshing, with very nice chestnut and floral aroma. Both soft and fragrant.
Recommended preparation: *Gaiwan*

GREEN TEAS

Mr Sakamoto's Okumidori and Saemidori Gyokuro
◐ Kagoshima, Japan
📋 Spring
Cultivar: Okumidori and Saemidori
Tea maker: Mr Sakemoto
Plucking standard: Machine harvested
Experience: Okumidori is strong, umami-rich and has a green scent. Saemidori is beautifully mild, sweet and slightly astringent.
Recommended preparation: *Kyusu*

Mr Osamu's Genmaicha
◐ Wazuka, Japan
📋 First season – May
Cultivar: Yabukita

Tea maker: Ueda Osamu

Plucking standard: Only the young tea leaves

Experience: Flavourful, lightly nutty. A smooth blend of *sencha* and toasted rice.

Recommended preparation: *Kyusu*

Mr Irie's Houjicha

⊙ Fukuoka, Japan

▧ Second harvest

Cultivar: Yabukita, Kanaya Midori

Tea maker: Mr Toshiro Irie

Plucking standard: firmly grown leaves

Experience: Roasted, nutty and savoury

Recommended preparation: *Kyusu*

Mr Irie's Sencha

⊙ Fukuoka, Japan

▧ First harvest

Cultivar: Yabukita, Saemidori

Tea maker: Mr Toshiro Irie

Plucking standard: young leaves

Experience: Stong and refreshing taste, remarkable umami, great balance between sweetness and bitterness

Recommended preparation: *Kyusu*

Nilgiri Green

⊙ Nr Ooty, Tamil Nadu, southern India

▧ June

Cultivar: No known cultivar name/ number. With small, thin leaves it is suitable for producing quality orthodox tea.

Tea maker: Murali Subramanian

Plucking standard: Two leaves and one bud

Experience: Sweet, smooth and

---

mildly astringent

Recommended preparation: Western teapot

Taiping Houkui

⊙ Houkong village, Taiping County, Anhui Province, China

▧ Spring

Cultivar: Local varietal

Tea maker: Mr Xiang

Plucking standard: One bud and three to four leaves

Experience: Fresh and vibrant

Recommended preparation: Tall, straight glass

OOLONG TEAS

Shanlinxi

⊙ Shibi, Yunlin County, Taiwan

▧ Winter

Cultivar: Qingxin Oolong

Tea maker: Mr Chen

Plucking standard: Hand picked

Experience: Gentle floral, crisp and naturally sweet

Recommended preparation: *Gongfu*

Oriental Beauty

⊙ Miaoli, Taiwan

▧ June and October

Cultivar: Chin Shin Dah Pan

Tea maker: Li-Min-Tseng

Plucking standard: Two leaves and one bud

Experience: Honey-sweet and mellow

Recommended preparation: *Gongfu*

Dong Ding

⊙ Nantou County, Taiwan

▧ September 2017

Cultivar: Jin Xuan Tres No 12 cultivar

Tea maker: Mrs Chen

Plucking standard: Mechanically harvested

Processing: Three-step multi-stage oven baking

Experience: Nutty, strong and deliciously woody

Recommended preparation: *Gongfu*

Mi Xian GABA oolong

Origin: Baguashan, Mingjian Township, Nantou County, Taiwan

▧ Spring

Cultivar: Jin Xuan Tres No 12

Tea maker: Mr Yu

Plucking standard: Mechanically harvested

Experience: Distinctive bug-bitten honey finish

Recommended preparation: *Gongfu*

Mr Wu's Rock Teas

⊙ Zheng Yan area of the Wuyi Mountains, China

▧ Spring, summer and autumn. Late April is considered best.

Cultivar: Tie Luo Han, Rou Gui, Qi Dan

Tea maker: Mr Wu

Plucking standard: Three to four leaves with stalk

Experience: Tie Luo Han: Strong, rich, full-bodied, warming and energizing Qi Dan: Smooth, multi-dimensional tea with a complex aftertaste

Recommended preparation: *Gongfu*

BLACK TEAS

Khongea Golden Tip Assam
◉ Hiloidari, Assam, India
🍃 June
Cultivar: Clonal P-126
Tea maker: Khongea
Plucking standard: Two leaves and one bud or three leaves and one bud
Experience: Rich, strong and malty
Recommended preparation: Western teapot

Kanoka Assam
◉ Dhekiajuli, Assam, India
🍃 June
Cultivar: TV17
Tea maker: Pallab
Plucking standard: Two leaves and one bud
Experience: Smooth, malty subtle honey flavour
Recommended preparation: Western teapot

Nilgiri Black
◉ Nr Ooty, Tamil Nadu, southern India
🍃 June
Cultivar: The plants are of 'China Plant' variety; no known cultivar name or number. With small, thin leaves, it is suitable for producing quality orthodox tea.
Tea maker: Murali Subramanian
Plucking standard: Two leaves and one bud
Experience: Smooth and flavoursome
Recommended preparation: Western teapot

Jamguri Assam Mist
◉ Golaghat, Assam, India
🍃 April
Cultivar: S3A3, T3E3, P126 and CP1
Tea maker: Jamguri Estate

Plucking standard: Two leaves and one bud
Experience: Lightly malty, sweet and bright
Recommended preparation: Western teapot

Glenburn First Flush Darjeeling
◉ Near Singritan, Darjeeling, West Bengal
🍃 Spring
Cultivar: Chinery and clonal cultivar
Tea maker: Glenburn
Plucking standard: Two leaves and one bud
Experience: Bright, sweet and refreshing
Recommended preparation: Western teapot

Ambootia Darjeeling: Sanjay Bansal
◉ Ambootia Garden, Darjeeling, India
🍃 June
Cultivar: TG 887
Tea maker: Ambootia
Plucking standard: Two leaves and one bud
Experience: A delicate tea with aromatic floral tones
Recommended preparation: Western teapot

Imboolpitiya Ceylon
◉ Central Province, Kandy district, Sri Lanka
🍃 Throughout the year
Cultivar: Available cultivars are TRI2023, TRI2024, TRI2025, TRI2026, DN, CH13 , N_2, old seedlings
Tea maker: E.M.D. Rajasekasa (manager)
Plucking standard: Fine plucking (two leaves and bud)
Experience: Full-bodied, bright and invigorating

Recommended preparation: Western teapot

High-Grown Ceylon Indulgashinna
◉ Nr Hatton, Sri Lanka
🍃 All year
Cultivar: CY9 and seedlings (small leaf type)
Tea maker: Gnanasekaran Rajaratnam (manager)
Plucking standard: Two leaves and one bud
Experience: Aromatic, flavoursome and light
Recommended preparation: Western teapot

Himalayan Hand Rolled: Sandakphu
◉ Jasbirey Village, Maipokhari, Ilam, East Nepal
🍃 May
Cultivar: A/V2
Tea maker: Chandra Bhushan
Plucking standard: One leaf and one bud
Experience: A light tea with flowery orchid aromas
Recommended preparation: Western teapot

Black Pearl: Sandakphu
◉ Jasbirey Village, Maipokhari, Ilam, East Nepal
🍃 April
Cultivar: Ilam
Tea maker: Chandra Bhushan
Plucking standard: One leaf and one bud
Experience: A robust tea with hints of sweet, dark fruit
Recommended preparation: *Gaiwan*

Ruby Vine: Sandakphu
◉ Jasbirey Village, Maipokhari, Ilam, East Nepal
🍃 March
Cultivar: 383

Tea maker: Chandra Bhushan

Plucking standard: Matured leaves

Experience: A bright, sweet tea with a hint of wine in the cup

Recommended preparation: *Gaiwan*

Yuchi Red Jade

🌏 Sun Moon Lake, China

🍂 August 2017

Cultivar: T-18

Tea maker: Mr Li

Plucking standard: Hand-picked

Experience: Smooth, fruity and malty

Recommended preparation: *Gongfu*

Lapsang Souchong

🌏 Ma Su Village, Tong Mu Guan, Wuyi Mountains, China

🍂 2009

Cultivar: Lao cong (old bush)

Tea maker: Mr Li He Sheng

Plucking standard: One bud and three leaves

Experience: Sweet, clean, fruity and pine-wood smoked

Recommended preparation: *Gaiwan*

Yunnan Golden Needles

🌏 Menglian, Puer Prefecture, Yunnan, China

🍂 April

Cultivar: Xing Jian

Tea maker: Mr Xu

Plucking standard: One leaf and one bud

Experience: Smooth, rich and biscuity

Recommended preparation: *Gaiwan*

Ancient Tree 2016 MengKu Dian Hong

🌏 East Banshan plot of the Snow Mountain Tea Factory, Menu, southwest Yunnan, China

🍂 April

Cultivar: 200 year-old trees

Tea makers: Mr Ni and Mrs Zhao

Plucking standard: Three to four leaves and one bud, although it depends on the coarseness of the leaf at the time of picking

Experience: Smooth with a light body but sweet taste and malty chocolate finish

Recommended preparation: *Gaiwan*

Keemun Maofeng special level

🌏 Likou Town, China

🍂 April to June

Cultivar: Qimen

Tea maker: Mr Li

Plucking standard: One leaf, one tip

Experience: Rich yet melow with fragrant cocoa tones

Recommended preparation: *Gaiwan*

Mr Irie's Koucha Black tea

🌏 Fukuoka, Japan

🍂 Second harvest

Cultivar: Saemidori

Tea maker: Mr Toshiro Irie

Plucking standard: Firmly grown leaves

Experience: Light, luxuriant fragrance. Light profile with low astringency.

Recommended preparation: *Kyusu*

Kenyan black: Emrok

🌏 Nandi County, Kenya

🍂 All year

Cultivar: Tea Clone TN14/3

Tea maker: Anand Varma

Plucking standard: Tender two leaves and a bud

Experience: Bold flavour, clear, bright infusion

Recommended preparation: *Western teapot*

Smallholder Black

🌏 Satemwa, Shire Highlands, Malawi

🍂 All year, but the best orthodox teas are produced after the rainy season from November to March

Cultivar: Endemic Malawian PC 150

Tea maker: Satemwa

Plucking standard: Two leaves and one bud

Experience: Soft aromatic with woody tones

Recommended preparation: *Western teapot*

DARK/PUER TEAS

Ancient Tree Mengku Sheng Puer

🌏 East Banshan, China

🍂 Picked March 25, 2016, compressed 15 May 2016

Cultivar: 400 year-old trees

Tea makers: Mr Ni and Mrs Zhao

Plucking standard: One bud and two leaves or one bud and three leaves

Experience: Smooth, complex and fruity

Recommended preparation: *Gongfu*

Vintage Shu Puer

🌏 West Banshan and East Banshan, China

🍂 Picked May 20 2015, fermented in January 2016 and compressed in August 2016

Cultivar: 100 year-old trees

Tea makers: Mr Ni and Mrs Zhao

Plucking standard: Bud and three or four leaves.

Experience: Smooth, rich and earthy

Recommended preparation: *Gongfu*

picture credits

The publishers would like to thank Howard Boyer, Katie Burden, Michelle and Rob Comins, Katharine Davies, Anette Kay, Andy Orchard, Satemwa, Hannah Thornton, Haydn West and Rachel Whiting for their contribution of images used in this book. Thanks also to Mariko Aruga for drawing the maps featured in this book. Where images are not credited to an individual photographer they are to be considered by Michelle and Rob Comins.

Every effort has been made to trace the copyright holders and obtain permission to reproduce this material. However, the publishers will be glad to rectify in future editions any inadvertent omissions brought to their attention.

Page 7 (from left to right) Clara, Esme, Michelle, Rob and Ruan Comins outside Comins Tea House in Sturminster Newton, Dorset, 2018. Photograph by Katharine Davies.

Page 19 Incredible Rock Formations Wuyi Mountains, China, 2017. Photograph by Howard Boyer.

Page 22 Mr Toshiro holding soil, Japan, 2017.

Page 27 (top left) Lalita: sardar at the Nuxalbari nursery and community leader, Nuxalbari Estate, Dooars, India, 2017; (top right) Mr Shen preparing his organic Long Jing, Zhejiang Province, 2017; (bottom) Michelle learning about the preparations in Jamguri from assistant manager Mr Sanjeev Singh, 2017.

Page 34 (top) Inside the Sandakphu Tea Factory, Jasibrey village, East Nepal, 2017; (bottom) Processing Sandakphu Snow Bird white tea, 2017.

Page 43 (top left) Freshly heated leaves at the start of the process, Tai Ping, 2017; (top right) Shaping the tea by hand, Tai Ping, 2017; (bottom left) Removing finished tea from the mesh, Tai Ping. 2017; (bottom right) The hand press, Tai Ping, 2017. Photographs by Howard Boyer.

Page 49 (top left) Nuxalbari; (top right) A tea picker in Yunnan, 2016; (centre) Michelle observing tea drying outside the factory of Mrs Zhao and Mr Ni, 2016; (bottom left) Mrs Zhao and Mr Ni's tea woks, 2016; (bottom right) The view wandering through the village adjacent to Mrs Zhao and Mr Ni's factory, 2016.

Page 53 Rob at work in our tea shop, 2018. Photograph by Katharine Davies.

Page 60 (top right) Walking through the villages with Mr Zheng on the way to the factory, 2016; (bottom right) Mr Zheng Fuding, 2016. Photographs by Haydn West.

Page 60 (centre) tea from Wuyi, 2017; (bottom left) A pathway through beautiful Wuyi, 2017. Photographs by Howard Boyer.

Page 61 (top) Mr Nan's village, 2016; (centre left) At lunch with Mr Nan, 2016; (bottom right) Michelle walking through the ancient tea forests, Jingmai, 2016. Photographs by Haydn West.

Page 61 (centre right) Leaf in transit, Wuyi, 2017; (bottom left) Trading in the Qimen tea market, Likou Town, 2017. Photographs by Howard Boyer.

Page 72 (top) Early morning in Mr Zheng's tea fields, Fuding, 2016. Photograph by Haydn West.

Page 72 (bottom left) Mr Wu. Photograph by Howard Boyer.

Page 72 (bottom right) 'The women rule this town'. From left to right is Sooha's mother (Du Xingg'er), aunt and amazing 90 year-old (plus) grandmother, Mei Cun village, Huangshan, 2018.

Page 73 (top left) Drinking Keemun in Qimen, 2017; (top right and centre right) Trading in the Qimen tea market, 2017; (bottom left) Michelle in conversation with Vincent, 2017. Photographs by Howard Boyer.

Page 73 (centre left) Chuanchuan.

Page 73 (bottom right) White tea drying at Mr Zheng's, 2016. Photograph by Haydn West.

Page 81 (top left) Mr Fan; (top right) Yu Xinrong in his studio Jingdezhen

2018; (centre left) Setting the table for tea with Liao Yi's Ramie cloth; (centre right) 'Zhi Ye' cup; (bottom) Xing Xiang studio.

Page 84 (top left) Traditional teahouse in Yame, 2017; (top right) Bags of unfinished Aracha tea waiting to be finished, 2017; (centre left) Koji Nakayama preparing a tea tasting, 2017; (centre right) Mr Sakamoto's tea field, Kagoshima, 2017; (bottom left) Koji Nakayama's immaculate factory, Yame 2017; (bottom right) Palets at a tea factory, Yame, 2017.

Page 85 Young tea bushes, Yame, 2017.

Page 93 (top left) Tea baskets, Kagoshima, October 2017; (top right) A tea field in Wazuka, 2017; (centre) Rob with the Sakamoto brothers, 2017; (bottom left) Akiho Horton; (bottom centre) Hanae; (bottom left) Tea scales at Koji Nakayama, 2017.

Page 104 (top) Mr Seo Jung Min's tea farm; (centre left) Jay shim with his family; (centre right) Soo Soo Choi making tea; (bottom) Mr Seo Jung Min's house.

Page 105 (top and bottom) Mr Seo Jung Min making tea.

Page 113 (top left) Seong Il Hong in his studio; (top right, bottom left and bottom right): Seong Il teapots.

Page 116 (top left) Yu Wen baking tea, Taiwan, October 2017; (top right) Bags in the tea fields at Jojo's – for four-season oolong, Miaoli, October 2017; (bottom left) Tea baking units at Yu Wen's place; (bottom right) Mr Yu in his office.

Page 117 (top left) Jojo making tea, October 2017; (top right) Taiwan green leaf hopper at Jojo's, October 2017; (bottom left) Withering area, Shanlinxi; (bottom right) Tea leaves and the oven at Jojo's factory.

Page 125 Leaf on the floor of Jojo's factory, Miaoli, October 2017.

Page 128 (top left) From leaf to cup: talking tea processing at Kanoka tea farm, 2017. Photograph by Hannah Thornton.

Page 128 (top right) Learning with

Pallab, Kanoka tea farm, 2017; (centre) Tea pickers in the Kanoka garden, 2017; (bottom) Tasting with Parveez at Glenburn, 2018. Photographs by Katie Thompson.

Page 129 (top) Michelle with Husna Tara from Glenburn and Khongea at their head office in Kolkata, 2017; (centre right) Skilled ladies sorting tea: Khongea Tea Factory, 2017.

Page 129 (bottom right) Walking with Bharwesh near Ghoom, 2018. Photograph by Andy Orchard.

Page 129 (centre left) Pallab in his factory, Assam, 2017. Photograph by Hannah Thornton.

Page 129 (bottom left) Inside the Kanoka factory. Photograph by Katie Thompson.

Page 140 (top) Looking down over Darjeeling.

Page 140 (bottom) Tea baskets at Kanoka Garden, 2017. Photograph by Katie Thompson.

Page 141 (top) Inside the Nuxalbari Factory, 2018;

Page 141 (centre left) Michelle tasting with Diwakar Khongea, 2017; (centre right) Khongea at night, 2017. Photographs by Katie Thompson.

Page 141 (bottom left) Michelle has a go at making tea with Pallab, Kanoka Garden, 2017; (bottom right) Michelle tasting at Khongea Factory with Diwakar and the team, 2017. Photographs by Hannah Thornton.

Page 145 (top) Michelle photographing the teas at Nuxalbari, 2018; (bottom) Looking over the tea fields in Dooars, 2018.

Page 148 (top left) Fresh leaves in transit at the Imboolypitiya garden, 2011; (top right) Mr Gnanasekaran Rajaratnam in the Idulgashinna factory, 2015; (bottom) Chance encounters on the road Imboolypitiya, 2011.

Page 149 (top left) Tea country on the road to Hatton, Sri Lanka, 2015; (top right) Michelle with the great Merrill Fernando, Dilmah headquarters, 2011; (centre) Tea stacked up in the factory

Imboolypitiya 2011; (bottom left) Roads lined with tea. On the road to Nuwara Eliya, 2015; (bottom right) Outside the Imboolypitiya factory, 2011.

Page 165 (top left) Talking tea with Sandip in the villages around the Gorkha tea factory, Ilam, Nepal, 2018; (top right) Michelle with the cooperative members at Sandakphu, 2018; (centre) The stunning Sandakphu tea factory, surely nowhere more perfect in the world, 2018; (centre right) Michelle tasting tea with Reggie at Kanyam on a misty day, 2017; (bottom left) Michelle with Chandra and Twistina at the Kathmandu tasting room; (bottom right) Bimala keeping a watchful eye on the tea, Sandakphu, 2018.

Page 165 (centre left) Processing tea at Sandakphu, 2017. Photograph by Andy Orchard.

Page 172 (top left) The view from the dam at Satemwa tea factory; (top right) Hand rolling the #107 Zomba Pearls white tea; (bottom) Satemwa sample room, where samples of each tea batch crafted is kept to monitor quality and traceability. Photographs by Anette Kay.

Page 173 (top) A plucking gang in on of the oldest fields (established in the 1920s) on Satemwa Tea Estates; (centre) Daily tasting and cupping session to evaluate the latest tea production by factory manager, Alfred Mwase and assistant factory manager, Alice Kambale; (bottom left) A group of women from the Msuwadzi smallholder association receiving new tea plants. Satemwa and the Msuwadzi smallholder farmers have a long-standing, sustainable partnership; (bottom right) Alexander Cathcart Kay (43) and his daughter Maia. Third and fourth generation tea farmers. Photographs by Anette Kay.

Page 176 (top left) Nick tasting tea at Emrok Estate, 2017; (top right) Rob and Chai in his unfinished factory, Kericho, 2017; (centre) Sacks of processed tea waiting for shipping at Emrok Estate, 2017; (centre right) Tea pickers at Emrok Tea

Estate, 2017; (bottom left) At the Tea Research Institute with Lilian, 2017; (bottom right) View of the Rift Valley from the road to Nairobi, 2017.

Page 177 (top) The orthodox tea production line at Emrok Tea Estate; (bottom left) Tasting tea with Jeremiah Kosgei, Emrok Tea Estate, 2017; (bottom right) Loading the freshly picked tea onto the conveyor system into Emrok Factory, 2017.

Page 181 Tea hut by the side of the road on the way to Kericho, 2017.

Page 192 (top left) Gong Fu tea service; (top right) Gaiwan tea service; (bottom left) Kyusu tea service. Photographs by Rachel Whiting.

Page 192 (bottom right) Seong Il's teapot.

index

thank you

We are extremely lucky to have the support of family and many friends around the world. Thanks to Michelle's mum for all those early cups of tea and to her mum and dad for all their support and for instilling a love of travel and adventure. Thanks to Rob's parents for their interest and encouragement of our business and of course to our siblings Karen, Amy and Laura and their partners. To our children, Ruen, Clara and Esme – may you read this and feel inspired to have your own adventures. Thanks to all the people who in the early days would visit us on weekends and get involved in washing up or watch the children while we worked (thanks Chris and Jane), who helped us with photos and beautiful illustrations for the website and beyond (thanks Mariko and Richard), and who turned up on the day of opening our Bath Tea House and never mentioned how impossible it had seemed that we would ever finish on time (thanks Steve, Jen and Sandra) or how terrible we looked (thanks Cathy and Oli). And then there are those who actively encourage you to go against the norm and who celebrate your 'alternativeness' (thanks, Erin and Tibo) and who don't mind you calling at 1am or at any other time for reassurance on the path you are taking (thanks Honor and Ethan).

Thanks of course to Stephanie Milner, our commissioning editor at Pavilion, for having faith and belief in the book, and all the team there for supporting us in sharing this story of tea. To Michelle Mac for her stunning design and editors Laura Gladwin and Nicola Graimes.

Thank you to our wonderful customers and team (a special mention to Heather and Antonia – what would we do without you; and Howard, Alicia, Genny, Denise, Andrew and Marina for your great friendship!) Thanks to our wholesale partners who have become friends and have lived with us through this journey since the first day we opened – too many to name – and continue to support us through their purchases, visits, friendship and counsel.

Finally, this book is dedicated to the world of tea, to all our partners around the world working tirelessly every day to produce teas that stop us in our tracks, open our minds and start conversations. For those who help us explore with an open mind and heart – who demonstrate endless patience with us – James and Ming in China, Philip in Taiwan, Nick and Sharon in Kenya, Yuta Kodama, Mr Yutaka Kinoshita, Akiho Horton, Joelle, Stephane and Tomoko in Japan. From the early kindness of Rajah, Merrill and the amazing Jane Pettigrew to the kindness, hospitality and patience of the dozens of tea farmers and experts we work with around the world today – we salute you all.

We're off to make tea now and we hope to see you soon. Rob and Michelle x

FURTHER READING

The authors would also like to acknowledge the texts consulted in the research for this book, including: *The Classic of Tea* by Carpenter, Francis Ross; *First Step to Chinese Puerh Tea* by Chan Kam Pong; *All the Tea in China* by Chow, Kit and Kramer, Ione; *The Tea Drinker's Handbook* by Delmas, Francois-xavier; *Tea* by Eden, T; *Tea* by Faulkner, Rupert; *The Way of Tea* by Aaron Fisher; *Great Teas of China* by Fong, Roy; *A Journey to the Tea Countries of China* by Fortune, Robert; *Tea* by Gascoyne, Marchand, Desharnais and Americi; *Tea* by Gebely, Tony; *Green Tea* by Hara, Yukihiko; *The Harney and Sons Guide to Tea* by Harney, Michael; *The Tea Enthusiast's Handbook* by Heiss, Mary Lou & Robert J.; *The Story of Tea* by Heiss, Mary Lou & Robert J.; *Tea* by Hincheldey, Christian; *Talking of Tea* by Huxley, Gervas; *Illustrated Dictionary of Famous Tea in China* by Jianrong, Wang and Wenjin, Zhou; *The Illustrated Book of Chinese Tea* by Jianrong, Wang and Danying, Guo; *All about Tea in China* by Jianrong, Wang and Danying, Guo (translated by Xiaolan, Qian); *The Book of Tea* by Kakuzo, Okakura; *The Classic of Tea, The Sequel to the Classic of Tea* (Volumes 1 and 2) by Library of Chinese Classics; *The Classics of Tea* by Lu Yu; *The True History of Tea* by Mair, Victor and Hoh, Erling; *Tea and Health* by Modder, W.W.D. and Amarakoon, A.M.T.; *The Ultimate Tea Lover's Treasury* by Norwood Pratt, James; *Tea Dictionary* by Norwood Pratt, James; *The Art of Tea* by Osho; *The Story of Tea* by Paul, E. Jaiwant; *A Social History of Tea* by Pettigrew, Jane; *Tea Classified* by Pettigrew, Jane; *To Think of Tea* by Repplier, Agnes; *For All the Tea in China* by Rose, Sarah; *Cha-No-Yu* by Sadler, A.L.; *Chai* by Sarin, Rekha and Kapoor, Rajan; *World Atlas of Tea* by Smith, Krisi; *Botanical Studies* (2009) 50: 477-485. 'The confirmation of Camellia formosensis (Theaceae) as an independent species based on DNA sequence analyses.' by SU,Mong-Huai, HSIEH, Chang-Fu and TSOU, Chih-Hua; *All About Tea* by Ukers, William H.; *The Evolution of the Tea Ceremony* byVarley, Paul; *The World of Caffeine* by Weinberg, Bennett Alan and Bealer Bonnie K.; *Tea* by Wilson, KC and Clifford, MN; *The Pictoral Album of Chinese Tea Art* by Wenjing, Zhou and Suna, Yue; *The J Thomas Story* by J Thomas and Co; *The China Tea Book* by Luo Jialin; *Chinese Tea Appreciation* by Chief Editor Wang Guangzhi; *CTTA Tea Digest* by Nisheeth Bijawat.